T0075650

Python Data Visualization Cookbook

Second Edition

Over 70 recipes, based on the principal concepts
of data visualization, to get you started with popular
Python libraries

Igor Milovanović

Dimitry Foures

Giuseppe Vettigli

BIRMINGHAM - MUMBAI

Python Data Visualization Cookbook
Second Edition

Copyright © 2015 Packt Publishing

All rights reserved. No part of this book may be reproduced, stored in a retrieval system, or transmitted in any form or by any means, without the prior written permission of the publisher, except in the case of brief quotations embedded in critical articles or reviews.

Every effort has been made in the preparation of this book to ensure the accuracy of the information presented. However, the information contained in this book is sold without warranty, either express or implied. Neither the authors, nor Packt Publishing, and its dealers and distributors will be held liable for any damages caused or alleged to be caused directly or indirectly by this book.

Packt Publishing has endeavored to provide trademark information about all of the companies and products mentioned in this book by the appropriate use of capitals. However, Packt Publishing cannot guarantee the accuracy of this information.

First published: November 2013

Second edition: November 2015

Production reference: 1261115

Published by Packt Publishing Ltd.
Livery Place
35 Livery Street
Birmingham B3 2PB, UK.

ISBN 978-1-78439-669-5

www.packtpub.com

Credits

Authors

Igor Milovanović

Dimitry Foures

Giuseppe Vettigli

Reviewer

Kostiantyn Kucher

Commissioning Editor

Akram Hussain

Acquisition Editor

Meeta Rajani

Content Development Editor

Mayur Pawanikar

Technical Editor

Anushree Arun Tendulkar

Copy Editor

Charlotte Carneiro

Project Coordinator

Nidhi Joshi

Proofreader

Safis Editing

Indexer

Rekha Nair

Graphics

Jason Monteiro

Production Coordinator

Manu Joseph

Cover Work

Manu Joseph

About the Authors

Igor Milovanović is an experienced developer, with strong background in Linux system knowledge and software engineering education, he is skilled in building scalable data-driven distributed software rich systems.

Evangelist for high-quality systems design who holds strong interests in software architecture and development methodologies, Igor is always persistent on advocating methodologies which promote high-quality software, such as test-driven development, one-step builds and continuous integration.

He also possesses solid knowledge of product development. Having field experience and official training, he is capable of transferring knowledge and communication flow from business to developers and vice versa.

Igor is most grateful to his girlfriend for letting him spent hours on the work instead with her and being avid listener to his endless book monologues. He thanks his brother for being the strongest supporter. He is thankful to his parents to let him develop in various ways and become a person he is today.

Dimitry Foures is a data scientist with a background in applied mathematics and theoretical physics. After completing his undergraduate studies in physics at ENS Lyon (France), he studied fluid mechanics at École Polytechnique in Paris where he obtained a first class master's. He holds a PhD in applied mathematics from the University of Cambridge. He currently works as a data scientist for a smart-energy startup in Cambridge, in close collaboration with the university.

Giuseppe Vettigli is a data scientist who has worked in the research industry and academia for many years. His work is focused on the development of machine learning models and applications to use information from structured and unstructured data. He also writes about scientific computing and data visualization in Python on his blog at http://glowingpython.blogspot.com.

About the Reviewer

Kostiantyn Kucher was born in Odessa, Ukraine. He received his master's degree in computer science from Odessa National Polytechnic University in 2012, and he has used Python as well as matplotlib and PIL for machine learning and image recognition purposes.

Since 2013, Kostiantyn has been a PhD student in computer science specializing in information visualization. He conducts his research under the supervision of Prof. Dr. Andreas Kerren with the ISOVIS group at the Computer Science department of Linnaeus University (Växjö, Sweden).

Kostiantyn was a technical reviewer for the first edition of this book.

www.PacktPub.com

Support files, eBooks, discount offers, and more

For support files and downloads related to your book, please visit www.PacktPub.com.

Did you know that Packt offers eBook versions of every book published, with PDF and ePub files available? You can upgrade to the eBook version at www.PacktPub.com and as a print book customer, you are entitled to a discount on the eBook copy. Get in touch with us at service@packtpub.com for more details.

At www.PacktPub.com, you can also read a collection of free technical articles, sign up for a range of free newsletters and receive exclusive discounts and offers on Packt books and eBooks.

https://www2.packtpub.com/books/subscription/packtlib

Do you need instant solutions to your IT questions? PacktLib is Packt's online digital book library. Here, you can search, access, and read Packt's entire library of books.

Why Subscribe?

- ▸ Fully searchable across every book published by Packt
- ▸ Copy and paste, print, and bookmark content
- ▸ On demand and accessible via a web browser

Free Access for Packt account holders

If you have an account with Packt at www.PacktPub.com, you can use this to access PacktLib today and view 9 entirely free books. Simply use your login credentials for immediate access.

Table of Contents

Preface

The best data is the data that we can see and understand. As developers and data scientists, we want to create and build the most comprehensive and understandable visualizations. It is not always simple; we need to find the data, read it, clean it, filter it, and then use the right tool to visualize it. This book explains the process of how to read, clean, and visualize the data into information with straight and simple (and sometimes not so simple) recipes.

How to read local data, remote data, CSV, JSON, and data from relational databases are all explained in this book.

Some simple plots can be plotted with one simple line in Python using matplotlib, but performing more advanced charting requires knowledge of more than just Python. We need to understand information theory and human perception aesthetics to produce the most appealing visualizations.

This book will explain some practices behind plotting with matplotlib in Python, statistics used, and usage examples for different charting features that we should use in an optimal way.

What this book covers

Chapter 1, *Preparing Your Working Environment*, covers a set of installation recipes and advice on how to install the required Python packages and libraries on your platform.

Chapter 2, *Knowing Your Data*, introduces you to common data formats and how to read and write them, be it CSV, JSON, XSL, or relational databases.

Chapter 3, *Drawing Your First Plots and Customizing Them*, starts with drawing simple plots and covers some customization.

Chapter 4, *More Plots and Customizations*, follows up from the previous chapter and covers more advanced charts and grid customization.

Chapter 5, *Making 3D Visualizations*, covers three-dimensional data visualizations such as 3D bars, 3D histograms, and also matplotlib animations.

Chapter 6, Plotting Charts with Images and Maps, deals with image processing, projecting data onto maps, and creating CAPTCHA test images.

Chapter 7, Using Right Plots to Understand Data, covers explanations and recipes on some more advanced plotting techniques such as spectrograms and correlations.

Chapter 8, More on matplotlib Gems, covers a set of charts such as Gantt charts, box plots, and whisker plots, and it also explains how to use LaTeX for rendering text in matplotlib.

Chapter 9, Visualizations on the Clouds with Plot.ly, introduces how to use Plot.ly to create and share your visualizations on its cloud environment.

What you need for this book

For this book, you will need Python 2.7.3 or a later version installed on your operating system.

Another software package used in this book is IPython, which is an interactive Python environment that is very powerful and flexible. This can be installed using package managers for Linux-based OSes or prepared installers for Windows and Mac OS X.

If you are new to Python installation and software installation in general, it is highly recommended to use prepackaged scientific Python distributions such as Anaconda, Enthought Python Distribution or Python(x, y).

Other required software mainly comprises Python packages that are all installed using the Python installation manager, pip, which itself is installed using Python's easy_install setup tool.

Who this book is for

Python Data Visualization Cookbook, Second Edition is for developers and data scientists who already use Python and want to learn how to create visualizations of their data in a practical way. If you have heard about data visualization but don't know where to start, this book will guide you from the start and help you understand data, data formats, data visualization, and how to use Python to visualize data.

You will need to know some general programming concepts, and any kind of programming experience will be helpful. However, the code in this book is explained almost line by line. You don't need math for this book; every concept that is introduced is thoroughly explained in plain English, and references are available for further interest in the topic.

Sections

In this book, you will find several headings that appear frequently (Getting ready, How to do it, How it works, There's more, and See also).

To give clear instructions on how to complete a recipe, we use these sections as follows:

Getting ready

This section tells you what to expect in the recipe, and describes how to set up any software or any preliminary settings required for the recipe.

How to do it...

This section contains the steps required to follow the recipe.

How it works...

This section usually consists of a detailed explanation of what happened in the previous section.

There's more...

This section consists of additional information about the recipe in order to make the reader more knowledgeable about the recipe.

See also

This section provides helpful links to other useful information for the recipe.

Conventions

In this book, you will find a number of styles of text that distinguish between different kinds of information. Here are some examples of these styles and an explanation of their meaning.

Code words in text, database table names, folder names, filenames, file extensions, pathnames, dummy URLs, user input, and Twitter handles are shown as follows: "We packed our little demo in the `DemoPIL` class, so that we can extend it easily, while sharing the common code around the demo function, `run_fixed_filters_demo`."

A block of code is set as follows:

```
def my_function(x):
    return x*x
```

When we wish to draw your attention to a particular part of a code block, the relevant lines or items are set in bold:

```
for a in range(10):
    print a
```

Any command-line input or output is written as follows:

```
$ sudo python setup.py install
```

Warnings or important notes appear in a box like this.

Tips and tricks appear like this.

Reader feedback

Feedback from our readers is always welcome. Let us know what you think about this book—what you liked or may have disliked. Reader feedback is important for us to develop titles that you really get the most out of.

To send us general feedback, simply send an e-mail to feedback@packtpub.com, and mention the book title via the subject of your message.

If there is a topic that you have expertise in and you are interested in either writing or contributing to a book, see our author guide on www.packtpub.com/authors.

Customer support

Now that you are the proud owner of a Packt book, we have a number of things to help you to get the most from your purchase.

Downloading the example code

You can download the example code files for all Packt books you have purchased from your account at http://www.packtpub.com. If you purchased this book elsewhere, you can visit http://www.packtpub.com/support and register to have the files e-mailed directly to you.

Downloading the color images of this book

We also provide you with a PDF file that has color images of the screenshots/diagrams used in this book. The color images will help you better understand the changes in the output. You can download this file from: http://www.packtpub.com/sites/default/files/downloads/PythonDataVisualizationCookbookSecondEdition_ColoredImages.pdf.

Errata

Although we have taken every care to ensure the accuracy of our content, mistakes do happen. If you find a mistake in one of our books—maybe a mistake in the text or the code—we would be grateful if you would report this to us. By doing so, you can save other readers from frustration and help us improve subsequent versions of this book. If you find any errata, please report them by visiting http://www.packtpub.com/submit-errata, selecting your book, clicking on the **errata submission form** link, and entering the details of your errata. Once your errata are verified, your submission will be accepted and the errata will be uploaded on our website, or added to any list of existing errata, under the Errata section of that title. Any existing errata can be viewed by selecting your title from http://www.packtpub.com/support.

Piracy

Piracy of copyright material on the Internet is an ongoing problem across all media. At Packt, we take the protection of our copyright and licenses very seriously. If you come across any illegal copies of our works, in any form, on the Internet, please provide us with the location address or website name immediately so that we can pursue a remedy.

Please contact us at copyright@packtpub.com with a link to the suspected pirated material.

We appreciate your help in protecting our authors, and our ability to bring you valuable content.

Questions

You can contact us at questions@packtpub.com if you are having a problem with any aspect of the book, and we will do our best to address it.

1

Preparing Your Working Environment

In this chapter, you will cover the following recipes:

- ▶ Installing matplotlib, NumPy, and SciPy
- ▶ Installing virtualenv and virtualenvwrapper
- ▶ Installing matplotlib on Mac OS X
- ▶ Installing matplotlib on Windows
- ▶ Installing Python Imaging Library (PIL) for image processing
- ▶ Installing a requests module
- ▶ Customizing matplotlib's parameters in code
- ▶ Customizing matplotlib's parameters per project

Introduction

This chapter introduces the reader to the essential tooling and their installation and configuration. This is necessary work and a common base for the rest of the book. If you have never used Python for data and image processing and visualization, it is advised not to skip this chapter. Even if you do skip it, you can always return to this chapter in case you need to install some supporting tools or verify what version you need to support the current solution.

Installing matplotlib, NumPy, and SciPy

This chapter describes several ways of installing **matplotlib** and required dependencies under Linux.

Getting ready

We assume that you already have Linux (preferably Debian/Ubuntu or RedHat/SciLinux) installed and Python installed on it. Usually, Python is already installed on the mentioned Linux distributions and, if not, it is easily installable through standard means. We assume that Python 2.7+ Version is installed on your workstation.

 Almost all code should work with Python 3.3+ Versions, but since most operating systems still deliver Python 2.7 (some even Python 2.6), we decided to write the Python 2.7 Version code. The differences are small, mainly in the version of packages and some code (xrange should be substituted with range in Python 3.3+).

We also assume that you know how to use your OS package manager in order to install software packages and know how to use a terminal.

The build requirements must be satisfied before matplotlib can be built.

matplotlib requires **NumPy**, **libpng**, and **freetype** as build dependencies. In order to be able to build matplotlib from source, we must have installed NumPy. Here's how to do it:

Install NumPy (1.5+ if you want to use it with Python 3) from http://www.numpy.org/

NumPy will provide us with data structures and mathematical functions for using it with large datasets. Python's default data structures such as tuples, lists, or dictionaries are great for insertions, deletions, and concatenation. NumPy's data structures support "vectorized" operations and are very efficient for use and for executions. They are implemented with big data in mind and rely on C implementations that allow efficient execution time.

 SciPy, building on top of NumPy, is the de facto standard's scientific and numeric toolkit for Python comprising a great selection of special functions and algorithms, most of them actually implemented in C and Fortran, coming from the well-known Netlib repository (http://www.netlib.org).

Perform the following steps for installing NumPy:

1. Install the Python-NumPy package:

```
sudo apt-get install python-numpy
```

2. Check the installed version:

```
$ python -c 'import numpy; print numpy.__version__'
```

3. Install the required libraries:

   ❑ **libpng 1.2**: PNG files support (requires zlib)

   ❑ **freetype 1.4+**: True type font support

```
$ sudo apt-get build-dep python-matplotlib
```

If you are using RedHat or a variation of this distribution (Fedora, SciLinux, or CentOS), you can use yum to perform the same installation:

```
$ su -c 'yum-builddep python-matplotlib'
```

How to do it...

There are many ways one can install matplotlib and its dependencies: from source, precompiled binaries, OS package manager, and with prepackaged Python distributions with built-in matplotlib.

Most probably the easiest way is to use your distribution's package manager. For Ubuntu that should be:

```
# in your terminal, type:
$ sudo apt-get install python-numpy python-matplotlib python-scipy
```

If you want to be on the bleeding edge, the best option is to install from source. This path comprises a few steps: get the source code, build requirements, and configure, compile, and install.

Download the latest source from code host SourceForge by following these steps:

```
$ cd ~/Downloads/
$ wget https://downloads.sourceforge.net/project/matplotlib/matplotlib/
matplotlib-1.3.1/matplotlib-1.3.1.tar.gz
$ tar xzf matplotlib-1.4.3.tar.gz
$ cd matplotlib-1.4.3
$ python setup.py build
$ sudo python setup.py install
```

Downloading the example code

You can download the example code files for all the Packt books you have purchased from your account at http://www.packtpub.com. If you purchased this book elsewhere, you can visit http://www.packtpub.com/support and register to have the files e-mailed directly to you.

How it works...

We use standard **Python Distribution Utilities**, known as **Distutils**, to install matplotlib from the source code. This procedure requires us to previously install dependencies, as we already explained in the *Getting ready* section of this recipe. The dependencies are installed using the standard Linux packaging tools.

There's more...

There are more optional packages that you might want to install depending on what your data visualization projects are about.

No matter what project you are working on, we recommend installing **IPython**—an **Interactive Python** shell where you already have matplotlib and related packages, such as NumPy and SciPy, imported and ready to play with. Please refer to IPython's official site on how to install it and use it—it is, though, very straightforward.

Installing virtualenv and virtualenvwrapper

If you are working on many projects simultaneously, or even just switching between them frequently, you'll find that having everything installed system-wide is not the best option and can bring problems in future on different systems (production) where you want to run your software. This is not a good time to find out that you are missing a certain package or you're having versioning conflicts between packages that are already installed on production system; hence, **virtualenv**.

virtualenv is an open source project started by Ian Bicking that enables a developer to isolate working environments per project, for easier maintenance of different package versions.

For example, you inherited legacy Django website based on Django 1.1 and Python 2.3, but at the same time you are working on a new project that must be written in Python 2.6. This is my usual case—having more than one required Python version (and related packages)— depending on the project I am working on.

virtualenv enables me to easily switch between different environments and have the same package easily reproduced if I need to switch to another machine or to deploy software to a production server (or to a client's workstation).

Getting ready

To install virtualenv, you must have a workable installation of Python and **pip**. Pip is a tool for installing and managing Python packages, and it is a replacement for `easy_install`. We will use pip through most of this book for package management. Pip is easily installed, as root executes the following line in your terminal:

```
# easy_install pip
```

virtualenv by itself is really useful, but with the help of **virtualenvwrapper**, all this becomes easy to do and also easy to organize many virtual environments. See all the features at `http://virtualenvwrapper.readthedocs.org/en/latest/#features`.

How to do it...

By performing the following steps, you can install the virtualenv and virtualenvwrapper tools:

1. Install virtualenv and virtualenvwrapper:

   ```
   $ sudo pip install virtualenv
   $ sudo pip install virtualenvwrapper
   # Create folder to hold all our virtual environments and export
   the path to it.
   $ export VIRTENV=~/.virtualenvs
   $ mkdir -p $VIRTENV
   # We source (ie. execute) shell script to activate the wrappers
   $ source /usr/local/bin/virtualenvwrapper.sh
   # And create our first virtual environment
   $ mkvirtualenv virt1
   ```

2. You can now install our favorite package inside `virt1`:

   ```
   (virt1)user1:~$ pip install matplotlib
   ```

3. You will probably want to add the following line to your `~/.bashrc` file:

   ```
   source /usr/loca/bin/virtualenvwrapper.sh
   ```

A few useful and most frequently used commands are as follows:

- `mkvirtualenv ENV`: This creates a virtual environment with the name `ENV` and activates it
- `workon ENV`: This activates the previously created `ENV`
- `deactivate`: This gets us out of the current virtual environment

pip not only provides you with a practical way of installing packages, but it also is a good solution for keeping track of the python packages installed on your system, as well as their version. The command `pip freeze` will print all the installed packages on your current environment, followed by their version number:

```
$ pip freeze
matplotlib==1.4.3
mock==1.0.1
nose==1.3.6
numpy==1.9.2
pyparsing==2.0.3
python-dateutil==2.4.2
pytz==2015.2
six==1.9.0
wsgiref==0.1.2
```

In this case, we see that even though we simply installed matplotlib, many other packages are also installed. Apart from `wsgiref`, which is used by pip itself, these are required dependencies of matplotlib which have been automatically installed.

When transferring a project from an environment (possibly a virtual environment) to another, the receiving environment needs to have all the necessary packages installed (in the same version as in the original environment) in order to be sure that the code can be properly run. This can be problematic as two different environments might not contain the same packages, and, worse, might contain different versions of the same package. This can lead to conflicts or unexpected behaviors in the execution of the program.

In order to avoid this problem, `pip freeze` can be used to save a copy of the current environment configuration. The command will save the output of the command to the file `requirements.txt`:

```
$ pip freeze > requirements.txt
```

In a new environment, this file can be used to install all the required libraries. Simply run:

```
$ pip install -r requirements.txt
```

All the necessary packages will automatically be installed in their specified version. That way, we ensure that the environment where the code is used is always the same. This is a good practice to have a virtual environment and a `requirements.txt` file for every project you are developing. Therefore, before installing the required packages, it is advised that you first create a new virtual environment to avoid conflicts with other projects.

The overall workflow from one machine to another is therefore:

- ▶ On machine 1:

```
$ mkvirtualenv env1
(env1)$ pip install matplotlib
(env1)$ pip freeze > requirements.txt
```

- ▶ On machine 2:

```
$ mkvirtualenv env2
(env2)$ pip install -r requirements.txt
```

Installing matplotlib on Mac OS X

The easiest way to get matplotlib on the Mac OS X is to use prepackaged python distributions such as **Enthought Python Distribution** (**EPD**). Just go to the EPD site, and download and install the latest stable version for your OS.

In case you are not satisfied with EPD or cannot use it for other reasons such as the versions distributed with it, there is a manual (read: harder) way of installing Python, matplotlib, and its dependencies.

Getting ready

We will use the **Homebrew** (you could also use MacPorts in the same way) project that eases the installation of all software that Apple did not install on your OS, including Python and matplotlib. Under the hood, Homebrew is a set of Ruby and Git that automate download and installation. Following these instructions should get the installation working. First, we will install Homebrew, and then Python, followed by tools such as virtualenv, then dependencies for matplotlib (NumPy and SciPy), and finally matplotlib. Hold on, here we go.

How to do it...

1. In your terminal, paste and execute the following command:

```
ruby -e "$(curl -fsSL https://raw.githubusercontent.com/Homebrew/
install/master/install)"
```

After the command finishes, try running brew update or brew doctor to verify that the installation is working properly.

2. Next, add the `Homebrew` directory to your system path, so the packages you install using Homebrew have greater priority than other versions. Open `~/.bash_profile` (or `/Users/[your-user-name]/.bash_profile`) and add the following line to the end of file:

   export PATH=/usr/local/bin:$PATH

3. You will need to restart the terminal so that it picks a new path. Installing Python is as easy as firing up another one liner:

   `brew install python --framework --universal`

   This will also install any prerequisites required by Python.

4. Now, you need to update your path (add to the same line):

   `export PATH=/usr/local/share/python:/usr/local/bin:$PATH`

5. To verify that the installation has worked, type `python --version` in the command line, you should see 2.7.3 as the version number in the response.

6. You should have pip installed by now. In case it is not installed, use `easy_install` to add pip:

   $ easy_install pip

7. Now, it's easy to install any required package; for example, `virtualenv` and `virtualenvwrapper` are useful:

   pip install virtualenv
   pip install virtualenvwrapper

8. The next step is what we really wanted to do all along—install matplotlib:

   pip install numpy
   brew install gfortran
   pip install scipy

9. Verify that everything is working. Call Python and execute the following commands:

   import numpy
   print numpy.__version__
   import scipy
   print scipy.__version__
   quit()

10. Install `matplotlib`:

    pip install matplotlib

Installing matplotlib on Windows

In this recipe, we will demonstrate how to install Python and start working with matplotlib installation. We assume Python was not previously installed.

Getting ready

There are two ways of installing matplotlib on Windows. The easiest way is by installing prepackaged Python environments, such as **EPD**, **Anaconda**, **SageMath**, and **Python(x,y)**. This is the suggested way to install Python, especially for beginners.

The second way is to install everything using binaries of precompiled matplotlib and required dependencies. This is more difficult as you have to be careful about the versions of NumPy and SciPy you are installing, as not every version is compatible with the latest version of matplotlib binaries. The advantage in this is that you can even compile your particular versions of matplotlib or any library to have the latest features, even if they are not provided by authors.

How to do it...

The suggested way of installing free or commercial Python scientific distributions is as easy as following the steps provided on the project's website.

If you just want to start using matplotlib and don't want to be bothered with Python versions and dependencies, you may want to consider using the **Enthought Python Distribution** (**EPD**). EPD contains prepackaged libraries required to work with matplotlib and all the required dependencies (SciPy, NumPy, IPython, and more).

As usual, we download Windows installer (`*.exe`) that will install all the code we need to start using matplotlib and all recipes from this book.

There is also a free scientific project Python(x,y) (`http://python-xy.github.io`) for Windows 32-bit system that contains all dependencies resolved, and is an easy (and free!) way of installing matplotlib on Windows. Since Python(x,y) is compatible with Python modules installers, it can be easily extended with other Python libraries. No Python installation should be present on the system before installing Python(x,y).

Let me shortly explain how we would install matplotlib using precompiled Python, NumPy, SciPy, and matplotlib binaries:

1. First, we download and install standard Python using the official `.msi` installer for our platform (x86 or x86-64).

2. After that, download official binaries for NumPy and SciPy and install them first.

3. When you are sure that NumPy and SciPy are properly installed. Then, we download the latest stable release binary for matplotlib and install it by following the official instructions.

There's more...

Note that many examples are not included in the Windows installer. If you want to try the demos, download the matplotlib source and look in the examples subdirectory.

Installing Python Imaging Library (PIL) for image processing

Python Imaging Library (**PIL**) enables image processing using Python. It has an extensive file format support and is powerful enough for image processing.

Some popular features of PIL are fast access to data, point operations, filtering, image resizing, rotation, and arbitrary affine transforms. For example, the histogram method allows us to get statistics about the images.

PIL can also be used for other purposes, such as batch processing, image archiving, creating thumbnails, conversion between image formats, and printing images.

PIL reads a large number of formats, while write support is (intentionally) restricted to the most commonly used interchange and presentation formats.

How to do it...

The easiest and most recommended way is to use your platform's package managers. For Debian and Ubuntu use the following commands:

```
$ sudo apt-get build-dep python-imaging
$ sudo pip install http://effbot.org/downloads/Imaging-1.1.7.tar.gz
```

How it works...

This way we are satisfying all build dependencies using the apt-get system but also installing the latest stable release of PIL. Some older versions of Ubuntu usually don't provide the latest releases.

On RedHat and SciLinux systems, run the following commands:

```
# yum install python-imaging
# yum install freetype-devel
# pip install PIL
```

There's more...

There is a good online handbook, specifically, for PIL. You can read it at http://www.pythonware.com/library/pil/handbook/index.htm or download the PDF version from http://www.pythonware.com/media/data/pil-handbook.pdf.

There is also a PIL fork, Pillow, whose main aim is to fix installation issues. Pillow can be found at http://pypi.python.org/pypi/Pillow and it is easy to install (at the time of writing, Pillow is the only choice if you are using OS X).

On Windows, PIL can also be installed using a binary installation file. Install PIL in your Python site-packages by executing .exe from http://www.pythonware.com/products/pil/.

Now, if you want PIL used in a virtual environment, manually copy the PIL.pth file and the PIL directory at C:\Python27\Lib\site-packages to your virtualenv site-packages directory.

Installing a requests module

Most of the data that we need now is available over HTTP or similar protocol, so we need something to get it. Python library requests make the job easy.

Even though Python comes with the urllib2 module for work with remote resources and supporting HTTP capabilities, it requires a lot of work to get the basic tasks done.

A requests module brings a new API that makes the use of web services seamless and pain free. Lots of the HTTP 1.1 stuff is hidden away and exposed only if you need it to behave differently than default.

How to do it...

Using pip is the best way to install `requests`. Use the following command for the same:

```
$ pip install requests
```

That's it. This can also be done inside your virtualenv, if you don't need requests for every project or want to support different requests versions for each project.

Just to get you ahead quickly, here's a small example on how to use requests:

```
import requests
r = requests.get('http://github.com/timeline.json')
print r.content
```

How it works...

We sent the `GET HTTP` request to a URI at `www.github.com` that returns a JSON-formatted timeline of activity on GitHub (you can see HTML version of that timeline at `https://github.com/timeline`). After the response is successfully read, the `r` object contains content and other properties of the response (response code, cookies set, header metadata, and even the request we sent in order to get this response).

Customizing matplotlib's parameters in code

The library we will use the most throughout this book is matplotlib; it provides the plotting capabilities. Default values for most properties are already set inside the configuration file for matplotlib, called `.rc` file. This recipe describes how to modify matplotlib properties from our application code.

Getting ready

As we already said, matplotlib configuration is read from a configuration file. This file provides a place to set up permanent default values for certain matplotlib properties, well, for almost everything in matplotlib.

How to do it...

There are two ways to change parameters during code execution: using the dictionary of parameters (`rcParams`) or calling the `matplotlib.rc()` command. The former enables us to load an already existing dictionary into `rcParams`, while the latter enables a call to a function using a tuple of keyword arguments.

If we want to restore the dynamically changed parameters, we can use `matplotlib.rcdefaults()` call to restore the standard matplotlib settings.

The following two code samples illustrate previously explained behaviors:

▶ An example for `matplotlib.rcParams`:

```
import matplotlib as mpl
mpl.rcParams['lines.linewidth'] = 2
mpl.rcParams['lines.color'] = 'r'
```

▶ An example for the `matplotlib.rc()` call:

```
import matplotlib as mpl
mpl.rc('lines', linewidth=2, color='r')
```

Both examples are semantically the same. In the second sample, we define that all subsequent plots will have lines with line width of 2 points. The last statement of the previous code defines that the color of every line following this statement will be red, unless we override it by local settings. See the following example:

```
import matplotlib.pyplot as plt
import numpy as np


t = np.arange(0.0, 1.0, 0.01)


s = np.sin(2 * np.pi * t)
# make line red
plt.rcParams['lines.color'] = 'r'
plt.plot(t,s)


c = np.cos(2 * np.pi * t)
# make line thick
plt.rcParams['lines.linewidth'] = '3'
plt.plot(t,c)


plt.show()
```

How it works...

First, we import `matplotlib.pyplot` and NumPy to allow us to draw sine and cosine graphs. Before plotting the first graph, we explicitly set the line color to red using the `plt.rcParams['lines.color'] = 'r'` command.

Next, we go to the second graph (cosine function) and explicitly set the line width to three points using the `plt.rcParams['lines.linewidth'] = '3'` command.

If we want to reset specific settings, we should call `matplotlib.rcdefaults()`.

In this recipe, we have seen how to customize the style of a matplotlib chart dynamically changing its configuration parameters. The `matplotlib.rcParams` object is the interface that we used to modify the parameters. It's global to the matplotlib packages and any change that we apply to it affects all the charts that we draw after.

Customizing matplotlib's parameters per project

This recipe explains where the various configuration files are that matplotlib uses and why we want to use one or the other. Also, we explain what is in these configuration files.

Getting ready

If you don't want to configure matplotlib as the first step in your code every time you use it (as we did in the previous recipe), this recipe will explain how to have different default configurations of matplotlib for different projects. This way your code will not be cluttered with configuration data and, moreover, you can easily share configuration templates with your co-workers or even among other projects.

How to do it...

If you have a working project that always uses the same settings for certain parameters in matplotlib, you probably don't want to set them every time you want to add a new graph code. Instead, what you want is a permanent file, outside of your code, which sets defaults for matplotlib parameters.

matplotlib supports this via its `matplotlibrc` configuration file that contains most of the changeable properties of matplotlib.

How it works...

There are three different places where this file can reside and its location defines its usage. They are:

- ▶ **Current working directory**: This is where your code runs from. This is the place to customize matplotlib just for your current directory that might contain your current project code. The file is named `matplotlibrc`.

- ▶ **Per user .matplotlib/matplotlibrc**: This is usually in the user's `$HOME` directory (under `Windows`, this is your `Documents and Settings` directory). You can find out where your configuration directory is using the `matplotlib.get_configdir()` command. Check the next command.

- ▶ **Per installation configuration file**: This is usually in your Python site-packages. This is a system-wide configuration, but it will get overwritten every time you reinstall matplotlib; so, it is better to use a per user configuration file for more persistent customizations. The best usage so far for me was to use this as a default template, if I mess up my user's configuration file or if I need fresh configuration to customize for a different project.

The following one liner will print the location of your configuration directory and can be run from shell:

```
$ python -c 'import matplotlib as mpl; print mpl.get_configdir()'
```

The configuration file contains settings for:

- ▶ **axes**: This deals with face and edge color, tick sizes, and grid display.
- ▶ **backend**: This sets the target output: `TkAgg` and `GTKAgg`.
- ▶ **figure**: This deals with dpi, edge color, figure size, and subplot settings.
- ▶ **font**: This looks at font families, font size, and style settings.
- ▶ **grid**: This deals with grid color and line settings.
- ▶ **legend**: This specifies how legends and text inside will be displayed.
- ▶ **lines**: This checks for line (color, style, width, and so on) and markers settings.
- ▶ **patch**: These patches are graphical objects that fill 2D space, such as polygons and circles; set linewidth, color, antialiasing, and so on.
- ▶ **savefig**: There are separate settings for saved figures. For example, to make rendered files with a white background.
- ▶ **text**: This looks for text color, how to interpret text (plain versus latex markup) and similar.

- ▶ **verbose**: This checks how much information matplotlib gives during runtime: silent, helpful, debug, and debug annoying.

- ▶ **xticks** and **yticks**: These set the color, size, direction, and label size for major and minor ticks for the *x* and *y* axes.

There's more...

If you are interested in more details for every mentioned setting (and some that we did not mention here), the best place to go is the website of the matplotlib project where there is up-to-date API documentation. If it doesn't help, user and development lists are always good places to leave questions. See the back of this book for useful online resources.

2

Knowing Your Data

In this chapter, we'll cover the following topics:

- ▶ Importing data from CSV
- ▶ Importing data from Microsoft Excel files
- ▶ Importing data from fixed-width data files
- ▶ Importing data from tab-delimited files
- ▶ Importing data from a JSON resource
- ▶ Exporting data to JSON, CSV, and Excel
- ▶ Importing and manipulating data with Pandas
- ▶ Importing data from a database
- ▶ Cleaning up data from outliers
- ▶ Reading files in chunks
- ▶ Reading streaming data sources
- ▶ Importing image data into NumPy arrays
- ▶ Generating controlled random datasets
- ▶ Smoothing the noise in real-world data

Introduction

This chapter covers basics about importing and exporting data from various formats. We first introduce how to import data by just using only the capabilities of the Python standard library; then we introduce the powerful Pandas library which is becoming the de facto standard in data manipulation in Python. Also we've covered the ways of cleaning data such as normalizing values, adding missing data, live data inspection, and usage of some similar tricks to get data correctly prepared for visualization.

Importing data from CSV

In this recipe, we'll work with the most common file format that you will encounter in the wild world of data—**CSV**. It stands for **Comma Separated Values**, which almost explains all the formatting there is. (There is also a header part of the file, but those values are also comma separated.)

Python has a module called csv that supports reading and writing CSV files in various dialects. Dialects are important because there is no standard CSV, and different applications implement CSV in slightly different ways. A file's dialect is almost always recognizable by the first look into the file.

Getting ready

What we need for this recipe is the CSV file itself. We'll use sample CSV data that you can download from ch02-data.csv.

We assume that sample data files are in the same folder as the code reading them.

How to do it...

The following code example demonstrates how to import data from a CSV file. We will perform the following steps for this:

1. Open the ch02-data.csv file for reading.
2. Read the header first.
3. Read the rest of the rows.
4. In case there is an error, raise an exception.
5. After reading everything, print the header and the rest of the rows.

This is shown in the following code:

```
import csv

filename = 'ch02-data.csv'

data = []
try:
    with open(filename) as f:
        reader = csv.reader(f)
        header = reader.next()
        data = [row for row in reader]
```

```
except csv.Error as e:
    print "Error reading CSV file at line %s: %s" % (reader.line_num,
e)
    sys.exit(-1)
if header:
    print header
    print '=================='

for datarow in data:
    print datarow
```

How it works...

First, we import the `csv` module in order to enable access to the required methods. Then, we open the file with data using the `with` compound statement and bind it to the object `f`. The context manager `with` statement releases us of care about the closing resource after we are finished manipulating those resources. It is a very handy way of working with resource-like files because it makes sure that the resource is freed (for example, that the file is closed) after the block of code is executed over it.

Then, we use the `csv.reader()` method that returns the `reader` object, which allows us to iterate over all rows of the read file. Every row is just a list of values and is printed inside the loop.

Reading the first row is somewhat different as it is the header of the file and describes the data in each column. This is not mandatory for CSV files and some files don't have headers, but they are a really nice way of providing minimal metadata about datasets. Sometimes though, you will find separate text or even CSV files that are just used as metadata describing the format and additional data about the data.

The only way to check what the first line looks like is to open the file and visually inspect it (for example, see the first few lines of the file)... This can be done efficiently on Linux using bash commands like `head` as shown here:

```
$ head some_file.csv
```

During iteration of data, we save the first row in `header` while we add every other row to the `data` list.

We can also check if the `.csv` file has a header or not using the method `csv.has_header`.

Should any errors occur during reading, `csv.reader()` will generate an error that we can catch and then print the helpful message to the user in order to help detection of errors.

There's more...

If you want to read about the background and reasoning for the `csv` module, the PEP-defined document *CSV File API* is available at `http://www.python.org/dev/peps/pep-0305/`.

If you have larger files that you want to load, it's often better to use well-known libraries like NumPy's `loadtxt()` that cope better with large CSV files.

The basic usage is simple as shown in the following code snippet:

```
import numpy
data = numpy.loadtxt('ch02-data.csv', dtype='string', delimiter=',')
```

Note that we need to define a delimiter to instruct NumPy to separate our data as appropriate. The function `numpy.loadtxt()` is somewhat faster than the similar function `numpy.genfromtxt()`, but the latter can cope better with missing data, and you are able to provide functions to express what is to be done during the processing of certain columns of loaded data files.

Currently, the csv module doesn't support Unicode, and so you must explicitly convert the read data into UTF-8 or ASCII printable. The official Python CSV documentation offers good examples on how to resolve data encoding issues.

In Python 3.3 and later versions, Unicode support is default and there are no such issues.

Importing data from Microsoft Excel files

Although Microsoft Excel supports some charting, sometimes you need more flexible and powerful visualization and need to export data from existing spreadsheets into Python for further use.

A common approach to importing data from Excel files is to export data from Excel into CSV-formatted files and use the tools described in the previous recipe to import data using Python from the CSV file. This is a fairly easy process if we have one or two files (and have Microsoft Excel or OpenOffice.org installed), but if we are automating a data pipe for many files (as part of an ongoing data processing effort), we are not in a position to manually convert every Excel file into CSV. So, we need a way to read any Excel file.

Python has decent support for reading and writing Excel files through the project `www.python-excel.org`. This support is available in the form of different modules for reading and writing and is platform-independent; in other words, we don't have to run it on Windows in order to read Excel files.

The Microsoft Excel file format changed over time, and support for different versions is available in different Python libraries. The latest stable version of XLRD is 0.90 at the time of this writing and it has support for reading `.xlsx` files.

Getting ready

First, we need to install the required module. For this example, we will use the module `xlrd`. We will use pip in our virtual environment, as shown in the following code:

```
$ mkvirtualenv xlrdexample
(xlrdexample)$ pip install xlrd
```

After successful installation, use the sample file `ch02-xlsxdata.xlsx`.

How to do it...

The following code example demonstrates how to read a sample dataset from a known Excel file. We will do this as shown in the following steps:

1. Open the file workbook.
2. Find the sheet by name.
3. Read the cells using the number of rows (`nrows`) and columns (`ncols`).
4. For demonstration purposes, we only print the read dataset.

This is shown in the following code:

```python
import xlrd

file = 'ch02-xlsxdata.xlsx'

wb = xlrd.open_workbook(filename=file)

ws = wb.sheet_by_name('Sheet1')

dataset = []

for r in xrange(ws.nrows):
    col = []
    for c in range(ws.ncols):
        col.append(ws.cell(r, c).value)
    dataset.append(col)

from pprint import pprint
pprint(dataset)
```

How it works...

Let's try to explain the simple object model that `xlrd` uses. At the top level, we have a workbook (the Python class `xlrd.book.Book`) that consists of one or more worksheets (`xlrd.sheet.Sheet`), and every sheet has a cell (`xlrd.sheet.Cell`) from which we can then read the value.

We load a workbook from a file using `open_workbook()`, which returns the `xlrd.book.Book` instance that contains all the information about a workbook like sheets. We access sheets using `sheet_by_name()`; if we need all sheets, we could use `sheets()`, which returns a list of the `xlrd.sheet.Sheet` instances. The `xlrd.sheet.Sheet` class has a number of columns and rows as attributes that we can use to infer ranges for our loop to access every particular cell inside a worksheet using the method `cell()`. There is an `xrld.sheet.Cell` class, though it is not something we want to use directly.

Note that the date is stored as a floating point number and not as a separate data type, but the `xlrd` module is able to inspect the value and try to infer if the data is in fact a date. So, we can inspect the cell type for the cell to get the Python date object. The module `xlrd` will return `xlrd.XL_CELL_DATE` as the cell type if the number format string looks like a date. Here is a snippet of code that demonstrates this:

```
from datetime import datetime
from xlrd import open_workbook, xldate_as_tuple
...
cell = sheet.cell(1, 0)
print cell
print cell.value
print cell.ctype
if cell.ctype == xlrd.XL_CELL_DATE:
    date_value = xldate_as_tuple(cell.value, book.datemode)
    print datetime(*date_value)
```

This field still has issues, so please refer to the official documentation and mailing list in case you require extensive work with dates.

There's more...

A neat feature of `xlrd` is its ability to load only parts of the file that are required in the memory. There is an `on_demand` parameter that can be passed as `True` value while calling `open_workbook` so that the worksheet will only be loaded when requested. See the following example of code snippet for this:

```
book = open_workbook('large.xls', on_demand=True)
```

We didn't mention writing Excel files in this section partly because there will be a separate recipe for that and partly because there is a different module for that—xlwt. You will read more about it in the *Exporting data to JSON, CSV, and Excel* recipe in this chapter.

If you need specific usage that was not covered with the module and examples explained earlier, here is a list of other Python modules on **PyPi** that might help you out with spreadsheets http://pypi.python.org/pypi?:action=browse&c=377.

Importing data from fixed-width data files

Log files from events and time series data files are common sources for data visualizations. Sometimes, we can read them using CSV dialect for tab-separated data, but sometimes they are not separated by any specific character. Instead, fields are of fixed widths and we can infer the format to match and extract data.

One way to approach this is to read a file line by line and then use string manipulation functions to split a string into separate parts. This approach seems straightforward, and if performance is not an issue, it should be tried first.

If performance is more important or the file to parse is large (hundreds of megabytes), using the Python module struct (http://docs.python.org/library/struct.html) can speed us up as the module is implemented in C rather than in Python.

Getting ready

As the module struct is part of the Python Standard Library, we don't need to install any additional software to implement this recipe.

How to do it...

We will use a pregenerated dataset with a million rows of fixed-width records. Here's what sample data looks like:

```
...
207152670 3984356804116 9532
427053180 1466959270421 5338
316700885 9726131532544 4920
138359697 3286515244210 7400
476953136 0921567802830 4214
213420370 6459362591178 0546
...
```

This dataset is generated using code that can be found in the repository for this chapter—ch02-generate_f_data.py.

Now we can read the data. We can use the following code sample. We will carry out the following steps for this:

1. Define the data file to read.

2. Define the mask for how to read the data.

3. Read line by line using the mask to unpack each line into separate data fields.

4. Print each line as separate fields.

This is shown in the following code snippet:

```
import struct
import string

datafile = 'ch02-fixed-width-1M.data'

# this is where we define how to
# understand line of data from the file
mask='9s14s5s'

with open(datafile, 'r') as f:
    for line in f:
        fields = struct.Struct(mask).unpack_from(line)
        print 'fields: ', [field.strip() for field in fields]
```

How it works...

We define our format mask according to what we have previously seen in the datafile. To see the file, we could have used Linux shell commands such as `head` or `more` or something similar.

String formats are used to define the expected layout of the data to extract. We use format characters to define what type of data we expect. So if the mask is defined as `9s15s5s`, we can read that as "a string of nine character width, followed by a string width of 15 characters and then again followed by a string of five characters."

In general, `c` defines the character (the `char` type in C) or a string of length 1, `s` defines a string (the `char []` type in C), `d` defines a float (the `double` type in C), and so on. The complete table is available on the official Python website at `http://docs.python.org/library/struct.html#format-characters`.

We then read the file line by line and extract (the `unpack_from` method) the line according to the specified format. Because we might have extraneous spaces before (or after) our fields, we use `strip()` to strip every extracted field.

For unpacking, we used the **object-oriented** (**OO**) approach using the `struct.Struct` class, but we could have as well used the non-object approach where the line would be as shown here:

```
fields = struct.unpack_from(mask, line)
```

The only difference is the usage of pattern. If we are to perform more processing using the same formatting mask, the OO approach saves us from stating that format in every call. Moreover, it gives us the ability to inherit the `struct.Struct` class in future, thus extending or providing additional functionality for specific needs.

Importing data from tab-delimited files

Another very common format of flat datafile is the tab-delimited file. This can also come from an Excel export but can be the output of some custom software we must get our input from.

The good thing is that usually this format can be read in almost the same way as CSV files as the Python module `csv` supports the so-called dialects that enable us to use the same principles to read variations of similar file formats, one of them being the tab- delimited format.

Getting ready

Now you're already able to read CSV files. If not, please refer to the *Importing data from CSV* recipe first.

How to do it...

We will reuse the code from the *Importing data from CSV* recipe, where all we need to change is the dialect we are using as shown in the following code:

```
import csv

filename = 'ch02-data.tab'

data = []
try:
    with open(filename) as f:
        reader = csv.reader(f, dialect=csv.excel_tab)
        header = reader.next()
        data = [row for row in reader]
except csv.Error as e:
    print "Error reading CSV file at line %s: %s" % (reader.line_num,
e)
    sys.exit(-1)
```

```
if header:
    print header
    print '=================='

for datarow in data:
    print datarow
```

How it works...

The dialect-based approach is very similar to what we already did in the *Importing data from CSV* recipe, except for the line where we instantiate the `csv` reader object, giving it the parameter `dialect` and specifying the `excel_tab` dialect that we want.

There's more...

A CSV-based approach will not work if the data is "dirty", that is, if there are certain lines not ending with just a new line character but have additional \t (*Tab*) markers. So we need to clean special lines separately before splitting them. The sample "dirty" tab-delimited file can be found in `ch02-data-dirty.tab`. The following code sample cleans data as it reads it:

```
datafile = 'ch02-data-dirty.tab'

with open(datafile, 'r') as f:
    for line in f:
        # remove next comment to see line before cleanup
        # print 'DIRTY: ', line.split('\t')

        # we remove any space in line start or end
        line = line.strip()

        # now we split the line by tab delimiter
        print line.split('\t')
```

We also see that there is another approach to do this—using the `split('\t')` function.

The advantage of using the `csv` module approach over `split()` is that we can reuse the same code for reading by just changing the dialect and detecting it with the file extension (`.csv` and `.tab`) or some other method (for example, using the `csv.Sniffer` class).

Importing data from a JSON resource

This recipe will show us how we can read the JSON data format. Moreover, we'll be using a remote resource in this recipe. It will add a tiny level of complexity to the recipe, but it will also make it much more useful because in real life we will encounter more remote resources than local ones.

JavaScript Object Notation (**JSON**) is widely used as a platform-independent format to exchange data between systems or applications.

A resource, in this context, is anything we can read, be it a file or a URL endpoint (which can be the output of a remote process/program or just a remote static file). In short, we don't care who produced a resource and how they did it; we just need it to be in a known format like JSON.

Getting ready

In order to get started with this recipe, we need the `requests` module installed and importable (in `PYTHONPATH`) in our virtual environment. We have installed this module in *Chapter 1, Preparing Your Working Environment*.

We also need Internet connectivity as we'll be reading a remote resource.

How to do it...

The following code sample performs reading and parsing of the recent activities' timeline from the GitHub (`http://github.com`) site. We will perform the following steps for this:

1. Define the GitHub URL of a JSON file with the details of a GitHub profile.
2. Get the contents from the URL using the `requests` module.
3. Read the content as JSON.

Here is the code for this:

```
import requests
from pprint import pprint
url = 'https://api.github.com/users/justglowing'
r = requests.get(url)
json_obj = r.json()pprint(json_obj)
```

How it works...

First, we use the "requests" module to fetch a remote resource. This is very straightforward as the "requests" module offers a simple API to define HTTP verbs, so we just need to issue one `get()` method call. This method retrieves data and request metadata and wraps it in the "Response" object, so we can inspect it. For this recipe, we are only interested in the `Response.json()` method, which automatically reads content (available at `Response.content`) and parses it as JSON and loads it into the JSON object.

Now that we have the JSON object, we can process the data. In order to do that, we need to understand what data looks like. We can achieve that understanding by opening the JSON resource using our favorite web browser or command-line tool such as `wget` or `curl`.

Another way is to fetch data from IPython and inspect it interactively. We can achieve that by running our program from IPython (using `%run program_name.py`). After execution, we are left with all variables that the program produced. List them all using `%who` or `%whos`.

Whatever method we use, we gain knowledge about the structure of the JSON data and the ability to see what parts of that structure we are interested in.

The JSON object is basically just a Python dictionary (or if stated in a more complex manner, a dictionary of dictionaries) and we can access parts of it using a well-known, key-based notation. In our example, the `.json` file contains the details of a GitHub profile and we can access the location of the user referencing `json_obj['location']`. If we compare the structure of the dictionary `json_obj` with that of the `.json` file, we see that each entry in the `.json` file corresponds to a key in the dictionary. This means that the entire content of the `.json` file is now into the dictionary (keep in mind that when you load a `.json` file, the order of the keys is not preserved!).

There's more...

The JSON format (specified by RFC 4627; refer to `http://tools.ietf.org/html/rfc4627.html`) became very popular recently as it is more human readable than XML and is also less verbose. Hence, it's lighter in terms of the syntaxes required to transfer data. It is very popular in the web application domain as it is native to JavaScript, the language used for most of today's rich Internet applications.

The Python JSON module has more capabilities than we have displayed here; for example, we could specialize the basic `JSONEncoder/JSONDecoder` class to transform our Python data into JSON format. The classical example uses this approach to JSON-ify the Python built-in type for complex numbers.

For simple customization, we don't have to subclass the `JSONDecoder/JSONEncoder` class as some of the parameters can solve our problems.

For example, `json.loads()` will parse a float as the Python type `float`, and most of the time it will be right. Sometimes, however, the float value in the `.json` file represents a price value, and this is better represented as a decimal. We can instruct the `json` parser to parse floats as decimal. For example, we have the following JSON string:

```
jstring = '{"name":"prod1","price":12.50}'
```

This is followed by these two lines of code:

```
from decimal import Decimal
json.loads(jstring, parse_float=Decimal)
```

The preceding two lines of code will generate this output:

```
{u'name': u'prod1', u'price': Decimal('12.50')}
```

Exporting data to JSON, CSV, and Excel

While as producers of data visualization, we are mostly using other people's data, importing and reading data are our major activities. We do need to write or export data that we produced or processed, whether it is for our or others' current or future use.

We will demonstrate how to use the previously mentioned Python modules to import, export, and write data to various formats such as JSON, CSV, and XLSX.

For demonstration purposes, we are using the pregenerated dataset from the *Importing data from fixed-width data files* recipe.

Getting ready

For the Excel writing part, we will need to install the `xlwt` module (inside our virtual environment) by executing the following command:

```
$ pip install xlwt
```

How to do it...

We will present one code sample that contains all the formats that we want to demonstrate: CSV, JSON, and XLSX. The main part of the program accepts the input and calls appropriate functions to transform data. We will walk through separate sections of code explaining its purpose, as shown here:

1. Import the required modules:

   ```
   import os
   import sys
   ```

```
import argparse

try:
    import cStringIO as StringIO
except:
    import StringIO
import struct
import json
import csv
```

2. Then, define the appropriate functions for reading and writing data:

```
def import_data(import_file):
    '''
    Imports data from import_file.
    Expects to find fixed width row
    Sample row: 161322597 0386544351896 0042
    '''
    mask = '9s14s5s'
    data = []
    with open(import_file, 'r') as f:
        for line in f:
            # unpack line to tuple
            fields = struct.Struct(mask).unpack_from(line)
            # strip any whitespace for each field
            # pack everything in a list and add to full dataset
            data.append(list([f.strip() for f in fields]))
    return data


def write_data(data, export_format):
    '''Dispatches call to a specific transformer and returns data
set.
    Exception is xlsx where we have to save data in a file.
    '''
    if export_format == 'csv':
        return write_csv(data)
    elif export_format == 'json':
        return write_json(data)
    elif export_format == 'xlsx':
        return write_xlsx(data)
    else:
        raise Exception("Illegal format defined")
```

3. We separately specify separate implementation for each data format (CSV, JSON, and XLSX):

```python
def write_csv(data):
    '''Transforms data into csv. Returns csv as string.
    '''
    # Using this to simulate file IO,
    # as csv can only write to files.
    f = StringIO.StringIO()
    writer = csv.writer(f)
    for row in data:
        writer.writerow(row)
    # Get the content of the file-like object
    return f.getvalue()


def write_json(data):
    '''Transforms data into json. Very straightforward.
    '''
    j = json.dumps(data)
    return j


def write_xlsx(data):
    '''Writes data into xlsx file.

    '''
    from xlwt import Workbook
    book = Workbook()
    sheet1 = book.add_sheet("Sheet 1")
    row = 0
    for line in data:
        col = 0
        for datum in line:
            print datum
            sheet1.write(row, col, datum)
            col += 1
        row += 1
        # We have hard limit here of 65535 rows
        # that we are able to save in spreadsheet.
        if row > 65535:
            print >> sys.stderr, "Hit limit of # of rows in one
sheet (65535)."
            break
    # XLS is special case where we have to
    # save the file and just return 0
    f = StringIO.StringIO()
    book.save(f)
    return f.getvalue()
```

4. Finally, we have the main code entry point, where we parse argument-like files from the command line to import data and export it to the required format:

```
if __name__ == '__main__':
    # parse input arguments
    parser = argparse.ArgumentParser()
    parser.add_argument("import_file", help="Path to a fixed-width
data file.")
    parser.add_argument("export_format", help="Export format:
json, csv, xlsx.")
    args = parser.parse_args()

    if args.import_file is None:
        print >> sys.stderr, "You must specify path to import
from."
        sys.exit(1)

    if args.export_format not in ('csv','json','xlsx'):
        print >> sys.stderr, "You must provide valid export file
format."
        sys.exit(1)

    # verify given path is accessible file
    if not os.path.isfile(args.import_file):
        print >> sys.stderr, "Given path is not a file: %s" %
args.import_file
        sys.exit(1)

    # read from formatted fixed-width file
    data = import_data(args.import_file)

    # export data to specified format
    # to make this Unix-like pipe-able
    # we just print to stdout
    print write_data(data, args.export_format)
```

How it works...

In one broad sentence, we import the fixed-width dataset (as defined in the *Importing data from fixed-width datafiles* recipe) and then export that to stdout, so we can catch that in a file or as an input to another program.

We call out the programmer from the command line giving two mandatory arguments: the input filename and the export data format (JSON, CSV, and XLSX).

If we successfully parse those arguments, we dispatch the input file reading to a function `import_data()`, which returns the Python data structure (list of lists) that we can easily manipulate to get to the appropriate export format.

We route our request inside the `write_data()` function, where we just forward a call to the appropriate function (for example, `write_csv()`).

For CSV, we obtain the `csv.writer()` instance that we use to write every line of data we iterate over.

We just return the given string as we will redirect this output from our program to another program (or just to copy in a file).

The JSON export is not required for this example as the `json` module provides us with the `dump()` method that happily reads our Python structure. Just as for CSV, we simply return and dump this output to `stdout`.

The Excel export requires more code as we need to create a more complex model of the Excel workbook and worksheet(s) that will hold the data. This activity is followed by a similar iterative approach. We have two loops— the outer one goes over every line in the source dataset iterated and the inner one iterates over every field in the given line.

After all this, we save the `Book` instance into a file-like stream that we can return to `stdout` and use it both in read files and the files consumed by the web service.

There's more...

This, of course, is just a small set of possible data formats that we could be exporting to. It is fairly easy to modify the behavior. Basically, two places need changes: the import and export functions. The function for import needs to change if we want to import a new kind of data source.

If we want to add a new export format, we need to first add functions that will return a stream of formatted data. Then, we need to update the `write_data()` function to add the new `elif` branch to have it call our new `write_*` function.

One thing we could also do is make this a Python package, so we can reuse it over more projects. In that case, we would like to make `import` more flexible and add some more configuration features for `import`.

Importing and manipulating data with Pandas

Until now we have seen how to import and export data using mostly the tools provided in the Python standard library. Now, we'll see how to do some of the operations shown above in just few lines using the Pandas library. Pandas is an open source, BSD-licensed library that simplifies the process of data import and manipulation thus providing data structures and parsing functions.

We will demonstrate how to import, manipulate and export data using Pandas.

Getting ready

To be able to use the code in this section, we need to install Pandas.This can be done again using pip as shown here:

```
pip install pandas
```

How to do it...

Here, we will import again the data `ch2-data.csv`, add a new column to the original data and export the result in csv, as shown in the following code snippet:

```
data = pd.read_csv('ch02-data.csv')
data['amount_x_2'] = data['amount']*2
data.to_csv('ch02-data_more.csv')
```

How it works...

First, we import Pandas in our environment and then we use the function `read_csv` on the file that we want to read. This function automatically parses the csv format and nicely organizes the data in an indexed structure called **DataFrame**. Then, we take the columns amount, we multiply each of its element by two and store the result in a new columns called *amount_x_2*. Finally, we save the result into a new file named `ch02-data_more.csv` using the method `to_csv`. A DataFrame is a Pandas object which represents a table and we can access its columns as shown in the following section

There's more...

DataFrames are very handy structures; they're designed to be fast and easy to access. Each column that they contain becomes an attribute of the object that represents the data frame. For example, we can print the values in the column amount of the object data defined earlier as shown here:

```
>>>print data.amount
>>>0 323 1 233 2 433 3 555 4 123 5 0 6 221 Name: amount, dtype: int64
```

We can also print the list of all the columns in a dataframe as shown in the following code:

```
>>>print data.columns
>>>Index([u'day', u'amount'], dtype='object')
```

Also, the function read_csv that we used to import the data has many parameters that we make use of to deal with messy files and parse particular data formats. For example, if the values of our files are delimited by spaces instead of commas, we can use the parameter delimiter to correctly parse the data. Here's an example of where we import data from a file, where the values are separated by a variable number of spaces and we specify our custom header:

```
pd.read_csv('ch02-data.tab', skiprows=1,
    delimiter=' *', names=['day','amount'])
```

Importing data from a database

Very often, our work on data analysis and visualization is at the consumer end of the data pipeline. We most often use the already produced data rather than producing the data ourselves. A modern application, for example, holds different datasets inside relational databases (or other databases like MongoDB), and we use these databases to produce beautiful graphs.

This recipe will show you how to use SQL drivers from Python to access data.

We will demonstrate this recipe using a SQLite database because it requires the least effort to set up, but the interface is similar to most other SQL-based database engines (MySQL and PostgreSQL). There are, however, differences in the SQL dialect that those database engines support. This example uses simple SQL language and should be reproducible on most common SQL database engines.

Getting ready

To be able to execute this recipe, we need to install the SQLite library as shown here:

```
$ sudo apt-get install sqlite3
```

Python support for SQLite is available by default, so we don't need to install anything Python-related. Just fire the following code snippet in IPython to verify that everything is present:

```
import sqlite3
sqlite3.version
sqlite3.sqlite_version
```

We get an output similar to this as shown here:

```
In [1]: import sqlite3


In [2]: sqlite3.version
Out[2]: '2.6.0'


In [3]: sqlite3.sqlite_version
Out[3]: '3.8.4.3'
```

Here, sqlite3.version gets us the version of the Python sqlite3 module, and sqlite_ version returns the system SQLite library version.

How to do it...

To be able to read from the database, we need to perform the following steps:

1. Connect to the database engine (or the file in the case of SQLite).
2. Run the query against the selected tables.
3. Read the result returned from the database engine.

I will not try to teach SQL here as there are many books on that particular topic. But just for the purpose of clarity, we will explain the SQL query in this code sample:

```
SELECT ID, Name, Population FROM City ORDER BY Population DESC LIMIT
1000
```

ID, Name, and Population are columns (fields) of the table City from which we select data. ORDER BY tells the database engine to sort our data by the Population column, and DESC means descending order. LIMIT allows us to get just the first 1,000 records found.

For this example, we will use the `world.sql` example table, which holds the world's city names and populations. This table has more than 5,000 entries.

First, we need to import this SQL file into the SQLite database. Here's is the code on how to do it:

```
import sqlite3
import sys

if len(sys.argv) < 2:
    print "Error: You must supply at least SQL script."
    print "Usage: %s table.db ./sql-dump.sql" % (sys.argv[0])
    sys.exit(1)

script_path = sys.argv[1]

if len(sys.argv) == 3:
    db = sys.argv[2]
else:
    # if DB is not defined
    # create memory database
    db = ":memory:"

try:
    con = sqlite3.connect(db)
    with con:
        cur = con.cursor()
        with open(script_path,'rb') as f:
            cur.executescript(f.read())
except sqlite3.Error as err:
    print "Error occurred: %s" % err
```

This reads the SQL file and executes the SQL statements against the opened SQLite db file. If we don't specify the filename, SQLite creates the database in the memory. The statements are then executed line by line.

If we encounter any errors, we catch exceptions and print the error message to the user.

After we have imported data into the database, we are able to query the data and do some processing. Here is the code to read the data from the database file:

```
import sqlite3
import sys

if len(sys.argv) != 2:
```

```
        print "Please specify database file."
        sys.exit(1)

    db = sys.argv[1]

    try:
        con = sqlite3.connect(db)
        with con:
            cur = con.cursor()
            query = 'SELECT ID, Name, Population FROM City ORDER BY
    Population DESC LIMIT 1000'
            con.text_factory = str
            cur.execute(query)

            resultset = cur.fetchall()

            # extract column names

            col_names = [cn[0] for cn in cur.description]
            print "%10s %30s %10s" % tuple(col_names)
            print "="*(10+1+30+1+10)

            for row in resultset:
                print "%10s %30s %10s" % row
    except sqlite3.Error as err:
        print "[ERROR]:", err
```

Here's an example of how to use the two preceding scripts:

```
$ python ch02-sqlite-import.py world.sql world.db
$ python ch02-sqlite-read.py world.db
        ID                             Name Population
========================================================
      1024                  Mumbai (Bombay)   10500000
      2331                            Seoul    9981619
       206                        S?o Paulo    9968485
      1890                         Shanghai    9696300
```

How it works...

First, we verify that the user has provided the database file path. This is just a quick check to ensure that we can proceed with the rest of the code.

Then, we try to connect to the database; if that fails, we catch `sqlite3.Error` and print it to the user.

If the connection is successful, we obtain a cursor using `con.cursor()`. A cursor is an iterator-like structure that enables us to traverse records of the result set returned from a database.

We define a query that we execute over the connection and we fetch the result set using `cur.fetchall()`. Had we expected just one result, we would have used just `fetchone()`.

List comprehension over `cur.description` allows us to obtain column names. description is a read-only attribute and returns more than we need for just column names, so we just fetch the first item from every column's 7-item tuple.

We then use simple string formatting to print the header of our table with column names. After that, we iterate over resultset and print every row in a similar manner.

There's more...

Databases are the most common sources of data today. We could not present everything in this short recipe, but we can suggest you where to look for more information.

The official Python documentation is the first place to look for an explanation about how to work with databases. The most common databases are open source databases, such as MySQL, PostgreSQL, and SQLite, and on the other end of the spectrum, there are enterprise database systems such as MS SQL, Oracle, and Sybase. Mostly Python has support for them and the interface is abstracted always, so you don't have to change your program if your underlying database changes, but some tweaks may be required. It depends on whether you have used the specifics of a particular database system. For example, Oracle supports a specific language PL/SQL that is not standard SQL, and some things will not work if your database changes from Oracle to MS SQL. Similarly, SQLite does not support specifics from MySQL data types or database engine types (**MyISAM** and **InnoDB**). Those things can be annoying, but having your code rely on standard SQL (available at `http://en.wikipedia.org/wiki/SQL:2011`) will make your code portable from one database system to another.

Cleaning up data from outliers

This recipe describes how to deal with datasets coming from the real world and how to clean them before doing any visualization.

We will present a few techniques, which are different in essence but have the same goal, to get the data cleaned.

Cleaning, however, should not be fully automatic. We need to understand the data as given and be able to understand what the outliers are and what the data points represent before we apply any of the robust modern algorithms made to clean the data. This is not something that can be defined in a recipe because it relies on vast areas such as statistics, knowledge of the domain, and a good eye (and then some luck).

Getting ready

We will use the standard Python modules we already know about, so no additional installation is required.

In this recipe, I will introduce a new. **Median absolute deviation** (**MAD**) in statistics represents a measure of the variability of a univariate (possessing one variable) sample of quantitative data. It is a measure of statistical dispersion. It falls into a group of robust statistics in a way that it is more resilient to outliers.

How to do it...

Here's one example that shows how to use MAD to detect outliers in our data. We will perform the following steps for this:

1. Generate normally distributed random data.
2. Add in a few outliers.
3. Use the function `is_outlier()` to detect the outliers.
4. Plot both the datasets (x and `filtered`) to see the difference.

Look at the following lines of code depicting this:

```
import numpy as np
import matplotlib.pyplot as plt

def is_outlier(points, threshold=3.5):
    """
    This returns a boolean array with "True" if points are outliers and
"False"
```

otherwise.

These are the data points with a modified z-score greater than this:

```
    # value will be classified as outliers.
    """
    # transform into vector
    if len(points.shape) == 1:
        points = points[:,None]

    # compute median value
    median = np.median(points, axis=0)

    # compute diff sums along the axis
    diff = np.sum((points - median)**2, axis=-1)
    diff = np.sqrt(diff)
    # compute MAD
    med_abs_deviation = np.median(diff)

    # compute modified Z-score
    # http://www.itl.nist.gov/div898/handbook/eda/section4/eda43.
htm#Iglewicz
    modified_z_score = 0.6745 * diff / med_abs_deviation

    # return a mask for each outlier
    return modified_z_score > threshold

# Random data
x = np.random.random(100)

# histogram buckets
buckets = 50

# Add in a few outliers
x = np.r_[x, -49, 95, 100, -100]

# Keep valid data points
# Note here that
# "~" is logical NOT on boolean numpy arrays
filtered = x[~is_outlier(x)]
# plot histograms
plt.figure()
```

```
plt.subplot(211)
plt.hist(x, buckets)
plt.xlabel('Raw')

plt.subplot(212)
plt.hist(filtered, buckets)
plt.xlabel('Cleaned')

plt.show()
```

Note that in NumPy, the ~ operator is overloaded to operate as a logical operator *and not* on Boolean arrays.

The preceding code produces two distinct histograms. The first one, which has been drawn using all the data, contains one main box with height 100 centered in 0.5 and three other very small boxes. This means that most of the samples were grouped in the first box and the other boxes just contain outliers. Indeed, in the second histogram, which has been drawn without the outliers, we can observe the details of the distribution of the data in the interval 0-1.

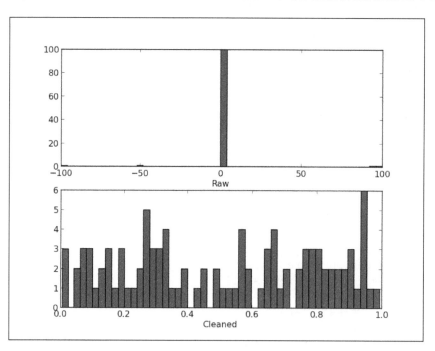

Another way to identify outliers is to visually inspect your data. In order to do so, we could create scatter plots, where we could easily spot values that are out of the central swarm or create a box plot, which will display the median, quartiles above and below the median, and points that are distant even from the extremes of the distribution of the data.

The box extends from the lower to the upper quartile values of the data, with a line at the median. The whiskers extend from the box to show the interquartile range. Flier points are those past the end of the whiskers.

Here's an example to demonstrate that:

```
from pylab import *

# fake up some data
spread= rand(50) * 100
center = ones(25) * 50

# generate some outliers high and low
flier_high = rand(10) * 100 + 100
flier_low = rand(10) * -100

# merge generated data set
data = concatenate((spread, center, flier_high, flier_low), 0)

subplot(311)
# basic plot
# 'gx' defining the outlier plotting properties
boxplot(data, 0, 'gx')

# compare this with similar scatter plot
subplot(312)
spread_1 = concatenate((spread, flier_high, flier_low), 0)
center_1 = ones(70) * 25
scatter(center_1, spread_1)
xlim([0, 50])

# and with another that is more appropriate for
# scatter plot
subplot(313)
center_2 = rand(70) * 50
scatter(center_2, spread_1)
xlim([0, 50])

show()
```

We can then see x-shaped markers representing outliers, as shown in the following table:

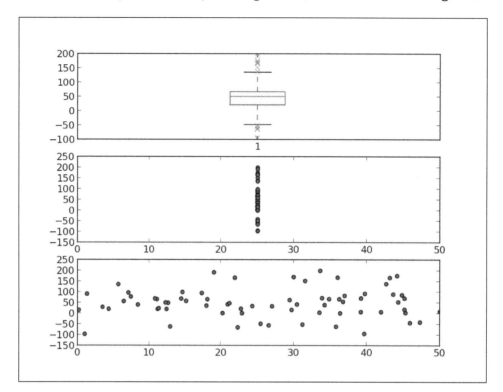

We can also see that the second plot showing a similar dataset in the scatter plot is not very intuitive because the x axis has all the values at 25 and we don't really distinguish between inliers and outliers.

The third plot, where we generated values on the x axis to be spread across the range from 0 to 50, gives us more visibility of the different values and we can see what values are outliers in terms of the y axis.

What if we have a dataset with missing values? We can use NumPy loaders to compensate for missing values, or we can write code to replace existing values with the ones we need for further use.

For example, we want to illustrate some dataset over the geographical map of USA and have values for state names that are not consistent in the dataset. For example, we have values OH, Ohio, OHIO, US-OH, and OH-USA all representing the state of Ohio in the USA. What we must do in this situation is that we need to inspect the dataset manually by loading it in a spreadsheet processor such as Microsoft Excel or OpenOffice.org Calc. Sometimes, it is easy enough to just print all the lines using Python. If the file is CSV or CSV-like, we can open it with any text editor and inspect the data directly.

After we have concluded what is present in the data, we can write Python code to group those similar values and replace them with the one value that is going to make further processing consistent. The usual way of doing this is to read in lines of the file using `readlines()` and use standard Python string manipulation functions to perform manipulations.

There's more...

There are special products, both commercial and non-commercial (such as **OpenRefine** available at `https://github.com/OpenRefine`) that provide some automation around transformation on "dirty" live datasets.

Manual work is still involved, depending on how noisy the data is and how great our understanding of that data is.

If you want to find out more about cleaning outliers and cleaning of data in general, look for statistical models and the sampling theory.

Reading files in chunks

Python is very good at handling reading and writing files or file-like objects. For example, if you try to load big files, say a few hundred MB, assuming you have a modern machine with at least 2 GB of RAM, Python will be able to handle it without any issue. It will not try to load everything at once, but play smart and load it as needed.

So even with decent file sizes, doing something as simple as the following code will work straight out of the box:

```
with open('/tmp/my_big_file', 'r') as bigfile:
    for line in bigfile:
        # line based operation, like 'print line'
```

But if we want to jump to a particular place in the file or do other nonsequential reading, we will need to use the handcrafted approach and use IO functions such as `seek()`, `tell()`, `read()`, and `next()` that allow enough flexibility for most users. Most of these functions are just bindings to C implementations (and are OS-specific), so they are fast, but their behavior can vary based on the OS we are running.

How to do it...

Depending on what our aim is, processing large files can sometimes be managed in chunks. For example, you could read 1,000 lines and process them using Python standard iterator-based approaches, as shown here:

```python
import sys

filename = sys.argv[1]   # must pass valid file name

with open(filename, 'rb') as hugefile:
    chunksize = 1000
    readable = ''
    # if you want to stop after certain number of blocks
    # put condition in the while
    while hugefile:
        # if you want to start not from 1st byte
        # do a hugefile.seek(skipbytes) to skip
        # skipbytes of bytes from the file start
        start = hugefile.tell()
        print "starting at:", start
        file_block = ''   # holds chunk_size of lines
        for _ in xrange(start, start + chunksize):
            line = hugefile.next()
            file_block = file_block + line
            print 'file_block', type(file_block), file_block
        readable = readable + file_block
        # tell where are we in file
        # file IO is usually buffered so tell()
        # will not be precise for every read.
        stop = hugefile.tell()
        print 'readable', type(readable), readable
        print 'reading bytes from %s to %s' % (start, stop)
        print 'read bytes total:', len(readable)

        # if you want to pause read between chucks
        # uncomment following line
        #raw_input()
```

We call this code from the Python command-line interpreter, giving the filename path as the first parameter:

```
$ python ch02-chunk-read.py myhugefile.dat
```

How it works...

We want to be able to read blocks of lines for processing without reading the whole file in the memory.

We open the file and read in lines in the inner for loop. The way we move through the file is by calling `next()` on the file object. This function reads the line from the file and moves the file pointer to the next line. We append lines in the `file_block` variable during the loop execution. In order to simplify the example code, we don't do any processing but just add `file_block` to complete the output variable readable.

We do some printing during execution just to illustrate the current state of certain variables.

The last comment line in the while loop `raw_input()` can be uncommented and we can pause the execution and read the printed lines above it.

There's more...

This recipe is, of course, just one of the possible approaches to reading large (huge) files. Other approaches could include specific Python or C libraries, but they all depend on what we aim to do with data and how we want to process it.

Parallel approaches like the MapReduce paradigm have become very popular recently as we get more processing power and memory for a low price.

Multiprocessing is also a feasible approach sometimes as Python has good library support for creating and managing threads with several libraries such as `multiprocessing`, `threading`, and `thread`.

If processing huge files is a repeated process for a project, we suggest building your data pipeline so that every time you need data ready in a specific format on the output end, you don't have to go to the source and do it manually.

Reading streaming data sources

What if the data that is coming from the source is continuous? What if we need to read continuous data? This recipe will demonstrate a simple solution that will work for many common real-life scenarios, but it is not universal and you will need to modify it if you hit a special case in your application.

How to do it...

In this recipe, we will show you how to read an ever-changing file and print the output. We will use the common Python module to accomplish this as shown here:

```python
import time
import os
import sys

if len(sys.argv) != 2:
    print >> sys.stderr, "Please specify filename to read"

filename = sys.argv[1]

if not os.path.isfile(filename):
    print >> sys.stderr, "Given file: \"%s\" is not a file" % filename

with open(filename,'r') as f:
    # Move to the end of file
    filesize = os.stat(filename)[6]
    f.seek(filesize)

    # endlessly loop
    while True:
        where = f.tell()
        # try reading a line
        line = f.readline()
        # if empty, go back
        if not line:
            time.sleep(1)
            f.seek(where)
        else:
            # , at the end prevents print to add newline, as
readline()
            # already read that.
            print line,
```

How it works...

The core of the code is inside the while True: loop. This loop never stops (unless we interrupt it by pressing *Ctrl + C* on our keyboard). We first move to the end of the file we are reading and then we try to read a line. If there is no line, that means nothing was added to the file after we checked it using seek(). So, we sleep for one second and then try again.

If there is a non-empty line, we print that out and suppress the new line character.

There's more...

We might want to read the last n lines. We could do that by going almost to the end of the file. We could go there by looking for the file, that is, with `file.seek(filesize - N * avg_line_len)`. Here, `avg_line_len` should be the approximation of average line length in that file (approximately 1,024). Then, we could use `readlines()` from that point to read line and then print just `[-N]` lines from that list.

The idea from this example can be used for various solutions. For example, the input has to be a file-like object or a remote HTTP-accessible resource. Thus, one can read the input from a remote service and continuously parse it and update live charts or update the intermediate queue, buffer, or database.

One particular module is very useful for stream handling—io. It is in Python from Version 2.6, is built as a replacement for the file module, and is a default interface in Python 3.x.

In some more complex data pipelines, we will need to enable some sort of message queues, where our incoming continuous data will have to be queued for some time before we are able to accept it. This enables us, as consumers of the data, to be able to pause processing if we are overloaded. Having data on the common message bus enables other clients on the project to consume the same data and not interfere with our software.

Importing image data into NumPy arrays

We are going to demonstrate how to do image processing using Python's libraries such as NumPy and SciPy.

In scientific computing, images are usually seen as n-dimensional arrays. They are usually two-dimensional arrays; in our examples, they are represented as a NumPy array data structure. Therefore, functions and operations performed on those structures are seen as matrix operations.

Images in this sense are not always two-dimensional. For medical or bio-sciences, images are data structures of higher dimensions such as 3D (having the z axis as depth or as the time axis) or 4D (having three spatial dimensions and a temporal one as the fourth dimension). We will not be using those in this recipe.

We can import images using various techniques; they all depend on what you want to do with image. Also, it depends on the larger ecosystem of tools you are using and the platform you are running your project on.

In this recipe, we will demonstrate several ways to use image processing in Python, mainly related to scientific processing and less on the artistic side of image manipulation.

Getting ready

In some examples in this recipe, we use the SciPy library, which you have already installed if you have installed NumPy. If you haven't, it is easily installable using your OS's package manager by executing the following command:

```
$ sudo apt-get install python-scipy
```

For Windows users, we recommend using prepackaged Python environments like EPD, which we discussed in *Chapter 1, Preparing Your Working Environment*.

If you want to install these using official source distributions, make sure you have installed system dependencies, such as:

 ▸ **BLAS and LAPACK**: `libblas` and `liblapack`
 ▸ **C and Fortran compilers**: `gcc` and `gfortran`

How to do it...

Whoever has worked in the field of digital signal processing or even attended a university course on this or a related subject must have come across Lena's image, the de facto standard image used for demonstrating image processing algorithms.

SciPy contains this image already packed inside the `misc.` module, so it is really simple for us to reuse that image. This is how you can read and show this image:

```python
import scipy.misc
import matplotlib.pyplot as plt

# load already prepared ndarray from scipy
lena = scipy.misc.lena()

# set the default colormap to gray
plt.gray()

plt.imshow(lena)
plt.colorbar()
plt.show()
```

This should open a new window with a figure displaying Lena's image in gray tones and axes. The color bar shows a range of values in the figure; here it shows 0—black to 255—white.

Further, we could examine this object with the following code:

```
print lena.shape
print lena.max()
print lena.dtype
```

The output for the preceding code is shown here:

```
(512, 512)
245
dtype('int32')
```

We see the following features in the image 512 points wide and 512 points high

- The max value in the whole array (that is, the image) is 245
- Every point is represented as a little endian 32-bit long integer

We could also read in an image using **Python Imaging Library** (**PIL**), which we installed in *Chapter 1, Preparing Your Working Environment.*

Here is the code to do that:

```
import numpy
import Image
import matplotlib.pyplot as plt

bug = Image.open('stinkbug.png')
arr = numpy.array(bug.getdata(), numpy.uint8).reshape(bug.size[1],
bug.size[0], 3)

plt.gray()
plt.imshow(arr)
plt.colorbar()
plt.show()
```

We should see something similar to Lena's image as shown in the following table:

This is useful if we are already tapping into an existing system that uses PIL as their default image loader.

How it works...

Other than just loading the images, what we really want to do is use Python to manipulate images and process them. For example, we want to be able to load a real image that consists of RGB channels, convert that into one channel `ndarray`, and later use array slicing to also zoom in to the part of the image. Here's the code to demonstrate how we are able to use NumPy and matplotlib to do that:

```
import matplotlib.pyplot as plt
import scipy
import numpy


bug = scipy.misc.imread('stinkbug1.png')

# if you want to inspect the shape of the loaded image
# uncomment following line
#print bug.shape

# the original image is RGB having values for all three
# channels separately. For simplicity, we convert that to greyscale
image
# by picking up just one channel.

# convert to gray
bug = bug[:,:,0]
```

`bug[:,:,0]` is called **array slicing**. This NumPy feature allows us to select any part of the multidimensional array. For example, let's see a one-dimensional array:

```
>>> a = array(5, 1, 2, 3, 4)
>>> a[2:3]
array([2])
>>> a[:2]
array([5, 1])
>>> a[3:]
array([3, 4])
```

For multidimensional arrays, we separate each dimension with a comma (,) as shown here:

```
>>> b = array([[1,1,1],[2,2,2],[3,3,3]])   # matrix 3 x 3
>>> b[0,:]   # pick first row
array([1,1,1])
>>> b[:,0]    # we pick the first column
array([1,2,3])
```

Have a look at the following code:

```
# show original image
plt.figure()
plt.gray()

plt.subplot(121)
plt.imshow(bug)

# show 'zoomed' region
zbug = bug[100:350,140:350]
```

Here we zoom into the particular portion of the whole image. Remember that the image is just a multidimensional array represented as a NumPy array. Zooming here means selecting a range of rows and columns from this matrix. So we select a partial matrix from rows 100 to 250 and columns 140 to 350. Remember that indexing starts at 0, so the row at coordinate 100 is the 101st row.

Take a look at the following code:

```
plt.subplot(122)
plt.imshow(zbug)

plt.show()
```

This will be displayed as shown here:

There's more...

For large images, we recommend using `numpy.memmap` for memory mapping of images. This will speed up manipulating the image data. Have a look at the following code as an example of this:

```
import numpy
file_name  = 'stinkbug.png'
image = numpy.memmap(file_name, dtype=numpy.uint8, shape = (375, 500))
```

Here we load part of a large file into memory, accessing it as a NumPy array. This is very efficient and allows us to manipulate file data structures as standard NumPy arrays without loading everything into memory. The argument shape defines the shape of the array loaded from the `file_name` argument, which is a file-like object. Note that this is a concept similar to Python's `mmap` argument (available at `http://docs.python.org/2/library/mmap.html`) but is different in a very important way. NumPy's `memmap` attribute returns an array-like object while Python's `mmap` returns a file-like object. So, the way we use them is very different yet very natural in each environment.

There are some specialized packages that just focus on image processing like scikit-image (available at `http://scikit-image.org/`); this is basically a free collection of algorithms for image processing built on top of NumPy/SciPy libraries. If you want to do edge detection, remove noise from an image, or find contours, scikit is the tool to use to look for algorithms. The best way to start is to look at the example gallery and find the example image and code (available at `http://scikit-image.org/docs/dev/auto_examples/`).

Generating controlled random datasets

In this recipe, we will show different ways of generating random number sequences and word sequences. Some of the examples use standard Python modules, and others use NumPy/SciPy functions.

We will go through some statistics terminology but will explain every term, so you don't have to have a statistical reference book with you while reading this recipe.

We generate artificial datasets using common Python modules. By doing so, we are able to understand distributions, variance, sampling, and similar statistical terminology. More importantly, we can use this fake data as a way to understand if our statistical method is capable of discovering models we want to discover. We can do that because we know the model in advance and verify our statistical method by applying it over our known data. In real life, we don't have that ability and there is always a percentage of uncertainty that we must assume, giving way to errors.

Getting ready

We don't need anything new installed on the system in order to exercise these examples. Having some knowledge of statistics is useful, although not required.

To refresh our statistical knowledge, here's a little glossary we will use in this and the following chapters:

- **Distribution or probability distribution**: This links the outcome of a statistical experiment with the probability of occurrence of that experiment.

- **Standard deviation**: This is a numerical value that indicates how individuals vary in comparison to a group. If they vary more, the standard derivation will be big, and in the opposite condition—if all the individual experiments are more or less the same across the whole group, the standard derivation will be small.

- **Variance**: This equals the square of standard derivation.

- **Population or statistical population**: This is a total set of all the potentially observable cases. For example, all the grades of all the students in the world if we are interested in getting the student average of the world.

- **Sample**: This is a subset of the population. We cannot obtain all the grades of all the students in the world, so we have to gather only a sample of data and model it.

How to do it...

We can generate a simple random sample using Python's module `random`. Here's an example of this:

```
import pylab
import random

SAMPLE_SIZE = 100

# seed random generator
# if no argument provided
# uses system current time
random.seed()

# store generated random values here
real_rand_vars = []

# pick some random values
real_rand_vars = [random.random() for val in xrange(SIZE)]
# create histogram from data in 10 buckets
pylab.hist(real_rand_vars, 10)
```

```
# define x and y labels
pylab.xlabel("Number range")
pylab.ylabel("Count")

# show figure
pylab.show()
```

This is a uniformly distributed sample. When we run this example, we should see something similar to the following plot:

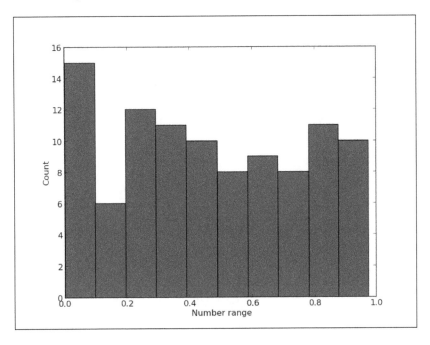

Try setting `SAMPLE_SIZE` to a big number (say `10000`) and see how the histogram behaves.

If we want to have values that range not from 0 to 1, but say from 1 to 6 (by simulating single dice throws), we could use `random.randint(min, max)`; here, `min` and `max` are the lower and upper inclusive bounds respectively. If what you want to generate are floats and not integers, there is a `random.uniform(min, max)` function to provide that.

In a similar fashion and using the same tools, we can generate a time series plot of fictional price growth data with some random noise, as shown here:

```
import pylab
import random
```

```
# days to generate data for
duration = 100
# mean value
mean_inc = 0.2

# standard deviation
std_dev_inc = 1.2

# time series
x = range(duration)
y = []
price_today = 0

for i in x:
    next_delta = random.normalvariate(mean_inc, std_dev_inc)
    price_today += next_delta
    y.append(price_today)

pylab.plot(x,y)
pylab.xlabel("Time")
pylab.xlabel("Time")
pylab.ylabel("Value")
pylab.show()
```

This code defines a series of 100 data points (fictional days). For every next day, we pick a random value from the normal distribution (`random.normalvariate()`) ranging from `mean_inc` to `std_dev_inc` and add that value to yesterday's price value (`price_today`).

If we wanted more control, we could use different distributions. The following code illustrates and visualizes different distributions. We will comment separate code sections as we present them. We start by importing required modules and defining a number of histogram buckets. We also create a figure that will hold our histograms as shown in the following lines of code:

```
# coding: utf-8
import random
import matplotlib
import matplotlib.pyplot as plt

SAMPLE_SIZE = 1000
# histogram buckets
buckets = 100


plt.figure()

# we need to update font size just for this example
matplotlib.rcParams.update({'font.size': 7})
```

To lay out all the required plots, we define a grid of six by two subplots for all the histograms. The first plot is a uniformly distributed random variable as seen in the following lines of code:

```
plt.subplot(621)
plt.xlabel("random.random")
# Return the next random floating point number in the range [0.0,
1.0).
res = [random.random() for _ in xrange(1, SAMPLE_SIZE)]
plt.hist(res, buckets)
```

For the second plot, we plot a uniformly distributed random variable as shown here:

```
plt.subplot(622)
plt.xlabel("random.uniform")
# Return a random floating point number N such that a <= N <= b for a
<= b and b <= N <= a for b < a.
# The end-point value b may or may not be included in the range
depending on floating-point rounding in the equation a + (b-a) *
random().
a = 1
b = SAMPLE_SIZE
res = [random.uniform(a, b) for _ in xrange(1, SAMPLE_SIZE)]
plt.hist(res, buckets)
```

Here is the third plot which is a triangular distribution:

```
plt.subplot(623)
plt.xlabel("random.triangular")

# Return a random floating point number N such that low <= N <= high
and with the specified  # mode between those bounds. The low and high
bounds default to zero and one. The mode
# argument defaults to the midpoint between the bounds, giving a
symmetric distribution.
low = 1
high = SAMPLE_SIZE
res = [random.triangular(low, high) for _ in xrange(1, SAMPLE_SIZE)]
plt.hist(res, buckets)
```

The fourth plot is a beta distribution. The condition on the parameters is that alpha and beta should be greater than zero. The returned values range between 0 and 1.

```
plt.subplot(624)
plt.xlabel("random.betavariate")
alpha = 1
beta = 10
res = [random.betavariate(alpha, beta) for _ in xrange(1, SAMPLE_
SIZE)]
plt.hist(res, buckets)
```

The fifth plot visualizes an exponential distribution. `lambd` is 1.0 divided by the desired mean. It should be non-zero (the parameter would be called lambda, but that is a reserved word in Python). The returned values range from 0 to positive infinity if `lambd` is positive, and from negative infinity to 0 if `lambd` is negative, as shown here:

```
plt.subplot(625)
plt.xlabel("random.expovariate")
lambd = 1.0 / ((SAMPLE_SIZE + 1) / 2.)
res = [random.expovariate(lambd) for _ in xrange(1, SAMPLE_SIZE)]
plt.hist(res, buckets)
```

Our next plot is the gamma distribution, where the condition on the parameters is that alpha and beta are greater than 0. The probability distribution function is shown here:

$$PDF(x) = \frac{x^{\alpha-1}e^{\frac{-x}{\beta}}}{\gamma(\alpha)\beta^{\alpha}}$$

Here's the code for the gamma distribution:

```
plt.subplot(626)
plt.xlabel("random.gammavariate")


alpha = 1
beta = 10
res = [random.gammavariate(alpha, beta) for _ in xrange(1, SAMPLE_SIZE)]
plt.hist(res, buckets)
```

Log normal distribution is our next plot. If you take the natural logarithm of this distribution, you'll get a normal distribution with the mean `mu` and the standard deviation `sigma`. `mu` can have any value; moreover, `sigma` must be greater than zero as shown here:

```
plt.subplot(627)
plt.xlabel("random.lognormvariate")
mu = 1
sigma = 0.5
res = [random.lognormvariate(mu, sigma) for _ in xrange(1, SAMPLE_SIZE)]
plt.hist(res, buckets)
```

The next plot is normal distribution, where `mu` is the mean and `sigma` is the standard deviation as shown here:

```
plt.subplot(628)
plt.xlabel("random.normalvariate")
mu = 1
sigma = 0.5
res = [random.normalvariate(mu, sigma) for _ in xrange(1, SAMPLE_
SIZE)]
plt.hist(res, buckets)
```

Here is the last plot which is the Pareto distribution and `alpha` is the shape parameter:

```
plt.subplot(629)
plt.xlabel("random.paretovariate")
alpha = 1
res = [random.paretovariate(alpha) for _ in xrange(1, SAMPLE_SIZE)]
plt.hist(res, buckets)

plt.tight_layout()
plt.show()
```

This was a big code example, but basically we pick 1,000 random numbers according to various distributions. These are common distributions used in different statistical branches (economics, sociology, bio-sciences, and so on).

We should see differences in the histogram based on the distribution algorithm used. Take a moment to understand the following nine plots:

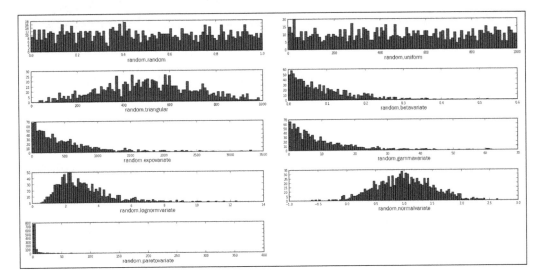

Use seed() to initialize the pseudo-random generator, so random() produces the same expected random values. This is sometimes useful and it is better than pregenerating random data and saving it to a file. The latter technique is not always feasible as it requires saving (possibly huge amounts of) data on a filesystem.

If you want to prevent any repeatability of your randomly generated sequences, we recommend using random.SystemRandom, which uses os.urandom underneath; os.urandom provides access to more entropy sources. If using this random generator interface, seed() and setstate() have no effect; hence these samples are not reproducible.

If we want to have some random words, the easiest way (on Linux) is probably to use /usr/share/dicts/words. We can see how that is done in the following example:

```
import random

with open('/usr/share/dict/words', 'rt') as f:
    words = f.readlines()
words = [w.rstrip() for w in words]

for w in random.sample(words, 5):
    print w
```

This solution is for Unix only and will not work on Windows (but, it will work on Mac OS). For Windows, you could use a file constructed from various free sources (Project Gutenberg, Wiktionary, British National Corpus, or http://norvig.com/big.txt by Dr Peter Norvig).

Smoothing the noise in real-world data

In this recipe, we introduce a few advanced algorithms to help with cleaning the data coming from real-world sources. These algorithms are well known in the signal processing world, and we will not go deep into mathematics but will just exemplify how and why they work and for what purposes they can be used.

Getting ready

Data that comes from different real-life sensors usually is not smooth and clean and contains some noise that we usually don't want to show on diagrams and plots. We want graphs and plots to be clear and to display information and cost viewers minimal efforts to interpret.

We don't need any new software installed because we are going to use some already familiar Python packages: NumPy, SciPy, and matplotlib.

How to do it...

The basic algorithm is based on using the rolling window (for example, convolution). This window rolls over the data and is used to compute the average over that window.

For our discrete data, we use NumPy's `convolve` function; it returns a discrete linear convolution of two one-dimensional sequences. We also use NumPy's `linspace` function, which generates a sequence of evenly spaced numbers for a specified interval.

The function `ones` defines an array or matrix (for example, a multidimensional array) where every element has the value 1. This helps with generating Windows for use in averaging.

How it works...

One simple and naive technique to smooth the noise in data we are processing is to average over some window (sample) and plot just that average value for the given window instead of all the data points. This is the basis for more advanced algorithms as shown here:

```python
from pylab import *
from numpy import *

def moving_average(interval, window_size):
    '''Compute convoluted window for given size
    '''
    window = ones(int(window_size)) / float(window_size)
    return convolve(interval, window, 'same')

t = linspace(-4, 4, 100)
y = sin(t) + randn(len(t))*0.1

plot(t, y, "k.")

# compute moving average
y_av = moving_average(y, 10)
plot(t, y_av,"r")
#xlim(0,1000)

xlabel("Time")
ylabel("Value")
grid(True)
show()
```

Here, we show how the smoothed line looks compared to the original data points (plotted as dots):

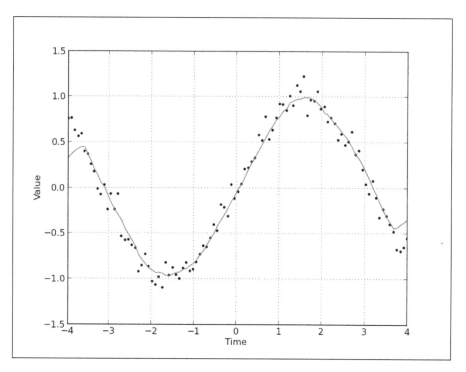

Following on this idea, we can jump ahead to an even more advanced example and use the existing SciPy library to make this window smoothing work even better.

The method we are going to demonstrate is based on convolution (summation of functions) of a scaled window with the signal (that is, data points). This signal is prepared in a clever way, adding copies of the same signal on both ends but reflecting it, so we minimize the boundary effect. This code is based on SciPy Cookbook's example that can be found here at `http://scipy-cookbook.readthedocs.org/`.

```
import numpy
from numpy import *
from pylab import *


# possible window type
WINDOWS = ['flat', 'hanning', 'hamming', 'bartlett', 'blackman']
# if you want to see just two window type, comment previous line,
# and uncomment the following one
# WINDOWS = ['flat', 'hanning']
```

```python
def smooth(x, window_len=11, window='hanning'):
    """
    Smooth the data using a window with requested size.
    Returns smoothed signal.

    x -- input signal
    window_len -- length of smoothing window
    window -- type of window: 'flat', 'hanning', 'hamming',
                  'bartlett', 'blackman'
                  flat window will produce a moving average smoothing.
    """

    if x.ndim != 1:
        raise ValueError, "smooth only accepts 1 dimension arrays."

    if x.size < window_len:
        raise ValueError, "Input vector needs to be bigger than window
size."

    if window_len < 3:
        return x

    if not window in WINDOWS:
        raise ValueError("Window is one of 'flat', 'hanning',
'hamming', "
                        "'bartlett', 'blackman'")
    # adding reflected windows in front and at the end
    s=numpy.r_[x[window_len-1:0:-1], x, x[-1:-window_len:-1]]
    # pick windows type and do averaging
    if window == 'flat': #moving average
        w = numpy.ones(window_len, 'd')
    else:
        # call appropriate function in numpy
        w = eval('numpy.' + window + '(window_len)')

    # NOTE: length(output) != length(input), to correct this:
    # return y[(window_len/2-1):-(window_len/2)] instead of just y.
    y = numpy.convolve(w/w.sum(), s, mode='valid')
    return y


# Get some evenly spaced numbers over a specified interval.
t = linspace(-4, 4, 100)
```

```
# Make some noisy sinusoidal
x = sin(t)
xn = x + randn(len(t))*0.1

# Smooth it
y = smooth(x)

# window size
ws = 31

subplot(211)
plot(ones(ws))

# draw on the same axes
hold(True)

# plot for every window
for w in WINDOWS[1:]:
    eval('plot('+w+'(ws) )')

# configure axis properties
axis([0, 30, 0, 1.1])

# add legend for every window
legend(WINDOWS)

title("Smoothing windows")

# add second plot
subplot(212)
# draw original signal
plot(x)

# and signal with added noise
plot(xn)

# smooth signal with noise for every possible windowing algorithm
for w in WINDOWS:
    plot(smooth(xn, 10, w))

# add legend for every graph
l=['original signal', 'signal with noise']
l.extend(WINDOWS)
```

```
legend(l)

title("Smoothed signal")

show()
```

We should see the following two plots to see how the windowing algorithm influences the noise signal. The top plot represents possible windowing algorithms and the bottom one displays every possible result from the original signal to the noised up signal and even the smoothed signal for every windowing algorithm. Try commenting possible window types and leave just one or two to gain better understanding.

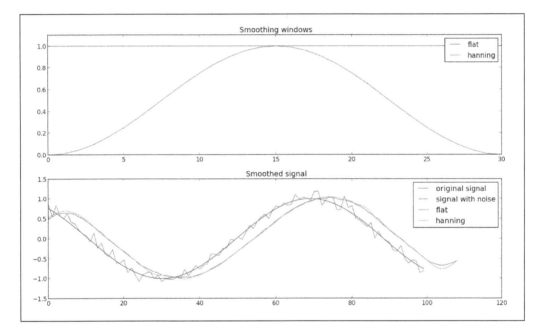

There's more...

Another very popular signal smoothing algorithm is **Median Filter**. The main idea of this filter is to run through the signal entry by entry, replacing each entry with the median of neighboring entries. This idea makes this filter fast and usable for one-dimensional datasets as well as for two-dimensional datasets (such as images).

In the following example, we use the implementation from the SciPy signal toolbox:

```
import numpy as np
import pylab as p
import scipy.signal as signal
```

```
# get some linear data
x = np.linspace (0, 1, 101)

# add some noisy signal
x[3::10] = 1.5

p.plot(x)
p.plot(signal.medfilt(x,3))
p.plot(signal.medfilt(x,5))

p.legend(['original signal', 'length 3','length 5'])
p.show ()
```

We see in the following plot that the bigger the window, the more our signal gets distorted as compared to the original but the smoother it looks:

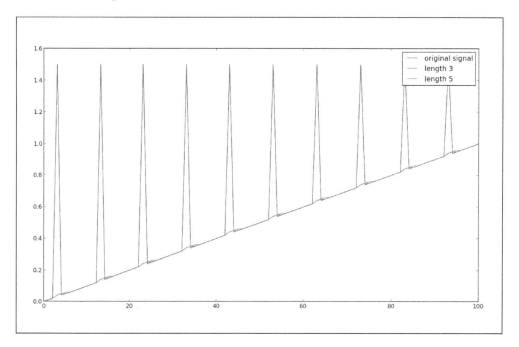

There are many more ways to smooth data (signals) that you receive from external sources. It depends a lot on the area you are working in and the nature of the signal. Many algorithms are specialized for a particular signal, and there may not be a general solution for every case you encounter.

There is, however, one important question: "When should you not smooth a signal?" One common situation where you should not smooth signals is prior to statistical procedures, such as least-squares curve fitting because all smoothing algorithms are at least slightly lousy and they change the signal shape. Also, smoothed noise may be mistaken for an actual signal.

3
Drawing Your First Plots and Customizing Them

In this chapter, we will go into a lot more detail and present most of the possibilities of matplotlib. We will cover the following points:

- ▶ Defining plot types – bar, line, and stacked charts
- ▶ Drawing simple sine and cosine plots
- ▶ Defining axis lengths and limits
- ▶ Defining plot line styles, properties, and format strings
- ▶ Setting ticks, labels, and grids
- ▶ Adding legends and annotations
- ▶ Moving spines to the center
- ▶ Making histograms
- ▶ Making bar charts with error bars
- ▶ Making pie charts count
- ▶ Plotting with filled areas
- ▶ Making stacked plots
- ▶ Drawing scatter plots with colored markers

Introduction

Although we have already drawn our first plots using matplotlib, we didn't go into the details about how they work, how to set them up, or what the possibilities with using matplotlib are. We explore and exercise most common types of data visualizations: line graphs, bar charts, histograms, pies, and variations thereof.

matplotlib is a powerful toolbox that satisfies almost all our needs for 2D and some 3D plotting needs as well. The best way the authors intend for you to learn matplotlib is through examples. When we need to draw a plot, we look for a similar example and try to change it to fit our needs. In this way, we are also going to present you with some useful examples and believe that this example will help you find a plot most similar to what you need.

Defining plot types – bar, line, and stacked charts

In this recipe, we will present different basic plots and what are they used for. Most of the plots described here are used daily, and some of them present the basis for understanding more advanced concepts in data visualization.

Getting ready

We start with some common charts from the `matplotlib.pyplot` library with just sample datasets; we start with basic charting and lay down the foundations of the following recipes.

How to do it...

We start by creating a simple plot in IPython. IPython is great because it allows us to interactively change plots and see the results immediately. You need to follow these steps for that:

1. Start IPython by typing the following code at the command prompt:

   ```
   $ ipython
   ```

2. Import the necessary functions:

   ```
   In [1]: from matplotlib.pyplot import *
   ```

3. Then type the matplotlib `plot` code:

   ```
   In [2]: plot([1,2,3,2,3,2,2,1])
   Out[2]: [<matplotlib.lines.Line2D at 0x412fb50>]
   ```

The plot should open in a new window displaying the default look of the plot and some supporting information as shown here:

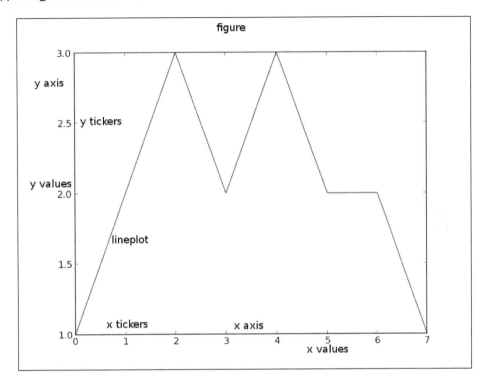

The basic plot in matplotlib contains the following elements:

- **x and y axes**: These are both horizontal and vertical axes.
- **x and y tickers**: These are little tickers denoting the segments of axes. There can be major and minor tickers.
- **x and y tick labels**: These represent values on particular axis.
- **Plotting area**: This is where the actual plots are drawn.

You will notice that the values we provided to `plot()` as y axis values. `plot()` provides default values for the x axis; they are linear values from **0** to **7** (the number of y values -1).

Now, try adding values for the x axis; as first argument to the `plot()` function again in the same IPython session, type the following script:

```
In [2]: plot([4,3,2,1],[1,2,3,4])
Out[2]: [<matplotlib.lines.Line2D at 0x31444d0>]
```

Note how IPython counts input and output lines (In [2] and Out [2]). This will help us remember where we are in the current session and enables more advanced features such as saving part of the session in a Python file. During data analysis, using IPython for prototyping is the fastest way to come to a satisfying solution and then save particular sessions into a file, to be executed later if you need to reproduce the same plot.

This will update the plot to look like this image:

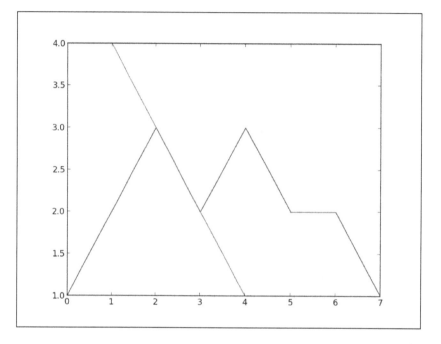

We see here how matplotlib expands the y axis to accommodate the new value range and automatically changes color of the second plot line to enable us to distinguish the new plot.

Unless we turn off the `hold` property (by calling `hold(False)`), all subsequent plots will draw over the same axes. This is the default behavior in `pylab` mode in IPython, while in regular Python scripts, `hold` is off by default.

Let us pack some more common plots and compare them over the same dataset. You can type this in IPython or run it from a separate Python script:

```python
from matplotlib.pyplot import *

# some simple data
x = [1,2,3,4]
y = [5,4,3,2]
# create new figure
figure()

# divide subplots into 2 x 3 grid
# and select #1
subplot(231)
plot(x, y)

# select #2
subplot(232)
bar(x, y)

    # horizontal bar-charts
subplot(233)
barh(x, y)

# create stacked bar charts
subplot(234)
bar(x, y)

# we need more data for stacked bar charts
y1 = [7,8,5,3]
bar(x, y1, bottom=y, color = 'r')

# box plot
subplot(235)
boxplot(x)

# scatter plot
subplot(236)
scatter(x,y)

show()
```

This is how it should turn out into graphs:

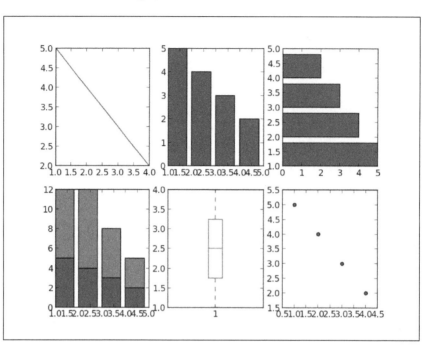

How it works...

With `figure()`, we create a new figure. If we supply a string argument such as `sample charts`, it will be the backend title of a window. If we call the `figure()` function with the same parameter (that can also be a number), we will make the corresponding figure active and all the following plotting will be performed on that figure.

Next, we divide the figure into a 2 x 3 grid using a `subplot(231)` call. We could call this using `subplot(2, 3, 1)`, where the first parameter is the number of rows, the second is the number of columns, and the third represents the plot number.

We continue and create a common charting type using simple calls to create vertical bar charts (`bar()`) and horizontal bars (`barh()`). For stacked bar charts, we need to tie two bar chart calls together. We do that by connecting the second bar chart with the previous using the parameter `bottom = y`.

Box plots are created using the `boxplot()` call, where the box extends from lower to upper quartiles with the line at the median value. We will return to box plots shortly.

We finally create a scatter plot to give you an idea of a point-based dataset. This is probably more appropriately used when we have thousands of data points in a dataset, but here we wanted to illustrate the difference in representations of the same dataset.

There's more...

We can return to box plots now as we need to explain the characteristics of this kind of plot.

A box plot presents, by default, the following elements:

- **Box**: This is a rectangle that covers the interquartile range
- **Median**: This is presented as a line inside each box
- **Whiskers**: These are vertical lines extending to the most extreme values (excluding outliers)
- **Fliers**: These are points beyond the whiskers, which are considered outliers

To illustrate this behavior, we will demonstrate plotting the same dataset in a box plot and a histogram as shown in the following code:

```
from pylab import *

dataset = [113, 115, 119, 121, 124,
           124, 125, 126, 126, 126,
           127, 127, 128, 129, 130,
           130, 131, 132, 133, 136]


subplot(121)
boxplot(dataset, vert=False)

subplot(122)
hist(dataset)

show()
```

That will give us the following plots:

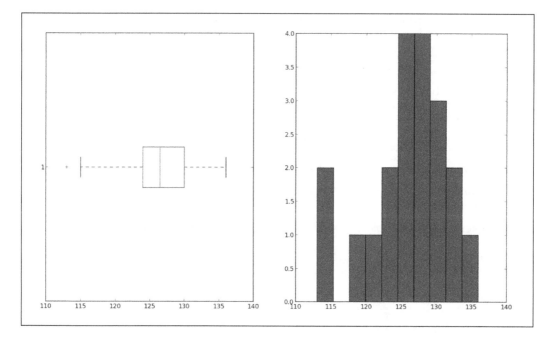

In the preceding comparison, we can observe a difference in representation of the same dataset in two different charts. The one on the left points toward the five mentioned statistical values, while the one on the right (the histogram) displays the grouping of the dataset in a given range.

Drawing simple sine and cosine plots

This recipe will go over basics of plotting mathematical functions and several things that are related to math graphs such as writing Greek symbols in labels and on curves.

Getting ready

The most common graph we will use is the line plot command, which draws the given (x,y) coordinates on a figure plot.

How to do it...

We start with computing sine and cosine functions over the same linear interval—from Pi to Pi with 256 points in between and we plot the values for *sin(x)* and *cos(x)* over the same plot as shown here:

```
import matplotlib.pyplot as pl
import numpy as np

x = np.linspace(-np.pi, np.pi, 256, endpoint=True)

y = np.cos(x)
y1 = np.sin(x)

pl.plot(x,y)
pl.plot(x, y1)

pl.show()
```

That will give us the following graph:

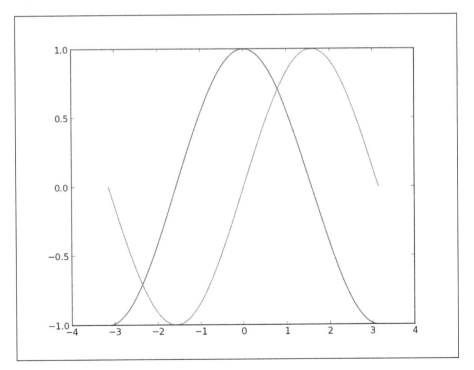

Following this simple plot, we can customize more to give more information and be more precise about axes and boundaries as shown here:

```
from pylab import *
import numpy as np

# generate uniformly distributed
# 256 points from -pi to pi, inclusive
x = np.linspace(-np.pi, np.pi, 256, endpoint=True)

# these are vectorised versions
# of math.cos, and math.sin in built-in Python maths
# compute cos for every x
y = np.cos(x)

# compute sin for every x
y1 = np.sin(x)

# plot cos
plot(x, y)

# plot sin
plot(x, y1)

# define plot title
title("Functions $\sin$ and $\cos$")

# set x limit
xlim(-3.0, 3.0)
# set y limit
ylim(-1.0, 1.0)

# format ticks at specific values
xticks([-np.pi, -np.pi/2, 0, np.pi/2, np.pi],
        [r'$-\pi$', r'$-\pi/2$', r'$0$', r'$+\pi/2$', r'$+\pi$'])
yticks([-1, 0, +1],
        [r'$-1$', r'$0$', r'$+1$'])

show()
```

That should give us a slightly nicer graph:

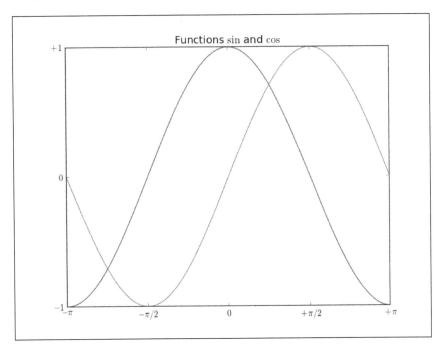

We see that we used expressions such as $\sin$ or $-\pi$ to write letters of the Greek alphabet in figures. This is LaTex syntax, which we will explore further in the following chapters. Here, we just illustrated how easy it is to make your math charts more readable for certain audiences.

Defining axis lengths and limits

This recipe will demonstrate a variety of useful axis properties around limits and lengths that we can configure in matplotlib.

Getting ready

For this recipe, we want to fire up IPython:

```
$ ipython
```

After this, we need to import the plotting functions right away:

```
from matplotlib.pylab import *
```

How to do it...

Start experimenting with various properties of axes. Just calling an empty `axis()` function will return the default values for the axis:

```
In [1]: axis()
Out[1]: (0.0, 1.0, 0.0, 1.0)
```

Note that if you are in interactive mode and are using a windowing backend, a figure with an empty axis will be displayed.

Here the values represent `xmin`, `xmax`, `ymin`, and `ymax` respectively. Similarly, we can set values for the x and y axes:

```
In [2]: l = [-1, 1, -10, 10]

In [3]: axis(l)
Out[3]: [-1, 1, -10, 10]
```

Again, if you are in an interactive mode, this will update the same figure. Furthermore, we can also update any value separately using keyword arguments (`**kwargs`), setting just `xmax` to a certain value.

How it works...

If we don't use `axis()` or other settings, matplotlib will automatically use minimum values that allow us to see all data points on one plot. If we set `axis()` limits to be less than the maximum values in a dataset, matplotlib will do as told and we will not see all points on the figure. This can be a source of confusion or even error, where we think we see everything we drew. One way to avoid this is to call `autoscale()` (`matplotlib.pyplot.autoscale()`), which will compute the optimal size of the axes to fit the data to be displayed.

If we want to add new axes to the same figure, we can use `matplotlib.pyplot.axes()`. We usually want to add some properties to this default call; for example, `rect`—which can have the attributes `left`, `bottom`, `width`, and `height` in normalized units (0, 1)—and maybe `axisbg`, which specifies the background color of axes.

There are also other properties that we can set for added axes such as `sharex`/`sharey`, which accepts values for other instances of axes and share the current axis (x/y) with other axes. Or parameter `polar` that defines whether we want to use polar axes.

Adding new axes can be useful; for example, to combine multiple charts on one figure if there is a need to tightly couple different views on the same data to illustrate its properties.

If we want to add just one line to the current figure, we can use `matplotlib.pyplot.axhline()` or `matplotlib.pyplot.axvline()`. The functions `axhilne()` and `axvline()` will draw horizontal and vertical lines across axes for given x and y data values respectively. They share similar parameters, the most important ones being y position, `xmin`, and `xmax` for `axhline()` and x position, `ymin`, and `ymax` for `axvline()`.

Let's see how it looks as a figure, continuing in the same IPython session:

```
In [3]: axhline()
Out[3]: <matplotlib.lines.Line2D at 0x414ecd0>


In [4]: axvline()
Out[4]: <matplotlib.lines.Line2D at 0x4152490>


In [5]: axhline(4)
Out[5]: <matplotlib.lines.Line2D at 0x4152850>
```

We should have a figure like the following plot:

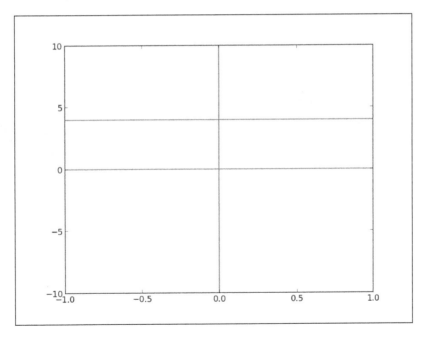

Here we see that just calling these functions without parameters makes them take default values and draw a horizontal line for y=0 (`axhline()`) and a vertical line for x=0 (`axvline()`).

Similar to these are two related functions that allow us to add a horizontal span (rectangle) across the axes. These are `matplotlib.pyplot.axhspan()` and `matplotlib.pyplot.axspan()`. The function `axhspan()` has `ymin` and `ymax` as required parameters that define how wide the horizontal span is. Analogous to this, `axvspan()` has `xmin` and `xmax` to define the width of the vertical span.

There's more...

Having a grid in a figure is turned off by default, but it can easily be switched on and customized. A default call to `matplotlib.pyplot.grid()` will toggle the grid's visibility. Other parameters for control are as shown here:

- `which`: This defines what grid tick type to draw (can be `major`, `minor`, or `both`)
- `axis`: This defines which set of grid lines are drawn (can be `both`, `x`, or `y`)

Axes are usually controlled via `matplotlib.pyplot.axis()`. Internally, axes are represented by several Python classes, the parent one is `matplotlib.axes.Axes`, which contains most methods to manipulate axes. A single axis is represented by the `matplotlib.axis.Axis` class, where the x axis uses `matplotlib.axis.XAxis` and the y axis uses the `matplotlib.axis.YAxis` class.

We don't need to use these to perform our recipe, but it is important to know where to look if more advanced axis control interests us and when we hit the limits of what is available via the `matplotlib.pyplot` namespace.

Defining plot line styles, properties, and format strings

This recipe shows how we can change various line properties such as styles, colors, or width. Having lines set up appropriately according to the information presented and distinct enough for target audiences (if the audience is a younger population, we may want to target them with more vivid colors; if they are older, we may want to use more contrasting colors) can make the difference between being barely noticeable and leaving a great impact on the viewer.

Getting ready

Although we stressed how important it is to aesthetically tune your presentation, we first must learn how to do it.

If you don't have a particular eye for color matching, there are free and commercial online tools that can generate color sets for you. One of the most well known is **Colorbrewer2**, which can be found at `http://colorbrewer2.org/`.

Some serious research has been conducted on the usage of color in data visualizations, but explaining that theory is out of the scope of this book. The material on the topic is a must read if you are working with more advanced visualizations daily.

How to do it...

Let's learn how to change line properties. We can change the lines in our plots using different methods and approaches.

The first and most common method is to define lines by passing keyword parameters to functions such as `plot()`:

```
plot(x, y, linewidth=1.5)
```

Because a call to `plot()` returns the line instance (`matplotlib.lines.Line2D`), we can use a set of setter methods on that instance to set various properties:

```
line, = plot(x, y)
line.set_linewidth(1.5)
```

Those who used MATLAB® will feel the need to use a third way of configuring line properties using the `setp()` function:

```
lines = plot(x, y)
setp(lines, 'linewidth', 1.5)
```

Another way to use `setp()` is this:

```
setp(lines, linewidth=1.5)
```

Whatever way you prefer to configure lines, choose one method and stay consistent for the whole project (or at least a file). This way, when you (or someone else in the future) come back to the code, it will be easier to make sense of it and change it.

How it works...

All the properties we can change for a line are contained in the `matplotlib.lines.Line2D` class. We list some of them in the following table:

Property		
Value type		**Description**
alpha	float	Sets the alpha value used for blending; not supported on all backends.
color or c	Any matplotlib color	Sets the color of the line.

dashes	Sequence of on/off ink in points	Sets the dash sequence, the sequence of dashes with on/off ink in points. If `seq` is empty or if `seq = (None, None)`, `linestyle` will be set to `solid`.
`label`	Any string	Sets the label to `s` for auto legend.
`linestyle` or `ls`	`['-'	'--'	'-.'	':'	'steps'	...]`	Sets the linestyle of the line (also accepts drawstyles).
`linewidth` or `lw`	`float` value in points	Sets the line width in points.
`marker`	`[7	4	5	6	'o'	'D'	'h'	'H'	'_'	''	'None'	' '	None	'8'	'p'	','	'+'	'.'	's'	'*'	'd'	3	0	1	2	'1'	'3'	'4'	'2'	'v'	'<'	'>'	'^'	'|'	'x'	'$...$'	tuple	Nx2 array]`	Sets the line marker.
`markeredgecolor` or `mec`	Any matplotlib color	Sets the marker edge color.
`markeredgewidth` or `mew`	`float` value in points	Sets the marker edge width in points.
`markerfacecolor` or `mfc`	Any matplotlib color	Set the marker face color.
`markersize` or `ms`	`float`	Set the marker size in points.
`solid_capstyle`	`['butt'	'round'	'projecting']`	Set the cap style for solid line styles.
`solid_joinstyle`	`['miter'	'round'	'bevel']`	Set the join style for solid line styles.
`visible`	`[True	False]`	Set the artist's visibility.
`xdata`	`np.array`	Set the data `np.array` for x.
`ydata`	`np.array`	Set the data `np.array` for y.

Zorder	Any number	Set the z axis order for the artist. Artists with lower `Zorder` values are drawn first.
		If x and y are axes going horizontal to the right and vertical to the top of the screen, the z axis is the one extending toward the viewer. So 0 value would be at the screen, 1, one layer above, and so on.

The following table shows some linestyles:

Linestyle	Description
`'_'`	Solid
`'--'`	Dashed
`'-.'`	Dash_dot
`':'`	Dotted
`'None', ' ', ''`	Draw nothing

The following table shows line markers:

Marker	Description
`'o'`	Circle
`'D'`	Diamond
`'h'`	Hexagon1
`'H'`	Hexagon2
`'_'`	Horizontal line
`'', 'None', ' ', None`	Nothing
`'8'`	Octagon
`'p'`	Pentagon
`','`	Pixel
`'+'`	Plus
`'.'`	Point
`'s'`	Square
`'*'`	Star
`'d'`	Thin_diamond
`'v'`	Triangle_down

Marker	Description
'<'	Triangle_left
'>'	Triangle_right
'^'	Triangle_up
'|'	Vertical line
'x'	X

Color

We can get all colors that matplotlib supports by calling `matplotlib.pyplot.colors()`; this will give the following results:

Alias	Color
B	Blue
G	Green
R	Red
C	Cyan
M	Magenta
Y	Yellow
K	Black
W	White

These colors can be used in different matplotlib functions that take color arguments.

If these basic colors are not enough and as we progress, they will not be enough.We can use two other ways of defining a color value. We can use an HTML hexadecimal string as shown here:

```
color = '#eeefff'
```

We can also use legal HTML color names (`'red'`, `'chartreuse'`). We can also pass an RGB tuple normalized to `[0, 1]`:

```
color = (0.3, 0.3, 0.4)
```

The argument color is accepted by a range of functions such as `title()`:

```
title('Title in a custom color', color='#123456')
```

Background color

By providing `axisbg` to a function such as `matplotlib.pyplot.axes()` or `matplotlib.pyplot.subplot()`, we can define the background color of an axis as shown here:

```
subplot(111, axisbg=(0.1843, 0.3098, 0.3098))
```

Setting ticks, labels, and grids

In this recipe, we will continue with setting axis and line properties and adding more data to our figure and charts.

Getting ready

Let's learn a bit about figures and subplots.

In matplotlib, `figure()` is used to explicitly create a figure, which represents a user interface window. Figures are created implicitly just by calling `plot()` or similar functions. This is fine for simple charts, but having the ability to explicitly create a figure and get a reference to its instance is very useful for more advanced use.

A figure contains one or more subplots. Subplots allow us to arrange plots in a regular grid. We already used `subplot()`, in which we specify the number of rows and columns and the number of the plot we are referring to.

If we want more control, we need to use axes instances from the `matplotlib.axes.Axes` class. They allow us to place plots at any location in the figure. An example of this would be to put a smaller plot inside a bigger one.

How to do it...

Ticks are part of figures. They consist of tick locators where ticks appear and tick formatters which show how ticks appear. There are major and minor ticks. Minor ticks are not visible by default. More importantly, major and minor ticks can be formatted and located independently of each other.

We can use `matplotlib.pyplot.locator_params()` to control the behavior of tick locators. Even though tick locations are usually determined automatically, we can control the number of ticks and use a tight view if we want to when plots are smaller:

```
from pylab import *

# get current axis
ax = gca()
```

```
# set view to tight, and maximum number of tick intervals to 10
ax.locator_params(tight=True, nbins = 10)

# generate 100 normal distribution values
ax.plot(np.random.normal(10, .1, 100))

show()
```

This should give us the following graph:

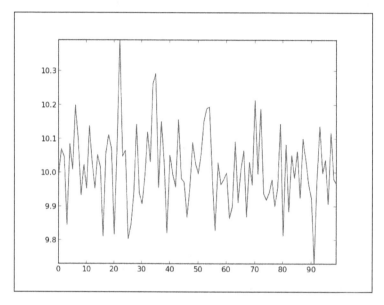

We see how the x and y axes are divided and what values are shown. We could have achieved the same setup using locator classes. Here we are saying "set the major locator to be a multiple of 10":

```
ax.xaxis.set_major_locator(matplotlib.ticker.MultipleLocator(10))
```

Tick formatters can similarly be specified. Formatters specify how the values (usually numbers) are displayed. For example, `matplotlib.ticker.FormatStrFormatter` simply specifies `'%2.1f'` or `'%1.1f cm'` as the string to be used as the label for the ticker.

Let's take a look at one example using dates.

 matplotlib represents dates in floating point values as the time in days passed since 0001-01-01 UTC plus 1. So, 0001-01-01 UTC 06:00 is 1.25.

Then we can use helper functions such as `matplotlib.dates.date2num()`, `matplotlib.dates.num2date()`, and `matplotlib.dates.drange()` to convert dates between different representations.

Let's see another example:

```
from pylab import *
import matplotlib as mpl
import datetime

fig = figure()

# get current axis
ax = gca()

# set some daterange
start = datetime.datetime(2013, 01, 01)
stop = datetime.datetime(2013, 12, 31)
delta = datetime.timedelta(days = 1)

# convert dates for matplotlib
dates = mpl.dates.drange(start, stop, delta)

# generate some random values
values = np.random.rand(len(dates))

ax = gca()

# create plot with dates
ax.plot_date(dates, values, linestyle='-', marker='')

# specify formater
date_format = mpl.dates.DateFormatter('%Y-%m-%d')

# apply formater
ax.xaxis.set_major_formatter(date_format)
```

```
# autoformat date labels
# rotates labels by 30 degrees by default
# use rotate param to specify different rotation degree
# use bottom param to give more room to date labels
fig.autofmt_xdate()

show()
```

The preceding code will give us the following graph:

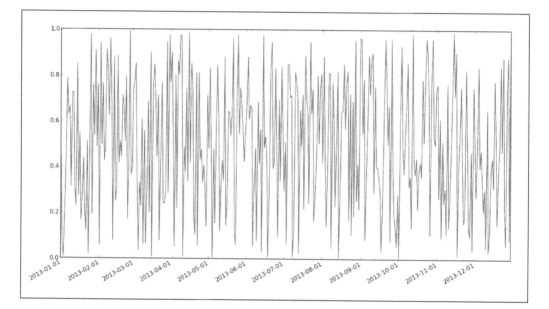

Adding legends and annotations

Legends and annotations explain data plots clearly and in context. By assigning each plot a short description about what data it represents, we are enabling an easier mental model in the reader's (viewer's) head. This recipe will show how to annotate specific points on our figures and how to create and position data legends.

Getting ready

How many times have you looked at a chart and wondered what the data represents? More often than not, newspapers and other daily and weekly publications create plots that don't contain appropriate legends, thus leaving the reader free to interpret the representation. This creates ambiguity for the readers and increases the possibility of error.

How to do it...

Let's demonstrate how to add legends and annotations with the following example:

```python
from matplotlib.pyplot import *

# generate different normal distributions
x1 =np.random.normal(30, 3, 100)
x2 = np.random.normal(20, 2, 100)
x3 = np.random.normal(10, 3, 100)

# plot them
plot(x1, label='plot')
plot(x2, label='2nd plot')
plot(x3, label='last plot')

# generate a legend box
legend(bbox_to_anchor=(0., 1.02, 1., .102), loc=3,
ncol=3, mode="expand", borderaxespad=0.)

# annotate an important value
annotate("Important value", (55,20), xycoords='data',
xytext=(5, 38),
arrowprops=dict(arrowstyle='->'))
show()
```

The preceding code will give us the following plot:

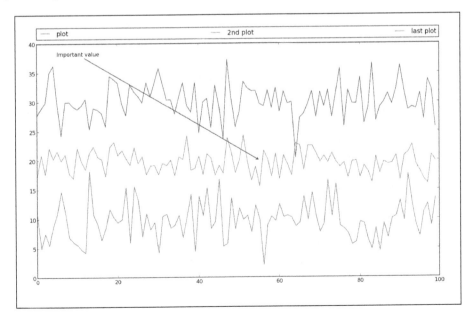

What we do is assign a string label with every plot, so `legend()` will try and determine what to add in the legend box.

We set the location of a legend box by defining the `loc` parameter. This is optional, but we want to specify a location where it is least likely for the legend box to be drawn over plot lines. Setting the location value to `0` is very useful as it automatically detects the location of the figure where the legend can fit with a minimum overlapping with the plot.

How it works...

All location parameter strings are given in the following table:

String	Number value
best	0
upper right	1
upper left	2
lower left	3
lower right	4
right	5
center left	6
center right	7
lower center	8
upper center	9
center	10

To not show the label in a legend, set the label to `_nolegend_`.

For the legend, we defined the number of columns with `ncol = 3` and set the location with `lower left`. We specified a bounding box (`bbox_to_anchor`) to start from position `(0., 1.02)` and to have a width of `1` and a height of `0.102`. These are normalized axis coordinates. Parameter `mode` is either `None` or `expand` to allow the legend box to expand horizontally filling the axis area. The parameter `borderaxespad` defines the padding between the axes and the legend border.

For annotations, we have defined a string to be drawn on a plot on a coordinate `xy`. The coordinate system is specified to be the same as the data one; therefore, coordinate system is `xycoord = 'data'`. The starting position for the text is defined by the value of `xytext`.

An arrow is drawn from `xytext` to `xy` coordinate and the `arrowprops` dictionary can define many properties for that arrow. For this example, we used `arrowstyle` to define arrow style.

Moving spines to the center

This recipe will demonstrate how to move spines to the center.

Spines define data area boundaries; they connect the axis tick marks. There are four spines. We can place them wherever we want; by default, they are placed on the border of the axis, hence we see a box around our data plot.

How to do it...

To move the spines to the center of the plot, we need to remove two spines, making them hidden (set `color` to `none`). After that, we move two others to coordinate (0,0). The coordinates are specified in data space coordinates.

The following code shows how to do this:

```python
import matplotlib.pyplot as plt
import numpy as np

x = np.linspace(-np.pi, np.pi, 500, endpoint=True)
y = np.sin(x)

plt.plot(x, y)

ax = plt.gca()

# hide two spines
ax.spines['right'].set_color('none')
ax.spines['top'].set_color('none')

# move bottom and left spine to 0,0
ax.spines['bottom'].set_position(('data',0))
ax.spines['left'].set_position(('data',0))

# move ticks positions
ax.xaxis.set_ticks_position('bottom')
ax.yaxis.set_ticks_position('left')

plt.show()
```

This is what the plot will look like:

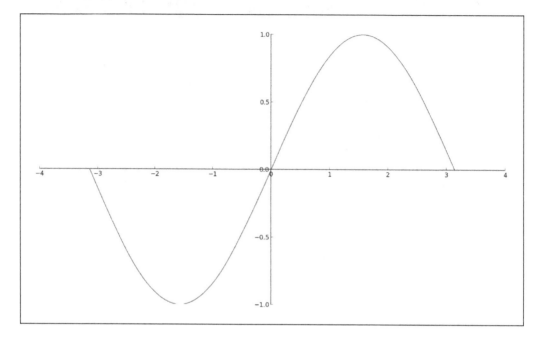

How it works...

This code is dependent on the plot that is drawn because we are moving spines to the location (0, 0) and are plotting a sine function on the interval where (0, 0) is in the middle of the plot.

Nevertheless, this demonstrated how to move spines to a particular location and how to get rid of spines we don't want to show.

There's more...

Furthermore, spines can be limited to end where the data ends (for example, using a `set_smart_bounds(True)` call). In this case, matplotlib tries to set bounds in a sophisticated way (for example, to handle inverted limits or to clip line to view if data extends past view).

Making histograms

Histograms are simple; yet it's important to get the right data into them. We will cover histograms in 2D for now.

Histograms are used to visualize estimations of distribution of data. Generally, we use a few terms when speaking of histograms. Vertical rectangles represent frequencies of data points within a particular interval called a bin. Bins are created at fixed intervals, so the total area of a histogram sums to the number of data points.

Instead of using absolute values of data, histograms can display relative frequencies of data. When this is the case, the total area equals 1.

Histograms are often used in image manipulation software as a way to visualize image properties such as distribution of light in a particular color channel. Further, these image histograms can be used in computer vision algorithms to detect peaks aiding in edge detections, image segmentation, and so on.

In *Chapter 5, Making 3D Visualizations*, we have recipes that deal with 3D histograms.

Getting ready

The number of bins is the value we want to get right, but it is hard to get them right as there are no strict rules on what is the optimal number of bins. There are different theories on how to calculate the number of bins, the simplest being the one based on a ceiling function, where the number of bins (k) is equal to the ceiling *(max(x) – min(x))/h,*where x is the dataset plotted and h is the desired bin width. This is just one option as the number of bins required to display data properly is dependent on real data distribution.

How to do it...

We create a histogram calling `matplotlib.pyplot.hist()` with a set of parameters. Here are some of the most useful ones:

- ▶ `bins`: This is either an integer number of bins or a sequence giving the bins. The default is `10`.
- ▶ `range`: This is the range of bins and is not used if bins are given as a sequence. Outliers are ignored and the default is `None`.
- ▶ `normed`: If the value for this is `True`, histogram values are normalized and form probability density. The default is `False`.

- ▶ histtype: This parameter allows us to specify the type of histogram that we want. The default value is 'bar' and the other options are shown here:
  - ❑ barstacked: This gives stacked-view histograms for multiple data
  - ❑ step: This creates a line plot that is left unfilled
  - ❑ stepfilled: This creates line plot that is filled by default

- ▶ align: This centers bars between bin edges. The default is mid. Other values are left and right.

- ▶ color: This specifies the color of the histogram. It may be a single value or have a sequence of colors. If multiple datasets are specified, the color sequence will be used in the same order. If not specified, a default line color sequence is used.

- ▶ orientation: This allows the creation of histograms that are horizontal by setting orientation to horizontal. The default is vertical.

The following code demonstrates how hist() is used:

```python
import numpy as np
import matplotlib.pyplot as plt

mu = 100
sigma = 15
x = np.random.normal(mu, sigma, 10000)

ax = plt.gca()

# the histogram of the data
ax.hist(x, bins=35, color='r')

ax.set_xlabel('Values')
ax.set_ylabel('Frequency')

ax.set_title(r'$\mathrm{Histogram:}\ \mu=%d,\ \sigma=%d$' % (mu,
sigma))

plt.show()
```

This creates a neat, red-colored histogram for our data sample:

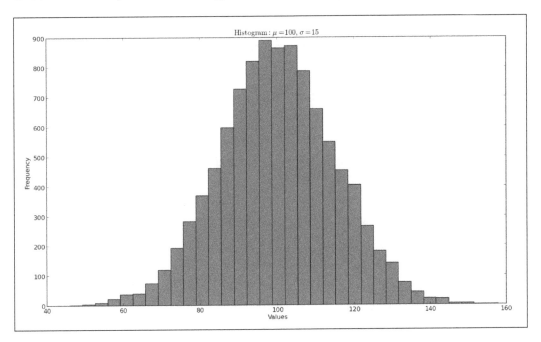

How it works...

We start by generating some normally distributed data. The histogram is plotted with the specified number of bins—35—and it is normalized by setting `normed` to `True` (or `1`); we set the `color` to red (`r`).

After that, we set labels and a title for the plot. Here we used the ability to write LaTeX expressions to write math symbols and mixed that with Python format strings.

Making bar charts with error bars

In this recipe, we will show how to create bar charts and how to draw error bars.

Getting ready

To visualize uncertainty of measurement in our dataset or to indicate the error, we can use error bars. Error bars can easily give an idea of how error free the dataset is. They can show one standard deviation, one standard error, or 95 percent confidence interval. There is no standard here, so always explicitly state what values (errors) error bars display. Most papers in the experimental sciences should contain error bars to present accuracy of the data.

How to do it...

Even though just two parameters are mandatory—`left` and `height`— we often want to use more than that. Here are some parameters we can use:

▸ `width`: This gives the width of the bars. The default value is `0.8`.

▸ `bottom`: If `bottom` is specified, the value is added to the height. The default is `None`.

▸ `edgecolor`: This gives the color of the bar edges.

▸ `ecolor`: This specifies the color of any error bar.

▸ `linewidth`: This gives width of bar edges; special values are `None` (use defaults) and `0` (when bar edges are not displayed).

▸ `orientation`: This has two values `vertical` and `horizontal`.

▸ `xerr` and `yerr`: These are used to generate error bars on the bar chart.

Some optional arguments (`color`, `edgecolor`, `linewidth`, `xerr`, and `yerr`) can be single values or sequences with the same length as the number of bars.

How it works...

Let's illustrate this using an example:

```
import numpy as np
import matplotlib.pyplot as plt

# generate number of measurements
x = np.arange(0, 10, 1)

# values computed from "measured"
y = np.log(x)

# add some error samples from standard normal distribution
xe = 0.1 * np.abs(np.random.randn(len(y)))

# draw and show errorbar
plt.bar(x, y, yerr=xe, width=0.4, align='center', ecolor='r',
color='cyan', label='experiment #1');

# give some explanations
plt.xlabel('# measurement')
plt.ylabel('Measured values')
plt.title('Measurements')
```

```
plt.legend(loc='upper left')

plt.show()
```

The preceding code will plot the following diagram:

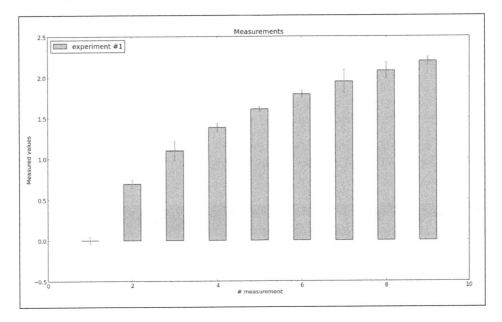

To be able to plot an error bar, we needed to have some measures (x); for every measure computed (y), we introduced errors (xe).

We used NumPy to generate and compute values; standard distributions are good enough for demonstration purposes, but if you happen to know your data distribution in advance, you can always make some prototype visualizations and try out different layouts to find the best options to present information.

Another interesting option to use if we are preparing visualizations for a black-and-white medium is hatch; it can have the following values:

Hatch value	Description
/	Diagonal hatching
\	Back diagonal
|	Vertical hatching
–	Horizontal
+	Crossed
x	Crossed diagonal

Hatch value	Description
o	Small circle
0	Large circle
.	Dot pattern
*	Star pattern

There's more...

What we have just used are error bars known as symmetrical error bars. If the nature of our dataset is such that errors are not the same in both directions (negative and positive), we can also specify them separately using asymmetrical error bars.

All we have to do differently is to specify `xerr` or `yerr` using a two-element list (such as a 2D array), where the first list contains values for negative errors and the second one for positive errors.

Making pie charts count

Pie charts are special in many ways, the most important being that the dataset they display must sum up to 100 percent or they are just not valid.

Getting ready

Pie charts represent numerical proportions, where the arc length of each segment is proportional to the quantity it represents.

They are compact and can look very aesthetically pleasing, but they have been criticized as they can be hard to compare. Another property of pie charts that does not work in their best interest is that pie charts are presented in a specific angle (perspective) and segments use certain colors that can skew our perception and influence our conclusion about information presented.

What we will show here is different ways to use pie charts to present data.

How to do it...

Here, we create a so-called **exploded** pie chart:

```
from pylab import *

# make a square figure and axes
figure(1, figsize=(6,6))
ax = axes([0.1, 0.1, 0.8, 0.8])

# the slices will be ordered
# and plotted counter-clockwise.
labels = 'Spring', 'Summer', 'Autumn', 'Winter'

# fractions are either x/sum(x) or x if sum(x) <= 1
x = [15, 30, 45, 10]

# explode must be len(x) sequence or None
explode=(0.1, 0.1, 0.1, 0.1)

pie(x, explode=explode, labels=labels,
autopct='%1.1f%%', startangle=67)

title('Rainy days by season')

show()
```

Pie charts look best if they are inside a square figure and have square axes.

Fractions of the whole sum of the pie chart are defined as $x/sum(x)$ or x if $sum(x) <= 1$. We get the explode effect by defining an explode sequence where each item represents the fraction of radius with which to offset each arc. We use the `autopct` parameter to format the labels that will be drawn inside the arcs; they can be a format string or a callable (function).

We can also use a Boolean shadow parameter to add a shadow effect to a pie chart.

If we don't specify `startangle`, the fractions will be ordered starting counterclockwise from the x axis (angle 0). If we specify `90` as the value of `startangle`, that will start the pie chart from the y axis.

This is the resulting pie chart:

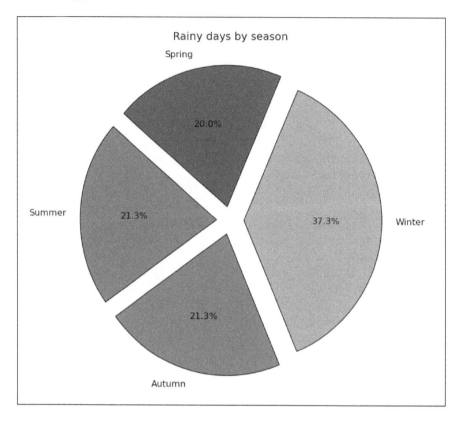

Plotting with filled areas

In this recipe, we will show you how to fill the area under a curve or in between two different curves.

Getting ready

Library matplotlib allows us to fill areas in between and under the curves with color so that we can display the value of that area to the spectator. Sometimes, it is necessary for readers (viewers) to comprehend the given specialization.

How to do it...

Here's one example of how to fill areas between two contours:

```
from matplotlib.pyplot import figure, show, gca
import numpy as np

x = np.arange(0.0, 2, 0.01)

# two different signals are measured
y1 = np.sin(2*np.pi*x)
y2 = 1.2*np.sin(4*np.pi*x)

fig = figure()
ax = gca()

# plot and
# fill between y1 and y2 where a logical condition is met
ax.plot(x, y1, x, y2, color='black')

ax.fill_between(x, y1, y2, where=y2>=y1, facecolor='darkblue',
interpolate=True)
ax.fill_between(x, y1, y2, where=y2<=y1, facecolor='deeppink',
interpolate=True)

ax.set_title('filled between')

show()
```

How it works...

After we have generated random signals for a predefined interval, we plot these two signals using a regular `plot()`. Then we call `fill_between()` with properties that are required and mandatory.

The function `fill_between()` is using x as the location from where to pick y values (y1, y2) and will then plot the polygon in certain defined colors.

We specify a condition to fill the curve with the `where` parameter, which accepts Boolean values (can be expressions) so that the fill happens only when the `where` condition is met.

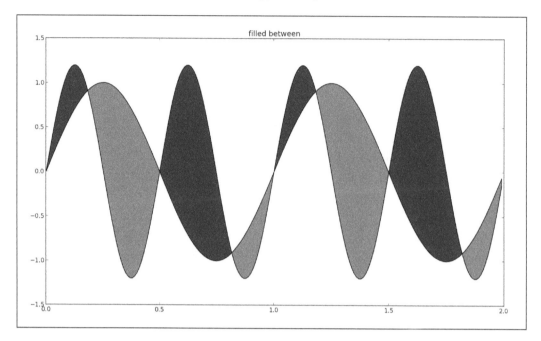

There's more...

Similar to other functions for plotting, this function also accepts many more parameters like `hatch` (to specify patterns to fill with instead of color) and line options (`linewidth` and `linestyle`).

There is also `fill_betweenx()`, which enables similar fill features, but it does so between horizontal curves.

The more general function `fill()` provides the ability to fill any polygon with a color or a hatch.

Making stacked plots

In this recipe, we will show you how to produce a **stacked plot**. Stacked plots are used when plotting a quantity which can be represented as the sum of several contributions. A stacked plot will allow us to represent not only the overall trend but also the trend of each individual components contributing to the total quantity.

Getting ready

We will consider the world's energy production as our total quantity and will represent the detailed break down in different energy sourced. We will represent the evolution of energy production type from 1973 to 2014. This data is contained in the file `ch03-energy-production.csv`. The data has been taken from `http://www.eia.gov/totalenergy/data/monthly/` and reshaped for the need of the recipe.

How to do it...

Here is the code to produce the stacked plot displayed further:

```python
import pandas as pd
import matplotlib.pyplot as plt

# We load the data with pandas.
df = pd.read_csv('ch03-energy-production.csv')

# We give names for the columns that we want to load. Different types
of energy have been ordered by total production values).
columns = ['Coal', 'Natural Gas (Dry)', 'Crude Oil', 'Nuclear Electric
Power',
  'Biomass Energy', 'Hydroelectric Power', 'Natural Gas Plant Liquids',
  'Wind Energy', 'Geothermal Energy', 'Solar/PV Energy']

# We define some specific colors to plot each type of energy produced.
colors = ['darkslategray', 'powderblue', 'darkmagenta', 'lightgreen',
'sienna',
  'royalblue', 'mistyrose', 'lavender', 'tomato', 'gold']

# Let's create the figure.
plt.figure(figsize = (12,8))
polys = plt.stackplot(df['Year'], df[columns].values.T, colors =
colors)

# The legend is not yet supported with stackplot. We will add it
manually.
rectangles= []
for poly in polys:
rectangles.append(plt.Rectangle((0, 0), 1, 1, fc=poly.get_facecolor()
[0]))
legend = plt.legend(rectangles, columns, loc = 3)
frame = legend.get_frame()
```

```
frame.set_color('white')

# We add some information to the plot.
plt.title('Primary Energy Production by Source', fontsize = 16)
plt.xlabel('Year', fontsize = 16)
plt.ylabel('Production (Quad BTU)', fontsize = 16)
plt.xticks(fontsize = 16)
plt.yticks(fontsize = 16)
plt.xlim(1973,2014)

# Finally we show the figure.
plt.show()
```

Here is the plot we obtain:

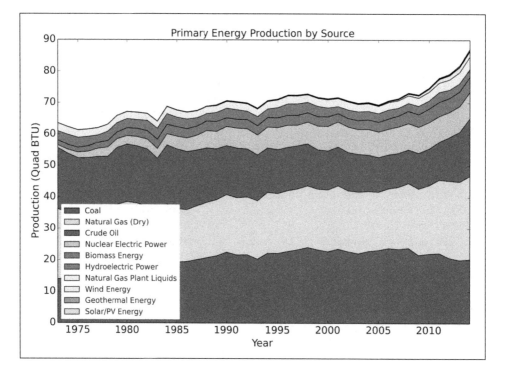

At a glance, we can see that the world's energy production is constantly increasing and has entered a faster growing phase since 2005. We can also analyze the evolution of each type of energy. Coal production is slowly decreasing while natural gas and crude oil productions are increasing. Nuclear production has also started to decrease. At the top of the stacked plot (which is more visible by zooming), we can see that renewable energies are still forming a negligible part of the global world's production. The stacked plot was the perfect tool to represent this dataset.

How it works...

The command `stackplot()` works just like the `plot()` command but can accept a multidimensional array as a second input. This array's first dimension is the number of filled areas to plot while the second dimension is the same as the first input array. In our case, the shape of `df['Year']` is (42,), while the shape of `df[columns].values.T` is (10,42). Note that we use the transpose operator `T` in order to have the second array in the right format. `stackplot()` creates a list of polygons that we store in the variable polys.

The legend is not yet supported with stacked plots. We therefore use the commands `plt.Rectangle()` to create the legend's rectangles. Each rectangle's colors is specified using `poly.get_facecolor()[0]`, where poly is an element of the list of polygons created by the `stackplot()` command.

Plotting the legend is then done simply using the command `legend()` with the rectangles as first arguments and the names of each corresponding type of energy source as second arguments. The third argument is used to specify the location of the legend. We set the background of the legend to white by first using the method `get_frame()` of the object legend, and then setting it's color to white with the frame's `set_color()` method.

Drawing scatter plots with colored markers

If you have two variables and want to spot the correlation between those, a scatter plot may be the solution to spot patterns.

This type of plot is also very usable as a start for more advanced visualization of multidimensional data (for example, to plot a scatter plot matrix).

Getting ready

Scatter plots display values for two sets of data. The data visualization is done as a collection of points not connected by lines. Each of them has its coordinates determined by the value of the variables. One variable is controlled (independent variable), while the other variable is measured (dependent variable) and is often plotted on the y axis.

How to do it...

Here's a code sample that plots two plots: one with uncorrelated data and the other with strong positive correlation:

```python
import matplotlib.pyplot as plt
import numpy as np

# generate x values
x = np.random.randn(1000)

# random measurements, no correlation
y1 = np.random.randn(len(x))

# strong correlation
y2 = 1.2 + np.exp(x)

ax1 = plt.subplot(121)
plt.scatter(x, y1, color='indigo', alpha=0.3, edgecolors='white',
label='no correl')
plt.xlabel('no correlation')
plt.grid(True)
plt.legend()

ax2 = plt.subplot(122, sharey=ax1, sharex=ax1)
plt.scatter(x, y2, color='green', alpha=0.3, edgecolors='grey',
label='correl')
plt.xlabel('strong correlation')
plt.grid(True)
plt.legend()

plt.show()
```

Here, we also use more parameters such as `color` for setting the color of the plot, `marker` for using as a point marker (the default is `circle`), `alpha` (alpha transparency), `edgecolors` (color of the marker edge), and `label` (for legend box).

These are the plots we get:

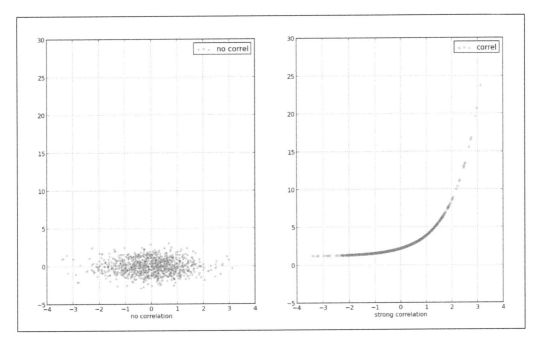

How it works...

A scatter plot is often used to identify potential association between two variables, and it's often drawn before working on a fitting regression function. It gives a good visual picture of the correlation, particularly for nonlinear relationships. matplotlib provides the scatter() function to plot x versus y—unidimensional array of the same length as a scatter plot.

4
More Plots and Customizations

In this chapter we will learn about:

- ▶ Setting the transparency and size of axis labels
- ▶ Adding a shadow to the chart line
- ▶ Adding a data table to the figure
- ▶ Using subplots
- ▶ Customizing grids
- ▶ Creating contour plots
- ▶ Filling an under-plot area
- ▶ Drawing polar plots
- ▶ Visualizing the filesystem tree using a polar bar
- ▶ Customizing matplotlib with style

Introduction

In this chapter, we will explore more advanced properties of the matplotlib library. We are going to introduce more options and will look at how to achieve certain visually pleasing results.

During this chapter, we will seek the solutions to some non-trivial problems with representing data when simple charts are not enough. We will try to use more than one type of graph or create hybrid graphs to cover advanced data structures and the representation required.

Setting the transparency and size of axis labels

The `Axes` label describes what the data in the figure represents and is quite important for the viewer's understanding of the figure itself. By providing labels to the axes background, we help the viewer comprehend the information in an appropriate way.

Getting ready

Before we dive into the code, it is important to understand how matplotlib organizes our figures.

At the top level, there is a `Figure` instance containing all that we see and some more (that we don't see). The figure contains, among other things, instances of the `Axes` class as a `Figure.axes` field. The `Axes` instances contain almost everything we care about: all the lines, points, ticks, and labels. So, when we call `plot()`, we are adding a line (`matplotlib.lines.Line2D`) to the `Axes.lines` list. If we plot a histogram (`hist()`), we are adding rectangles to the list of `Axes.patches` ("patches" is the term inherited from MATLAB®, and it represents the "patch of color" concept).

An instance of `Axes` also holds references to the `XAxis` and `YAxis` instances, which in turn refer to the *x* axis and *y* axis, respectively. The `XAxis` and `YAxis` instances manage the drawing of the axis, labels, ticks, tick labels, locators, and formatters. We can reference these through `Axes.xaxis` and `Axes.yaxis`, respectively. We don't have to go all the way down to `XAxis` or `YAxis` instances to get to the labels as matplotlib gives us a helper method (practically a shortcut) that enables iterations via these labels: `matplotlib.pyplot.xlabel()` and `matplotlib.pyplot.ylabel()`.

How to do it...

We will now create a new figure, in which we will:

1. Create a plot with some random generated data.

2. Add the `title` and `axes` labels.

3. Add alpha settings.

4. Add shadow effects to the title and axes labels.

   ```
   import matplotlib.pyplot as plt
   from matplotlib import patheffects
   import numpy as np
   data = np.random.randn(70)
   ```

```
fontsize = 18
plt.plot(data)

title = "This is figure title"
x_label = "This is x axis label"
y_label = "This is y axis label"

title_text_obj = plt.title(title, fontsize=fontsize,
verticalalignment='bottom')

title_text_obj.set_path_effects([patheffects.
withSimplePatchShadow()])

# offset_xy -- set the 'angle' of the shadow
# shadow_rgbFace -- set the color of the shadow
# patch_alpha -- setup the transparency of the shadow

offset_xy = (1, -1)
rgbRed = (1.0,0.0,0.0)
alpha = 0.8

# customize shadow properties
pe = patheffects.withSimplePatchShadow(offset_xy = offset_xy,
shadow_rgbFace = rgbRed,
patch_alpha = alpha)
# apply them to the xaxis and yaxis labels
xlabel_obj = plt.xlabel(x_label, fontsize=fontsize, alpha=0.5)
xlabel_obj.set_path_effects([pe])

ylabel_obj = plt.ylabel(y_label, fontsize=fontsize, alpha=0.5)
ylabel_obj.set_path_effects([pe])

plt.show()
```

How it works...

We already know all the familiar imports, parts that generate data, and basic plotting techniques, so we will skip those. If you are not able to decipher the first few lines of the example, please refer to *Chapter 2*, *Knowing Your Data*, and *Chapter 3*, *Drawing Your First Plots and Customizing Them*, where these concepts are already explained.

After we have plotted the dataset, we are ready to add titles and labels, and to customize their appearance.

First, we add the title. Then, we define the font size and vertical alignment of the title text to be bottom aligned. The default shadow effect is added to the title if we are using `matplotlib.patheffects.withSimplePatchShadow()` with no parameters. The default values for the parameters are: `offset_xy=(2,-2)`, `shadow_rgbFace=None`, and `patch_alpha=0.7`. The other values are `center`, `top`, and `baseline`, but we choose `bottom` as the text will have some shadowing. In the next line, we add the shadow effect. The path effects are part of the matplotlib module `matplotlib.patheffects` that supports `matplotlib.text.Text` and `matplotlib.patches.Patch`.

We now want to add different settings of the shadow to both the x and y axes. First, we customize the position (offset) of the shadow to the parent object, and then we set the color of the shadow. The color is here represented in triples (3-tuple) of float values between 0.0 and 1.0, for each of the RGB channels. For example, our red color is represented as (`1.0`, `0.0`, `0.0`) (all red, no green and no blue).

The transparency (or alpha) is set up as a normalized value, and we also want to set this up here to be different from the default.

With all the settings present, we instantiate `matplotlib.patheffects.withSimplePatchShadow` and hold the reference to it in the variable `pe` to reuse it few lines later.

To be able to apply the shadow effect, we need to get to the `label` object. This is simple enough because `matplotlib.pyplot.xlabel()` returns a reference to the object (`matplotlib.text.Text`) that we then use to call `set_path_effects([pe])`.

We finally show the plot and can feel proud of our work.

There's more...

If you are not satisfied with the effects that `matplotlib.patheffects` currently offers, you can inherit the `matplotlib.patheffects._Base` class and override the `draw_path` method. Take a look at the code and comments on how to do this here:

`https://github.com/matplotlib/matplotlib/blob/master/lib/matplotlib/patheffects.py#L47`

Adding a shadow to the chart line

To be able to distinguish one particular plot line in the figure or just to fit in the overall style of the output our figure is in, we sometimes need to add a shadow effect to the chart line (or histogram, for that matter). In this recipe, you will be learning how to add a shadow effect to the plot's chart lines.

Getting ready

To add shadows to the lines or rectangles in our charts, we need to use the transformation framework built in matplotlib and located in `matplotlib.transforms`.

To understand how it all works, we need to explain what transformations are available in matplotlib and how they work.

Transformations know how to convert the given coordinates from their coordinate system into display. They also know how to convert them from display coordinates into their own coordinate system.

The following table summarizes the existing coordinate systems and what they represent:

Coordinate system	Transformation object	Description
Data	Axes.transData	Represents the user's data coordinate system.
Axes	Axes.transAxes	Represents the Axes coordinate system, where (0,0) represents the bottom-left end of the axes and (1,1) represents the upper-right end of the axes.
Figure	Figure.transFigure	This is the Figure coordinate system, where (0,0) represents the bottom-left end of the figure and (1,1) represents the upper-right end of the figure.
Display	None	Represents the pixel coordinate system of the user display, where (0,0) represents the bottom-left of the display, and tuple (width, height) represents the upper-right of the display, where width and height are in pixels.

Note how the display does not have a value in the column. This is because the default coordinate system is Display, so coordinates are always in pixels relative to your display coordinate systems. This is not very useful, and most often we want them normalized into Figure or Axes or a Data coordinate system.

This framework enables us to transform the current object into an offset object, that is, to place that object shifted a certain distance from the original object.

We will use this framework to create our desired effect on the plotted sine wave.

How to do it...

Here is the code recipe to add shadowing to the plotted chart. The code is explained in the section that follows.

```python
import numpy as np
import matplotlib.pyplot as plt
import matplotlib.transforms as transforms

def setup(layout=None):
    assert layout is not None

    fig = plt.figure()
    ax = fig.add_subplot(layout)
    return fig, ax

def get_signal():
    t = np.arange(0., 2.5, 0.01)
    s = np.sin(5 * np.pi * t)
    return t, s

def plot_signal(t, s):
    line, = axes.plot(t, s, linewidth=5, color='magenta')
    return line

def make_shadow(fig, axes, line, t, s):
    delta = 2 / 72.  # how many points to move the shadow
    offset = transforms.ScaledTranslation(delta, -delta, fig.dpi_
scale_trans)
    offset_transform = axes.transData + offset

    # We plot the same data, but now using offset transform
    # zorder -- to render it below the line
    axes.plot(t, s, linewidth=5, color='gray',
            transform=offset_transform,
            zorder=0.5 * line.get_zorder())

if __name__ == "__main__":
    fig, axes = setup(111)
    t, s = get_signal()
    line = plot_signal(t, s)

    make_shadow(fig, axes, line, t, s)

    axes.set_title('Shadow effect using an offset transform')
    plt.show()
```

How it works...

We start reading the code from the bottom, after the `if __name__` check. First, we create the figure and axes in `setup()`; after that, we obtain a signal (or generate data—sine wave). We plot the basic signal in `plot_signal()`. Then, we make the shadow transformation and plot the shadow in `make_shadow()`.

We use the offset effect to create an offset object underneath and just a few points away from the original object.

The original object is a simple sine wave that we plot using the standard function `plot()`.

To add to this offset transformation, matplotlib contains helper transformation— `matplotlib.transforms.ScaledTranslation`.

The values for `dx` and `dy` are defined in points, and as the point is 1/72 inches, we move the offset object 2 pt right and 2pt down.

 If you want to learn more about how we converted the point to 1/72 inches, read more in this Wikipedia article: `http://en.wikipedia.org/wiki/Point_%28typography%29`.

We can use `matplotlib.transforms.ScaledTransformation(xtr, ytr, scaletr)`; here, `xtr` and `ytr` are translation offsets and `scaletr` is a transformation callable to scale `xtr` and `ytr` at transformation time and before display. The most common use case for this is transforming from points to display space—for example—to DPI so that the offset always stays at the same place no matter what the actual output—be it the monitor or printed material. The callable we use for this is already built in, and is available at `Figure.dpi_scale_trans`.

We then plot the same data with the applied transformation.

There's more...

Using transforms to add shadows is just one and not the most popular use case of this framework. To be able to do more with the transformation framework, you will need to learn the details of how the transformation pipeline works and what the extension points are (what classes to inherit and how). This easy enough because matplotlib is open source, and even if some code is not well documented, there is a source you can read from and use or change, thus contributing to the overall quality and usefulness of matplotlib.

Adding a data table to the figure

Although matplotlib is mainly a plotting library, it helps us with small errands when we are creating a chart, such as having a neat data table beside our beautiful chart. In this recipe, you will be learning how to display a data table alongside the plots in the figure.

Getting ready

It is important to understand why we are adding a table to a chart. The main intention of plotting data visually is to explain the otherwise not understandable (or hardly understandable) data values. Now, we want to add that data back. It is not wise just to cram a big table with values underneath the chart.

But, carefully picked, maybe the summed or highlighted values from the whole, a charted dataset can identify important parts of the chart or emphasize the important values for those places where the exact value (for example, yearly sales in USD) is important (or even required).

How to do it...

Here's the code to add a sample table to our figure:

```
import matplotlib.pyplot as plt
import numpy as np

plt.figure()
ax = plt.gca()
y = np.random.randn(9)

col_labels = ['col1','col2','col3']
row_labels = ['row1','row2','row3']
table_vals = [[11, 12, 13], [21, 22, 23], [28, 29, 30]]
row_colors = ['red', 'gold', 'green']
my_table = plt.table(cellText=table_vals,
colWidths=[0.1] * 3,
rowLabels=row_labels,
colLabels=col_labels,
rowColours=row_colors,
loc='upper right')

plt.plot(y)
plt.show()
```

The previous code snippet gives a plot such as the following:

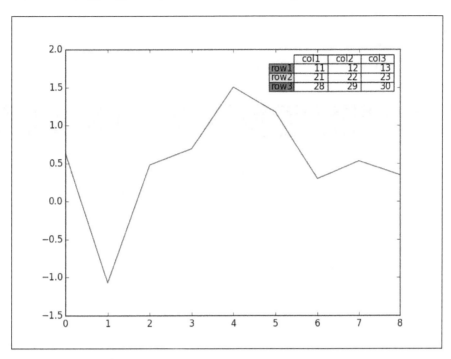

How it works...

Using `plt.table()`, we create a table of cells and add it to the current axes. The table can have (optional) row and column headers. Each table cell contains either patch or text. The column widths and row heights for the table can be specified. The return value is a sequence of objects (text, line, and patch instances) that the table is made of.

The basic function signature is:

```
table(cellText=None, cellColours=None,
cellLoc='right', colWidths=None,
rowLabels=None, rowColours=None, rowLoc='left',
colLabels=None, colColours=None, colLoc='center',
loc='bottom', bbox=None)
```

The function instantiates and returns the `matplotlib.table.Table` instance. This is usually the case with matplotlib; there's just one way to add the table to the figure. The object-oriented interface can be directly accessed. We can use the `matplotlib.table.Table` class directly to fine-tune our table before we add it onto our `axes` instance with `add_table()`.

There's more...

You can have more control if you directly create an instance of `matplotlib.table.Table` and configure it before you add it to the `axes` instance. You can add the `table` instance to `axes` using `Axes.add_table(table)`, where `table` is an instance of `matplotlib.table.Table`.

Using subplots

If you are reading this book from the beginning, you are probably familiar with the `subplot` class, a descendant of `axes` that lives on the regular grid of `subplot` instances. We are going to explain and demonstrate how to use subplots in advanced ways.

In this recipe, you will be learning how to create custom subplot configurations on our plots.

Getting ready

The base class for subplots is `matplotlib.axes.SubplotBase`. These subplots are `matplotlib.axes.Axes` instances, but provide helper methods for generating and manipulating a set of `Axes` within a figure.

There is a class `matplotlib.figure.SubplotParams`, which holds all the parameters for `subplot`. The dimensions are normalized to the width or height of the figure. As we already know, if we don't specify any custom values, they will be read from the `rc` parameters.

The scripting layer (`matplotlib.pyplot`) holds a few helper methods to manipulate subplots.

`matplotlib.pyplot.subplots` is used for the easy creation of common layouts of subplots. We can specify the size of the grid—the number of rows and columns of the subplot grid.

We can create subplots that share the *X* or *Y* axes. This is achieved using `sharex` or the `sharey` keyword argument. The `sharex` argument can have the `True` value, in which case the *X* axis is shared among all the subplots. The tick labels will be invisible on all but the last row of plots. They can also be defined as String, with enumerated values of `row`, `col`, `all`, or `none`. The `all` value is the same as `True`, and the value `none` is the same as `False`. If the value `row` is specified, each subplot row shares the *X* axis. If the value `col` is specified, each subplot column shares the *X* axis. This helper returns tuple `fig, ax`, where `ax` is either an axis instance or, if more than one subplot is created, an array of axis instances.

`matplotlib.pyplot.subplots_adjust` is used to tune the subplot layout. The keyword arguments specify the coordinates of the subplots inside the figure (`left`, `right`, `bottom`, and `top`) normalized to figure size. White space can be specified to be left between the subplots using the `wspace` and `hspace` arguments for width and height amounts, respectively.

How to do it...

1. We will show you an example of using yet another helper function in the matplotlib toolkit—`subplot2grid`. We define the grid's geometry and the subplot location. Note that this location is 0-based not 1-based as we are used to in `plot.subplot()`. We can also use `colspan` and `rowspan` to allow the subplot to span multiple columns and rows in a given grid. For example, we will create a figure, add various subplot layouts using `subplot2grid`, and reconfigure the tick label size.

2. Show the plot:

```
import matplotlib.pyplot as plt

plt.figure(0)
axes1 = plt.subplot2grid((3, 3), (0, 0), colspan=3)
axes2 = plt.subplot2grid((3, 3), (1, 0), colspan=2)
axes3 = plt.subplot2grid((3, 3), (1, 2))
axes4 = plt.subplot2grid((3, 3), (2, 0))
axes5 = plt.subplot2grid((3, 3), (2, 1), colspan=2)

# tidy up tick labels size
all_axes = plt.gcf().axes
for ax in all_axes:
forticklabel in ax.get_xticklabels() + ax.get_yticklabels():
ticklabel.set_fontsize(10)

plt.suptitle("Demo of subplot2grid")
plt.show()
```

When we execute the previous code, the following plot is created:

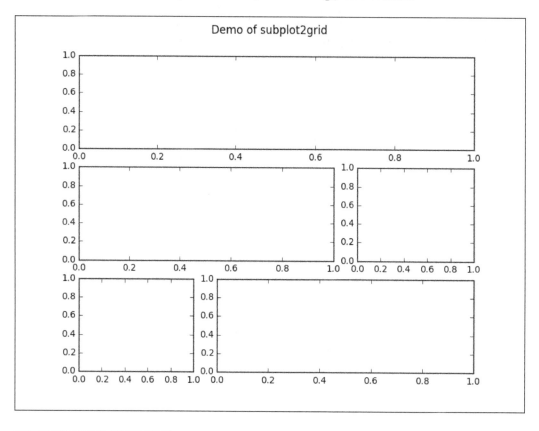

How it works...

We provide `subplot2grid` with a shape, location (`loc`), and optionally, `rowspan` and `colspan`. The important difference here is that the location is indexed from 0, and not from 1, as in `figure.add_subplot`.

There's more...

To give an example of another way, you can customize the current `axes` or `subplot`:

```
axes = fig.add_subplot(111)
rectangle = axes.patch
rectangle.set_facecolor('blue')
```

Here we see that every `axes` instance contains a field patch referencing the `rectangle` instance, thus representing the background of the current `axes` instance. This instance has properties that we can update, hence updating the current `axes` background. We can change its color, but we can also load an image to add a watermark protection, for example.

It is also possible to create a patch first and then just add it to the `axes` background:

```
fig = plt.figure()
axes = fig.add_subplot(111)
rect = matplotlib.patches.Rectangle((1,1), width=6, height=12)
axes.add_patch(rect)
# we have to manually force a figure draw
axes.figure.canvas.draw()
```

Customizing grids

A grid is usually handy to have under lines and charts as it helps the human eye spot differences in patterns and compare plots visually in the figure. To be able to set up how visibly, how frequently, and in what style the grid is displayed—or whether it is displayed at all—we should use `matplotlib.pyplot.grid`.

In this recipe, you will be learning how to turn the grid on and off and how to change the major and minor ticks on a grid.

Getting ready

The most frequent grid customization is reachable in the `matplotlib.pyplot.grid` helper function.

To see the interactive effect of this, you should run the following under `ipython`. The basic call to `plt.grid()` will toggle the grid visibility in the current interactive session started by the last `IPythonPyLab` environment:

```
In [1]: plt.plot([1,2,3,3.5,4,4.3,3])
Out[1]: [<matplotlib.lines.Line2D at 0x3dcc810>]
```

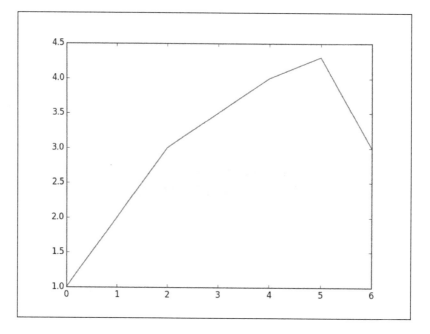

Now, we can toggle the grid on the same figure:

```
In [2]: plt.grid()
```

We turn the grid back on, as shown in the following plot:

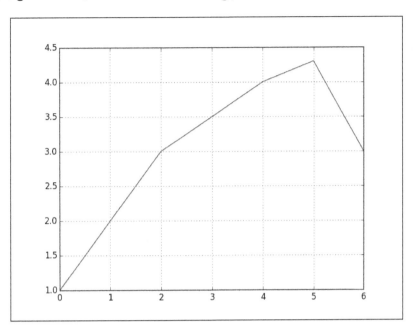

We then turn it off again:

```
In [3]: plt.grid()
```

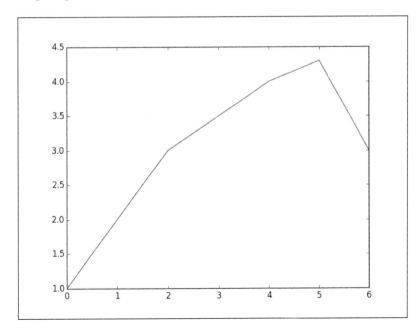

Apart from just turning it on and off, we can further customize the grid's appearance.

We can manipulate the grid with just major ticks, or just minor ticks, or both; hence, the value of function argument `which` can be `'major'`, `'minor'`, or `'both'`. Similarly, we can control the horizontal and vertical ticks separately using the argument `axis` that can have values `'x'`, `'y'`, or `'both'`.

All the other properties are passed via `kwargs` and represent a standard set of properties that a `matplotlib.lines.Line2D` instance can accept, such as `color`, `linestyle`, and `linewidth`; here is an example:

```
ax.grid(color='g', linestyle='--', linewidth=1)
```

How to do it...

This is nice, but we want to be able to customize more. In order to do that, we need to reach deeper into matplotlib and into `mpl_toolkits` and find the `AxesGrid` module that allows us to make grids of axes in an easy and manageable way:

```python
import numpy as np
import matplotlib.pyplot as plt
from mpl_toolkits.axes_grid1 import ImageGrid
from matplotlib.cbook import get_sample_data


def get_demo_image():
    f = get_sample_data("axes_grid/bivariate_normal.npy",
asfileobj=False)
    # z is a numpy array of 15x15
    Z = np.load(f)
    return Z, (-3, 4, -4, 3)


def get_grid(fig=None, layout=None, nrows_ncols=None):
    assert fig is not None
    assert layout is not None
    assert nrows_ncols is not None

    grid = ImageGrid(fig, layout, nrows_ncols=nrows_ncols,
                axes_pad=0.05, add_all=True, label_mode="L")
    return grid


def load_images_to_grid(grid, Z, *images):
    min, max = Z.min(), Z.max()
    for i, image in enumerate(images):
```

```
        axes = grid[i]
        axes.imshow(image, origin="lower", vmin=min, vmax=max,
                    interpolation="nearest")

if __name__ == "__main__":
    fig = plt.figure(1, (8, 6))
    grid = get_grid(fig, 111, (1, 3))
    Z, extent = get_demo_image()

    # Slice image
    image1 = Z
    image2 = Z[:, :10]
    image3 = Z[:, 10:]

    load_images_to_grid(grid, Z, image1, image2, image3)

    plt.draw()
    plt.show()
```

The given code will render the following plot:

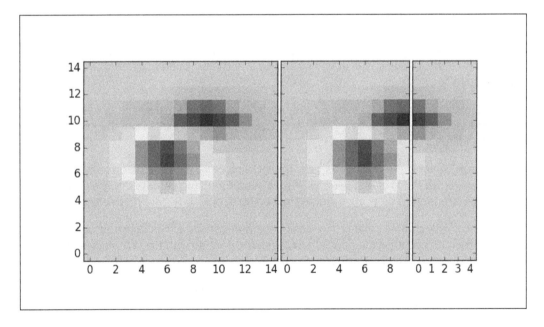

How it works...

In the `get_demo_image` function, we loaded data from the sample data directory that comes with matplotlib.

The list `grid` holds our `axes` grid (in this case, `ImageGrid`).

The variables `image1`, `image2`, and `image3` hold sliced data from Z that we have split over multiple axes in the list `grid`.

Looping over all the grids, we are plotting data from `im1`, `im2`, and `im3` using the standard `imshow()` call, while matplotlib takes care that everything is neatly rendered and aligned.

Creating contour plots

A contour plot displays the **isolines** of a matrix. Isolines are curves where a function of two variables has the same value.

In this recipe, you will learn how to create contour plots.

Getting ready

Contours are represented as contour plots of the matrix z, where z is interpreted as height with respect to the *XY* plane. z is of minimum size 2 and must contain at least two different values.

The problem with contour plots is that if they are coded without labeling the isolines, they are rendered pretty useless as we cannot decode the high points from the low points or find local minimas.

Here, we need to label the contour as well. The labeling of isolines can be done by using either labels (`clabel()`) or `colormaps`. If your output medium permits the use of color, `colormaps` are preferred because viewers will be able to decode data more easily.

The other risk with contour plots is in choosing the number of isolines to plot. If we choose too many, the plot becomes too dense to decode, and if we go with too few isolines, we lose information and can perceive data differently.

The `contour()` function will automatically guess how many isolines to plot, but we also have the ability to specify our own number.

In matplotlib, we draw contour plots using `matplotlib.pyplot.contour`.

There are two similar functions: `contour()` draws contour lines, and `contourf()` draws filled contours. We are going to demonstrate only `contour()`, but almost everything is applicable to `contourf()`. They understand almost the same arguments as well.

The `contour()` function can have different call signatures, depending on what data we have and/or what the properties that we want to visualize are.

Call signature	Description
`contour(Z)`	Plots the contour of `Z` (array). The level values are chosen automatically.
`contour(X,Y,Z)`	Plots the contour of `X`, `Y`, and `Z`. The arrays `X` and `Y` are (x, y) surface coordinates.
`contour(Z,N)` `contour(X,Y,Z,N)`	Plots the contour of `Z`, where the number of levels is defined by `N`. The level values are automatically chosen.
`contour(Z,V)` `contour(X,Y,Z,V)`	Plots the contour lines with levels at the values specified in `V`.
`contourf(..., V)`	Fills the `len(V)-1` regions between the level values in sequence `V`.
`contour(Z, **kwargs)`	Uses keyword arguments to control common line properties (colors, line width, origin, color map, and so on).

There exist certain constraints on the dimensionality and shape of `X`, `Y`, and `Z`. For example, `X` and `Y` can be of two dimensions and of the same shape as `Z`. If they are of one dimension, such that the length of `X` is equal to the number of columns in `Z`, then the length of `Y` will be equal to the number of rows in `Z`.

How to do it...

In the following code example, we will:

1. Implement a function to act as a mock signal processor.
2. Generate some linear signal data.
3. Transform the data into suitable matrices for use in matrix operations.
4. Plot contour lines.
5. Add contour line labels.
6. Show the plot.

```
import numpy as np
import matplotlib as mpl
import matplotlib.pyplot as plt
defprocess_signals(x,y):
return (1 - (x ** 2 + y ** 2)) * np.exp(-y ** 3 / 3)
```

```
x = np.arange(-1.5, 1.5, 0.1)
y = np.arange(-1.5, 1.5, 0.1)

# Make grids of points
X,Y = np.meshgrid(x, y)

Z = process_signals(X, Y)

# Number of isolines
N = np.arange(-1, 1.5, 0.3)

# adding the Contour lines with labels
CS = plt.contour(Z, N, linewidths=2, cmap=mpl.cm.jet)
plt.clabel(CS, inline=True, fmt='%1.1f', fontsize=10)
plt.colorbar(CS)

plt.title('My function: $z=(1-x^2+y^2) e^{-(y^3)/3}$')
plt.show()
```

This will give us the following chart:

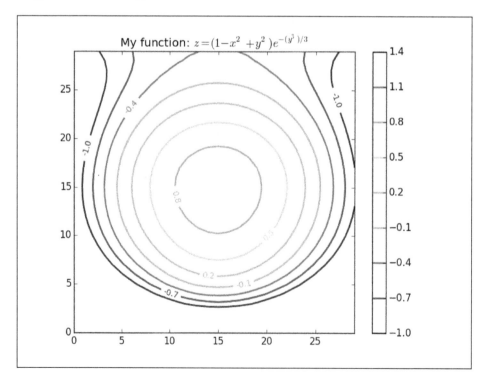

How it works...

We reached for little helpers from `numpy` to create our ranges and matrices.

After we evaluated `my_function` into Z, we simply called `contour`, providing Z and the number of levels for isolines.

At this point, try experimenting with the third parameter in the `N arange()` call. For example, instead of `N = np.arange(-1, 1.5, 0.3)`, try changing `0.3` to `0.1` or `1` to experience how the same data is seen differently, depending on how we encode the data in a contour plot.

We also added a color map by simply giving it CS (a `matplotlib.contour.QuadContourSet` instance).

Filling an under-plot area

The basic way to draw a filled polygon in matplotlib is to use `matplotlib.pyplot.fill`. This function accepts similar arguments as `matplotlib.pyplot.plot`—multiple x and y pairs and other Line2D properties. This function returns the list of patch instances that were added.

In this recipe, you will learn how to shade certain areas of plot intersections.

Getting ready

matplotlib provides several functions to help us plot filled figures, apart from plotting functions that are inherently plotting closed filled polygons, such as `histogram ()`, of course.

We already mentioned one—`matplotlib.pyplot.fill`—but there are the `matplotlib.pyplot.fill_between()` and `matplotlib.pyplot.fill_betweenx()` functions too. These functions fill the polygons between two curves. The main difference between `fill_between()` and `fill_betweenx()` is that the latter fills between the x axis values, whereas the former fills between the y axis values.

The `fill_between` function accepts argument x—an x axis array of data—and y1 and y2—the y axis arrays of the data. Using arguments, we can specify conditions under which the area will be filled. This condition is the Boolean condition, usually specifying the y axis value ranges. The default value is `None`—meaning, to fill everywhere.

How to do it...

To start off with a simple example, we will fill the area under a simple function:

```python
import numpy as np
import matplotlib.pyplot as plt
from math import sqrt

t = range(1000)
y = [sqrt(i) for i in t]
plt.plot(t, y, color='red', lw=2)
plt.fill_between(t, y, color='silver')
plt.show()
```

The preceding code gives us the following plot:

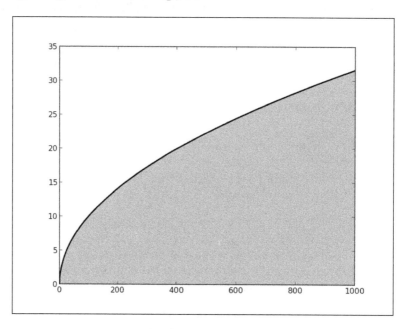

This is fairly straightforward and gives an idea of how `fill_between()` works. Note how we needed to plot the actual function line (using `plot()`, of course), where `fill_between()` just draws a polygonal area filled with color ("silver").

We will demonstrate another recipe here. It will involve more conditioning for the fill function. The following is the code for the example:

```python
import matplotlib.pyplot as plt
import numpy as np
```

```
x = np.arange(0.0, 2, 0.01)
y1 = np.sin(np.pi*x)
y2 = 1.7*np.sin(4*np.pi*x)

fig = plt.figure()
axes1 = fig.add_subplot(211)
axes1.plot(x, y1, x, y2, color='grey')
axes1.fill_between(x, y1, y2, where=y2<=y1, facecolor='blue',
interpolate=True)
axes1.fill_between(x, y1, y2, where=y2>=y1, facecolor='gold',
interpolate=True)
axes1.set_title('Blue where y2<= y1. Gold-color where y2>= y1.')
axes1.set_ylim(-2,2)

# Mask values in y2 with value greater than 1.0
y2 = np.ma.masked_greater(y2, 1.0)
axes2 = fig.add_subplot(212, sharex=axes1)
axes2.plot(x, y1, x, y2, color='black')
axes2.fill_between(x, y1, y2, where=y2<=y1, facecolor='blue',
interpolate=True)
axes2.fill_between(x, y1, y2, where=y2>=y1, facecolor='gold',
interpolate=True)
axes2.set_title('Same as above, but mask')
axes2.set_ylim(-2,2)
axes2.grid('on')

plt.show()
```

The preceding code will render the following plot:

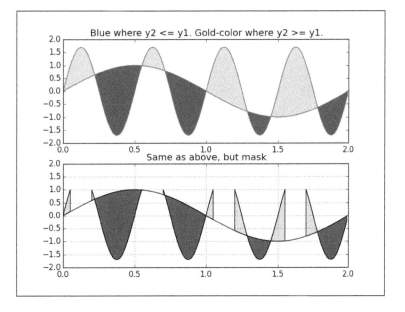

How it works...

For this example, we first created two sinusoidal functions that overlap at certain points.

We also created two subplots to compare the two variations that render filled regions.

In both cases, we used `fill_between()` with an argument, `where`, that accepts an *N*-length Boolean array and will fill regions where the value equals `True`.

The bottom subplot illustrates `mask_greater`, which masks an array at values greater than a given value. This is a function from the `numpy.ma` package to handle missing or invalid values. We turned the grid on the bottom axes to make it easier to spot this.

Drawing polar plots

If the data is already represented using polar coordinates, we can also display it using polar figures. Even if the data is not in polar coordinates, we should consider converting it to polar form and draw on polar plots.

To decide whether we want to do this, we need to understand what the data represents and what we are hoping to display to the end user. Imagining what the user will read and decode from our figures usually leads us to the best visualizations.

Polar plots are commonly used to display information that is radial in nature. For example, in sun path diagrams—we see the sky in radial projection and the radiation maps of antennas radiate differently at different angles. You can learn more about this at `http://www.astronwireless.com/topic-archives-antenna-radiation-patterns.asp`.

In this recipe, you will learn how to change the coordinate system used in the plot and to use the polar coordinate system instead.

Getting ready

To display data in polar coordinates, we must have appropriate data values. In the polar coordinate system, a point is described with radius distance (usually denoted by r) and angle (usually `theta`). The angle can be in radians or degrees, but matplotlib uses degrees.

Similarly enough to the function `plot()`, to draw polar plots, we will use the `polar()` function, which accepts two same-length arrays of parameters, `theta` and `r`, for the angle array and radius array, respectively. The function also accepts other formatting arguments, the same as those used by `plot()` one does.

We also need to tell matplotlib that we want axes in the polar coordinate system. This is done by providing the `polar=True` argument to the `add_axes` or `add_subplot` functions.

Additionally, to set other properties on the figure, such as grids on radii or angles, we need to use `matplotlib.pyplot.rgrids()` to toggle radial grid visibility or to set up labels. Similarly, we use `matplotlib.pyplot.thetagrid()` to configure angle ticks and labels.

How to do it...

Here is one recipe that demonstrates how to plot polar bars:

```
import numpy as np
import matplotlib.cm as cm
import matplotlib.pyplot as plt

figsize = 7
colormap = lambda r: cm.Set2(r / 20.)
N = 18 # number of bars

fig = plt.figure(figsize=(figsize,figsize))
ax = fig.add_axes([0.2, 0.2, 0.7, 0.7], polar=True)

theta = np.arange(0.0, 2*np.pi, 2*np.pi/N)
radii = 20*np.random.rand(N)
width = np.pi/4*np.random.rand(N)
bars = ax.bar(theta, radii, width=width, bottom=0.0)
for r, bar in zip(radii, bars):
bar.set_facecolor(colormap(r))
bar.set_alpha(0.6)

plt.show()
```

The preceding code snippet will give us the following plot:

How it works...

First, we create a square figure and add the polar axes to it. The figure does not have to be square, but then our polar plot will be ellipsoidal.

We then generate random values for a set of angles (theta) and a set of polar distances (radii). Since we have drawn bars, we also need a set of widths for each bar, so we also generate a set of widths. `matplotlib.axes.bar` accepts an array of values (as almost all the drawing functions in matplotlib do), so we don't have to loop over this generated dataset; we just need to call the bar once with all the arguments passed to it.

In order to make every bar easily distinguishable, we have to loop over each bar added to `ax` (Axes) and customize its appearance (face-color and transparency).

Visualizing the filesystem tree using a polar bar

We want to show in this recipe how to solve a "real-world" task—how to use matplotlib to visualize our directory occupancy.

In this recipe, you will learn how to visualize a filesystem tree with relative sizes.

Getting ready

We all have big hard drives that sometimes contain stuff that we usually forget about. It would be nice to see what is inside such a directory, and what the biggest file inside it is.

Although there are many more sophisticated and elaborate software products for this job, we want to demonstrate how this is achievable using Python and matplotlib.

How to do it...

Let's perform the following steps:

1. Implement a few helper functions to deal with folder discovery and internal data structures.
2. Implement the main function, `draw()`, that does the plotting.
3. Implement the main program body that verifies the user input arguments:

```
import os
import sys
```

```python
import matplotlib.pyplot as plt
import matplotlib.cm as cm
import numpy as np

def build_folders(start_path):
    folders = []

    for each in get_directories(start_path):
        size = get_size(each)
        if size >= 25 * 1024 * 1024:
            folders.append({'size' : size, 'path' : each})

    for each in folders:
        print "Path: " + os.path.basename(each['path'])
        print "Size: " + str(each['size'] / 1024 / 1024) + " MB"
    return folders

def get_size(path):
    assert path is not None

    total_size = 0
    for dirpath, dirnames, filenames in os.walk(path):
        for f in filenames:
            fp = os.path.join(dirpath, f)
            try:
                size = os.path.getsize(fp)
                total_size += size
                #print "Size of '{0}' is {1}".format(fp, size)
            except OSError as err:
                print str(err)
                pass
    return total_size

def get_directories(path):
    dirs = set()
    for dirpath, dirnames, filenames in os.walk(path):
        dirs = set([os.path.join(dirpath, x) for x in dirnames])
        break # we just want the first one
    return dirs

def draw(folders):
    """ Draw folder size for given folder"""
    figsize = (8, 8)  # keep the figure square
```

```
        ldo, rup = 0.1, 0.8  # leftdown and right up normalized
        fig = plt.figure(figsize=figsize)
        ax = fig.add_axes([ldo, ldo, rup, rup], polar=True)

        # transform data
        x = [os.path.basename(x['path']) for x in folders]
        y = [y['size'] / 1024 / 1024 for y in folders]
        theta = np.arange(0.0, 2 * np.pi, 2 * np.pi / len(x))
        radii = y

        bars = ax.bar(theta, radii)
        middle = 90/len(x)
        theta_ticks = [t*(180/np.pi)+middle for t in theta]
        lines, labels = plt.thetagrids(theta_ticks, labels=x, frac=0.5)
        for step, each in enumerate(labels):
            each.set_rotation(theta[step]*(180/np.pi)+ middle)
            each.set_fontsize(8)

        # configure bars
        colormap = lambda r:cm.Set2(r / len(x))
        for r, each in zip(radii, bars):
            each.set_facecolor(colormap(r))
            each.set_alpha(0.5)

        plt.show()
```

4. Next, we will implement the main program body where we verify the input arguments given by the user when the program is called from the command line:

```
if __name__ == '__main__':
    if len(sys.argv) is not 2:
        print "ERROR: Please supply path to folder."
        sys.exit(-1)

    start_path = sys.argv[1]

    if not os.path.exists(start_path):
        print "ERROR: Path must exits."
        sys.exit(-1)

    folders = build_folders(start_path)

    if len(folders) < 1:
        print "ERROR: Path does not contain any folders."
```

```
        sys.exit(-1)

    draw(folders)
```

5. You need to run the following from the command line:

   $ pythonch04_rec11_filesystem.py /usr/

6. It will produce a plot similar to this one:

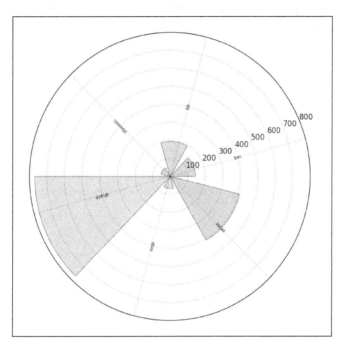

How it works...

We will start from the bottom of the code, after `if __name__ == '__main__'` because this is the place where our program starts.

Using the module `sys`, we pick up the command-line arguments; they represent the path to the directory we want to visualize.

The function `build_folders` builds the list of dictionaries, each containing the size and path that it found inside the given `start_path`. This function calls `get_directories`, which returns a list of all the subdirectories in `start_path`. Later, for each directory found, we calculated the sizes in bytes using the `get_size` function.

For debugging purposes, we print our dictionary so that we are able to compare the figure against what our data looks like.

After we have built the folders as a list of dictionaries, we pass them to a function, `draw`, that performs all the work of transforming the data to the right dimensions (here, we are using the polar coordinate system), constructing the polar figure, and drawing all the bars, ticks, and labels.

Strictly speaking, we should divide this job into smaller functions, especially if this code is to be further developed.

Customizing matplotlib with style

The default style configuration of matplotlib is made to satisfy the requirements of a wide audience, but this means that we always have to spend some time customizing the details that we care about. In this recipe, we want to show how to create custom and reusable styles for matplotlib so that we make our changes only once.

Getting ready

All the styles that matplotlib can use are stored in a directory called `stylelib`, under the configuration directory of matplotlib. To check the path of this directory, we can use the `get_configdir()` method:

```
In [1]: import matplotlib

In [2]: matplotlib.get_configdir()
Out[2]: u'~/.matplotlib'
```

In this directory we will store the files that specify our custom styles.

How to do it...

First, we will create the file that contains all the specifications of our style:

```
axes.titlesize : 12
lines.linewidth : 2
xtick.labelsize : 8
ytick.labelsize : 8
figure.facecolor: white
figure.edgecolor: 555555
xtick.color: 555555

axes.color_cycle: E54A22, 3A89BE
                  # E24A33 : red
                  # 348ABD : blue

axes.facecolor: EEEEEE
```

This style must be saved in the matplotlib `config` directory under the `stylelib` directory with the name `mystyle.mplstyle`. Right after creating this file we can use the style:

```
import matplotlib.pyplot as plt
import matplotlib
import numpy as np

plt.style.use('mystyle')

x = np.linspace(-2*np.pi, 2*np.pi, 100)
plt.title('sin(x)')
plt.xlabel('x')
plt.ylabel('y')
plt.plot(x, np.sin(x))
plt.plot(x, np.cos(x))
plt.show()
```

The result is as follows:

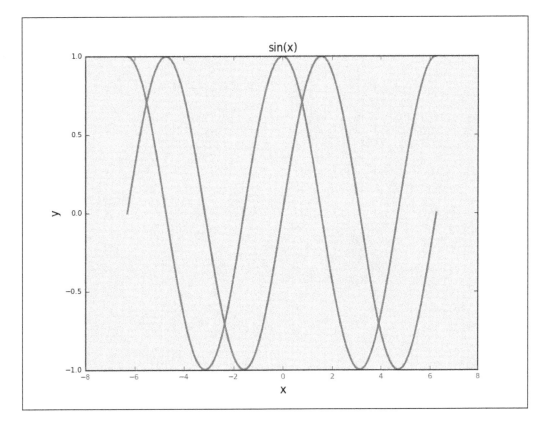

How it works...

Each line in the file `mystyle.mplstyle` modifies one of the elements of the matplotlib style. In the first line, we set the size of the font of the title of the figure to `12`, in the second one we set the width of the lines to `2`, and so on. The style is activated by passing a string with the name of the style to be used to the `matplotlib.style.use()` method, the name of the style is specified by the filename, and we can check all the styles available by printing `plt.style.string.available`.

5
Making 3D Visualizations

You will learn the following recipes in this chapter:

- ▸ Creating 3D bars
- ▸ Creating 3D histograms
- ▸ Animating in matplotlib
- ▸ Animating with OpenGL

Introduction

Visualization in 3D is sometimes effective and sometimes inevitable. Here, we present some examples that will satisfy most frequent requirements.

The content of this chapter will introduce and explain some topics on 3D visualizations.

Creating 3D bars

Although matplotlib is mainly focused on plotting and mainly in two dimensions, there are different extensions that enable us to plot over geographical maps, to integrate more with Excel, and plot in 3D. These extensions are called toolkits in the matplotlib world. A toolkit is a collection of specific functions focused on one topic, such as plotting in 3D.

Popular toolkits are Basemap, GTK Tools, Excel Tools, Natgrid, AxesGrid, and mplot3d.

We will explore more about mplot3d in this recipe. Toolkit `mpl_toolkits.mplot3d` provides some basic 3D plotting. Plots supported are scatter, surf, line, and mesh plots. Although this is not the best 3D plotting library, it comes with matplotlib, and we are already familiar with the interface.

Getting ready

Basically, we still need to create a figure and add the desired axes to it. The difference is that we are now specifying a 3D projection for the figure and the axes we are adding are `Axes3D`.

Now, we can use almost the same functions for plotting. Of course, the difference is the argument, for we now have three axes, which we need to provide data for.

For example, the `mpl_toolkits.mplot3d.Axes3D.plot` function specifies the `xs`, `ys`, `zs`, and `zdir` arguments. All others are transferred directly to `matplotlib.axes.Axes.plot`. We will explain these specific arguments:

  ▶ `xs`, `ys`: These are the coordinates for the *X* and *Y* axes.

  ▶ `zs`: This is the value(s) for the *Z* axis. There can be one value for all the points, or one for each point.

  ▶ `zdir`: This chooses what the *Z*-axis dimension (usually this is `zs`, but can also be `xs` or `ys`) will be.

> There is a method `rotate_axes` in the `mpl_toolkits.mplot3d.art3d` module that contains 3D artist code and functions to convert 2D artists into 3D, which can be added to `Axes3D` to reorder coordinates so that the axes are rotated with `zdir` along. The default value is z. Prepending the axis with a '-' does the inverse transform, so `zdir` can be x, -x, y, -y, z, or -z.

How to do it...

This is the code to demonstrate the concept explained here:

```
import random

import numpy as np
import matplotlib as mpl
import matplotlib.pyplot as plt
import matplotlib.dates as mdates

from mpl_toolkits.mplot3d import Axes3D

mpl.rcParams['font.size'] = 10

fig = plt.figure()
```

```
ax = fig.add_subplot(111, projection='3d')

for z in [2011, 2012, 2013, 2014]:
    xs = xrange(1,13)
    ys = 1000 * np.random.rand(12)

    color = plt.cm.Set2(random.choice(xrange(plt.cm.Set2.N)))
    ax.bar(xs, ys, zs=z, zdir='y', color=color, alpha=0.8)

ax.xaxis.set_major_locator(mpl.ticker.FixedLocator(xs))
ax.yaxis.set_major_locator(mpl.ticker.FixedLocator(ys))


ax.set_xlabel('Month')
ax.set_ylabel('Year')
ax.set_zlabel('Sales Net [usd]')

plt.show()
```

This code produces the following figure:

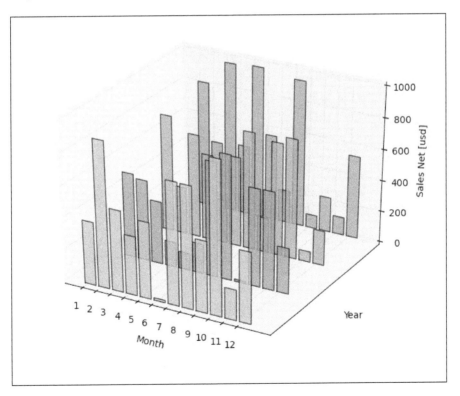

How it works...

We had to do the same prep work as in the 2D world. The difference here is that we needed to specify what "kind of backend". Then we generate random data for supposedly 4 years of sale (2011-2014).

We needed to specify *Z* values to be the same for the 3D axis.

We picked the color randomly from the color-map set, and then we associated each *Z*-order collection of xs, ys pairs that would be used to render the bar series.

There's more...

The other plot from 2D matplotlib is available here—for example, scatter()—which has a similar interface to plot(), but with increased size of the point marker. We are also familiar with contour, contourf, and bar.

New types that are available only in 3D are wireframe, surface, and tri-surface plots.

For example, this code example plots a tri-surface plot of popular Pringle functions or, more mathematically, a hyperbolic paraboloid:

```
from mpl_toolkits.mplot3d import Axes3D
from matplotlib import cm
import matplotlib.pyplot as plt
import numpy as np

n_angles = 36
n_radii = 8

# An array of radii
# Does not include radius r=0, this is to eliminate duplicate points
radii = np.linspace(0.125, 1.0, n_radii)

# An array of angles
angles = np.linspace(0, 2*np.pi, n_angles, endpoint=False)

# Repeat all angles for each radius
angles = np.repeat(angles[...,np.newaxis], n_radii, axis=1)

# Convert polar (radii, angles) coords to cartesian (x, y) coords
# (0, 0) is added here. There are no duplicate points in the (x, y)
plane
x = np.append(0, (radii*np.cos(angles)).flatten())
```

```
y = np.append(0, (radii*np.sin(angles)).flatten())

# Pringle surface
z = np.sin(-x*y)

fig = plt.figure()
ax = fig.gca(projection='3d')

ax.plot_trisurf(x, y, z, cmap=cm.jet, linewidth=0.2)

plt.show()
```

The code will give the following output:

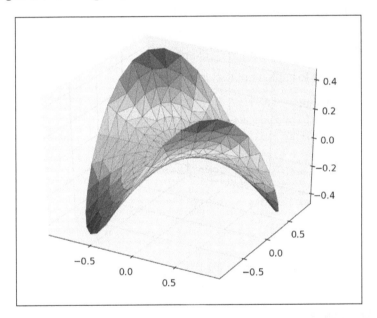

Creating 3D histograms

Similarly to 3D bars, we might want to create 3D histograms. These are useful for easily spotting correlation between three independent variables. They can be used to extract information from images in which the third dimension could be the intensity of a channel in the *x*, *y* space of the image under analysis.

In this recipe, you will learn how to create 3D histograms.

Getting ready

To recall, a histogram represents the number of occurrences of some value in a particular column—usually called bin. A 3D histogram, then, represents the number of occurrences in a grid. This grid is rectangular, over two variables represented by the data in the two columns.

How to do it...

For this computation we will:

1. Use NumPy's help, as it has a function for computing the histogram of two variables.
2. Generate x and y from normal distributions, but with different parameters, to be able to distinguish the correlation in the resulting histogram.
3. Plot the scatter plot of the same dataset, to demonstrate how different the display of the scatter plot is to the 3D histogram.

Here is the code sample to implement the described steps:

```python
import numpy as np
import matplotlib.pyplot as plt
import matplotlib as mpl

from mpl_toolkits.mplot3d import Axes3D

mpl.rcParams['font.size'] = 10

samples = 25

x = np.random.normal(5, 1, samples)
y = np.random.normal(3, .5, samples)

fig = plt.figure()
ax1 = fig.add_subplot(211, projection='3d')

# compute two-dimensional histogram
hist, xedges, yedges = np.histogram2d(x, y, bins=10)

# compute location of the x,y bar positions
elements = (len(xedges) - 1) * (len(yedges) - 1)
xpos, ypos = np.meshgrid(xedges[:-1]+.25, yedges[:-1]+.25)

xpos = xpos.flatten()
ypos = ypos.flatten()
```

```
zpos = np.zeros(elements)

# make every bar the same width in base
dx = .1 * np.ones_like(zpos)
dy = dx.copy()

# this defines the height of the bar
dz = hist.flatten()

ax1.bar3d(xpos, ypos, zpos, dx, dy, dz, color='b', alpha=0.4)
ax1.set_xlabel('X Axis')
ax1.set_ylabel('Y Axis')
ax1.set_zlabel('Z Axis')

# plot the same x,y correlation in scatter plot
# for comparison
ax2 = fig.add_subplot(212)
ax2.scatter(x, y)
ax2.set_xlabel('X Axis')
ax2.set_ylabel('Y Axis')

plt.show()
```

This code will give the following output:

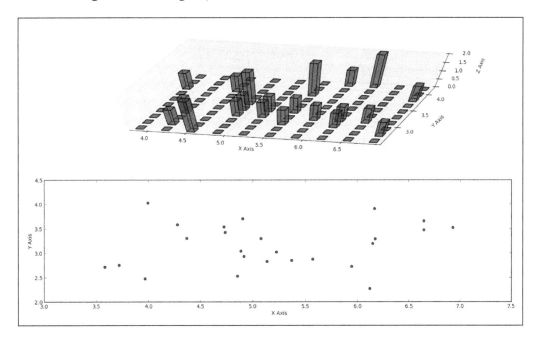

How it works...

We prepare a computer histogram using `np.histogram2d`, which returns our histogram (hist) and *x* and *y* bin edges.

Because for the `bard3d` function we need coordinates in `x`, `y` space, we need to compute the common matrix coordinates, and for that we use `np.meshgrid` that combines `x` and `y` positional vectors into a 2D space grid (matrix). This we can use to plot bars in the *XY* plane locations.

Variables `dx` and `dy` represent the width of the base of each bar, and as we want to make this constant, we give it a 0.1 point value for every position in the *xy* plane.

The value in the *Z*-axis (`dz`) is actually our computer histogram (in the variable `hist`) that represents the count of common *x* and *y* samples at a particular bin.

The scatter plot displays the 2D axes that also visualize the correlation between two similar distributions, but with a different set of starting parameters.

Sometimes, 3D gives us more information and better explains what the data is showing. More often, however, 3D visualizations are more confusing than 2D, and it is advisable to think twice before choosing them over 2D.

Animating in matplotlib

In this recipe, we will explore how to animate our figures. Sometimes it is more descriptive to have pictures moving in animations to explain what happens if we change the values of variables. Our main library has limited but usually sufficient animation capabilities and we will explain how to use them.

Getting ready

The framework for animation is added to standard matplotlib from version 1.1 and its main class is `matplotlib.animation.Animation`. This class is the base class, which is to be subclassed for specific behavior, as is the case with the classes already provided: `TimedAnimation`, `ArtistAnimation`, and `FuncAnimation`.

Class name (parent class)	Description
`Animation` (object)	This class wraps the creation of an animation using matplotlib. It is only a base class which should be subclassed to provide the required behavior.

Class name (parent class)	Description
TimedAnimation(Animation)	The Animation subclass supports time-based animation, drawing a new frame every *interval* milliseconds.
ArtistAnimation(TimedAnimation)	Before calling this function, all plotting should have taken place and the relevant artists saved.
FuncAnimation(TimedAnimation)	Makes an animation by repeatedly calling a function, passing in (optional) arguments.

In order to be able to save animations in a video file, we must have the `ffmpeg` or `mencoder` installer. Installation of these packages varies depending on the OS used, and changes by different releases, so we must leave it to the dear reader to Google the valid information.

How to do it...

Here is the code listing to demonstrate some matplotlib animations:

```python
import numpy as np
from matplotlib import pyplot as plt
from matplotlib import animation

fig = plt.figure()
ax = plt.axes(xlim=(0, 2), ylim=(-2, 2))
line, = ax.plot([], [], lw=2)

def init():
    """Clears current frame."""
    line.set_data([], [])
    return line,


def animate(i):
    """Draw figure.
    @param i: Frame counter
    @type i: int
    """
    x = np.linspace(0, 2, 1000)
    y = np.sin(2 * np.pi * (x - 0.01 * i)) * np.cos(22 * np.pi * (x -
0.01 * i))
    line.set_data(x, y)
    return line,


# This call puts the work in motion
```

```
# connecting init and animate functions and figure we want to draw
animator = animation.FuncAnimation(fig, animate, init_func=init,
                                   frames=200, interval=20, blit=True)#
set blit to False if you're under OS X!

# This call creates the video file.
# Temporary, every frame is saved as PNG file
# and later processed by ffmpeg encoder into MPEG4 file
# we can pass various arguments to ffmpeg via extra_args
animator.save('basic_animation.mp4', fps=30,
              extra_args=['-vcodec', 'libx264'],
              writer='ffmpeg_file')
plt.show()
```

This will create the basic_animation.mp4 file in the folder you started this file from, and also displays a figure window with the running animation. The video file can be opened with most modern video players that support the MPEG-4 format. The figure (frame) should look like this:

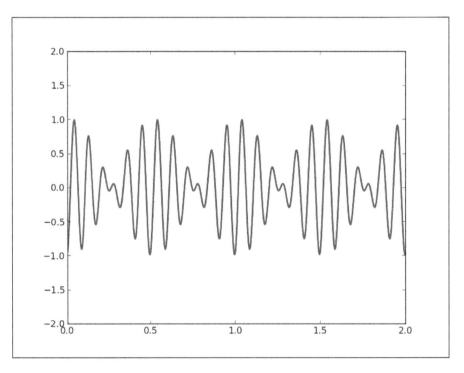

How it works...

Most important are the `init()`, `animate()`, and `save()` functions. We first construct `FuncAnimate` by passing two callback functions to it, `init` and `animate`. Then, we call the `save` method to save our video file. More details on each function are in the following table:

Function name	Usage
`init`	Passed to `matplotlib.animation.FuncAnimation` constructor via parameter `init_func` to clear the frame before the next frame is drawn.
`animate`	Passed to `matplotlib.animation.FuncAnimation` constructor via `func` parameter.
	The figure we want to animate is passed via `fig` argument, which is passed under the hood to the `matplotlib.animation.Animation` constructor to connect animation events with the figure we want to draw. This function gets (optional) parameters from `frames`—usually iterable, representing the number of frames.
`matplotlib.animation.Animation.save`	Saves a movie file by drawing every frame. It creates temporary image files before processing them through the encoder (`ffmpeg` or `mencoder`) to create a video file. This function also accepts various parameters that configure video output, including metadata (author...), codec to use, and resolution/size. One of the parameters is – which defines what video encoder to use. Currently supported are `ffmpeg`, `ffmpeg_file`, and `mencoder`.

There's more...

The usage of `matplotlib.animation.ArtistAnimation` differs from `FuncAnimation` in that we must draw each artist beforehand and then instantiate the `ArtistAnimation` class with all the different frames of the artist. `ArtistAnimation` is a kind of a wrapper of the `matplotlib.animation.TimedAnimation` class that draws frames every *N* milliseconds, thus supporting time-based animation.

 For Mac OS X users, animation framework can unfortunately be troublesome on this platform, and sometimes simply does not work. This will improve with future releases of matplotlib.

Animating with OpenGL

The motivation to use OpenGL stems from limitations of CPU processing power when we are faced with the task of visualizing millions of data points and doing it fast (sometimes even in real time).

Modern computers have powerful GPUs that are made for fast visualization-related computations (such as games), and there is no reason why they can't be used for science-related visualizations.

Actually, there is at least one drawback of writing hardware-accelerated software that is hardware dependent. Modern graphics cards require proprietary drivers which are sometimes not available on the target platform/machine (the user's laptop, for example). Even when available, sometimes installing the required dependencies on-site is not what you want to spend your time on, while all you want is to present your findings and demonstrate your research results. This is not a showstopper but you should bear this in mind, and measure the benefits and costs of introducing this complexity in your project.

With the caveats explained, we can say yes to hardware-accelerated visualizations and to OpenGL, which is the industry standard for accelerated graphics.

We will be using OpenGL as it is cross-platform, so the examples should work as presented on Linux, Mac, or Windows, provided you have the required hardware and OS-level drivers installed.

Getting ready

If you have never used OpenGL, we will now try to give a quick introduction, although to really understand OpenGL, at least one complete book needs to be read. OpenGL is a specification, not an implementation, so OpenGL itself doesn't have any code, while the implementations are libraries developed according to this specification. These are shipped with your operating system or by vendors of graphics cards such as NVidia or AMD/ATI.

Moreover, OpenGL is concerned only with graphics rendering and not animation, timing, or other "complex" things that are left for additional libraries to pick up.

Basics of animating with OpenGL

Since OpenGL is a rendering library, it does not know what objects we draw on a screen. It doesn't care if we draw a cat, a ball, a line, or all of these objects. So, to move a rendered object, we need to clear and draw the whole image again. To animate something, we need a loop that draws and redraws everything very quickly and displays it to a user, so that the user thinks he/she sees an animation.

Installing OpenGL on a machine is a platform-dependent process. On the Mac OS X, OpenGL implementation is part of the OS upgrade, but development libraries (so called headers) are part of the Xcode development package.

On Windows, the best way would be to install the vendor's latest graphics drivers for your graphic card. OpenGL may work without them, but you will probably be left without the latest features with stock drivers.

On Linux, if you are not against installing closed source software, there are vendor-specific drivers downloadable either from the distro's own software manager or from the vendor site as an installable binary. Standard implementations are almost always Mesa3D—the best known OpenGL implementation, which uses Xorg to provide support for OpenGL for Linux, FreeBSD, and similar operating systems.

On Debian/Ubuntu, you should install the following packages and their dependencies:

```
$ sudo apt-get install libgl1-mesa-dev libgl-mesa-dri
```

After this, you should be ready to use some development libraries and/or frameworks to actually write OpenGL-backed applications.

We are focused here on Python, so we will overview some of the Python's most used libraries and frameworks that are built on top of OpenGL. We will mention matplotlib and its current and future support for OpenGL:

- ▸ **Mayavi**: This is a library specialized for 3D
- ▸ **Pyglet**: This is a pure Python library for graphics
- ▸ **Glumpy**: This is a fast rendering library built on top of NumPy

How to do it...

Specialized project Mayavi is a full-featured 3D graphics library, which is mainly used for advanced 3D rendering. It comes with already mentioned Python packages like EPD (though not with a free license), which is a recommended way of installing it on Windows and Mac OS X. On Linux, it can also be easily installed using pip:

```
$ pip install mayavi
```

Mayavi can be used as a development library/framework or as an application. The Mayavi application comprises a visual editor for easy data exploration and somewhat interactive visualization.

As a library, it can be used in a similar way to `matplotlib`—either from the   script interface or as a full object-oriented library. Most of that interface is inside the `mlab` module, to be able to use that interface. For example, simple animation with Mayavi can be done as follows:

```python
import numpy
from mayavi.mlab import *

# Produce some nice data.
n_mer, n_long = 6, 11
pi = numpy.pi
dphi = pi/1000.0
phi = numpy.arange(0.0, 2*pi + 0.5*dphi, dphi, 'd')
mu = phi*n_mer
x = numpy.cos(mu)*(1+numpy.cos(n_long*mu/n_mer)*0.5)
y = numpy.sin(mu)*(1+numpy.cos(n_long*mu/n_mer)*0.5)
z = numpy.sin(n_long*mu/n_mer)*0.5

# View it.
l = plot3d(x, y, z, numpy.sin(mu), tube_radius=0.025,
colormap='Spectral')

# Now animate the data.
ms = l.mlab_source
for i in range(100):
    x = numpy.cos(mu)*(1+numpy.cos(n_long*mu/n_mer +
                                    numpy.pi*(i+1)/5.)*0.5)
    scalars = numpy.sin(mu + numpy.pi*(i+1)/5)
    ms.set(x=x, scalars=scalars)
```

This code will produce the following window with rotating figure:

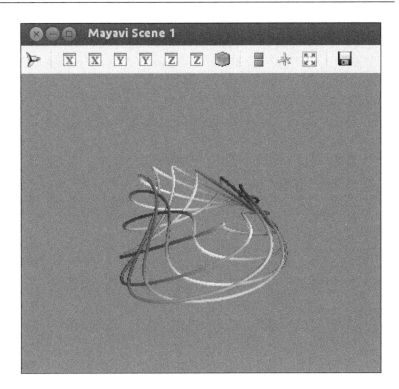

How it works...

We generate a dataset and create set of functions for *x*, *y*, and *z* to be used in the `plot3d` function for start position of the figure.

We then import the `mlab_source` object that enables us to manipulate our plot on the level of points and scalars. We then use this feature to set particular points and scalars in `for` loop to create a rotation animation with 100 frames.

There's more...

If you want to experiment more, the easiest way to do so is to load IPython, import `mayavi.mlab`, and run some `test_*` functions.

To see what is going on, you can use IPython's ability to inspect and explore Python source, as follows:

```
In [1]: import mayavi.mlab

In [2]: mayavi.mlab.test_simple_surf??
Type:        function
```

```
String Form:<function test_simple_surf at 0x641b410>
File:        /usr/lib/python2.7/dist-packages/mayavi/tools/helper_
functions.py
Definition: mayavi.mlab.test_simple_surf()
Source:
def test_simple_surf():
    """Test Surf with a simple collection of points."""
    x, y = numpy.mgrid[0:3:1,0:3:1]
    return surf(x, y, numpy.asarray(x, 'd'))
```

We can see here how, by adding two question marks after the function name ("??"), IPython found the source of the function and showed it to us. This is true exploratory computing, and is often used within the visualization community, because it is a fast way to get to know your data and code.

6

Plotting Charts with Images and Maps

This chapter contains recipes that will cover:

- ▸ Processing images with PIL
- ▸ Plotting with images
- ▸ Displaying images with other plots in the figure
- ▸ Plotting data on a map using Basemap
- ▸ Plotting data on a map using the Google Map API
- ▸ Generating CAPTCHA images

Introduction

This chapter explores how to work with images and maps. Python has some well-known image libraries that allow us to process images in both aesthetic and scientific ways.

First, we will introduce the capabilities of PIL (and its friendly fork Pillow), by demonstrating how to process images by applying filters and resizing them.

Furthermore, we will show you how to use image files as annotation for our matplotlib charts.

To deal with data visualization of geospatial datasets, we will cover the functionality of Python's available libraries and public APIs that we can use with map-based visual representations.

The final recipe shows how Python can create CAPTCHA test images.

Processing images with PIL

Why use Python for image processing if we can use **WIMP** (http://en.wikipedia.org/wiki/WIMP_(computing)) or **WYSIWYG** (http://en.wikipedia.org/wiki/WYSIWYG) to achieve the same goal? Python is used because we want to create an automated system to process images in real time without human support, thus optimizing the image pipeline.

Getting ready

Note that the PIL coordinate system assumes that the (0,0) coordinate is in the upper-left corner.

The `Image` module has a useful class and instance method for performing basic operations over a loaded image object (`im`):

- `im = Image.open(filename)`: This opens a file and loads the image into the `im` object.

- `im.crop(box)`: This crops the image inside the coordinates defined by `box`. `box` defines the left, upper, right, and lower pixel coordinates (for example, `box = (0, 100, 100,100))`.

- `im.filter(filter)`: This applies a filter on the image and returns a filtered image.

- `im.histogram()`: This returns a histogram list for this image, where each item represents the number of pixels. The number of items in the list is 256 for single channel images, but if the image is not a single channel image, there can be more items in the list. For an RGB image, the list contains 768 items (one set of 256 values for each channel).

- `im.resize(size, filter)`: This resizes the image and uses a filter for resampling. The possible filters are `NEAREST`, `BILINEAR`, `BICUBIC`, and `ANTIALIAS`. The default is `NEAREST`.

- `im.rotate(angle, filter)`: This rotates an image in the counter clockwise direction.

- `im.split()`: This splits the bands of an image and returns a tuple of individual bands. Useful for splitting an RGB image into three single band images.

- `im.transform(size, method, data, filter)`: This applies transformation on a given image using data and a filter. Transformation can be `AFFINE`, `EXTENT`, `QUAD`, and `MESH`. You can read more about transformation in the official documentation. Data defines the box in the original image where the transformation will be applied.

The `ImageDraw` module allows us to draw over the image, where we can use functions such as `arc`, `ellipse`, `line`, `pieslice`, `point`, and `polygon` to modify the pixels of the loaded image.

The `ImageChops` module contains a number of image channel operations (hence the name `Chops`) that can be used for image composition, painting, special effects, and other processing operations. Channel operations are allowed only for 8-bit images. Here are some interesting channel operations:

- ► `ImageChops.duplicate(image)`: This copies the current image into a new `image` object
- ► `ImageChops.invert(image)`: This inverts an `image` and returns a copy
- ► `ImageChops.difference(image1, image2)`: This is useful for verification that images are the same without visual inspection

The `ImageFilter` module contains the implementation of the kernel class that allows the creation of custom convolution kernels. This module also contains a set of healthy common filters that allows the application of well-known filters (`BLUR` and `MedianFilter`) to our image.

There are two types of filters provided by the `ImageFilter` module: **fixed image enhancement filters** and **image filters** that require certain arguments to be defined, for example, the size of kernel to be used.

We can easily get the list of all fixed filter names in IPython:

```
In [1]: import ImageFilter
In [2]: [ f for f in dir(ImageFilter) if f.isupper()]
Out[2]:
['BLUR',
 'CONTOUR',
 'DETAIL',
 'EDGE_ENHANCE',
 'EDGE_ENHANCE_MORE',
 'EMBOSS',
 'FIND_EDGES',
 'SHARPEN',
 'SMOOTH',
 'SMOOTH_MORE']
```

The next example shows how we can apply all currently supported fixed filters on any supported image:

```
import os
import sys
from PIL import Image, ImageChops, ImageFilter


class DemoPIL(object):
    def __init__(self, image_file=None):
```

```
            self.fixed_filters = [ff for ff in dir(ImageFilter) if
    ff.isupper()]

            assert image_file is not None
            assert os.path.isfile(image_file) is True
            self.image_file = image_file
            self.image = Image.open(self.image_file)

        def _make_temp_dir(self):
            from tempfile import mkdtemp
            self.ff_tempdir = mkdtemp(prefix="ff_demo")

        def _get_temp_name(self, filter_name):
            name, ext = os.path.splitext(os.path.basename(self.image_
    file))
            newimage_file = name + "-" + filter_name + ext
            path = os.path.join(self.ff_tempdir, newimage_file)
            return path

        def _get_filter(self, filter_name):
            # note the use Python's eval() builtin here to return function
    object
            real_filter = eval("ImageFilter." + filter_name)
            return real_filter

        def apply_filter(self, filter_name):
            print "Applying filter: " + filter_name
            filter_callable = self._get_filter(filter_name)
            # prevent calling non-fixed filters for now
            if filter_name in self.fixed_filters:
                temp_img = self.image.filter(filter_callable)
            else:
                print "Can't apply non-fixed filter now."
            return temp_img

        def run_fixed_filters_demo(self):
            self._make_temp_dir()
            for ffilter in self.fixed_filters:
                temp_img = self.apply_filter(ffilter)
                temp_img.save(self._get_temp_name(ffilter))
            print "Images are in: {0}".format((self.ff_tempdir),)

    if __name__ == "__main__":
        assert len(sys.argv) == 2
```

```
        demo_image = sys.argv[1]
        demo = DemoPIL(demo_image)
        # will create set of images in temporary folder
        demo.run_fixed_filters_demo()
```

We can run this easily from the command prompt:

$ pythonch06_rec01_01_pil_demo.py image.jpeg

We packed our little demo in the `DemoPIL` class, so we can extend it easily while sharing the common code around the `run_fixed_filters_demo` demo function. Common code here includes opening the image file, testing if the file is really a file, creating a temporary directory to hold our filtered images, building the filtered image filename, and printing useful information to the user. This way the code is organized in a better manner, and we can easily focus on our demo function, without touching other parts of the code.

This demo will open our image file and apply every fixed filter available in `ImageFilter` to it and save that new filtered image in a unique temporary directory. At the end of the process, the script prints the path of the temporary directory used so that we can check the output of the filters.

As an optional exercise, try extending this demo class to perform other filters available in `ImageFilter` on the given image.

How to do it...

The example in this section shows how we can process all the images in a certain folder. We specify a target path, and the program that reads all the image files in that target path (images folder) resizes them to a specified ratio (0.1 in this example), and saves each one in a target folder called `thumbnail_folder`:

```
import os
import sys
from PIL import Image


class Thumbnailer(object):
    def __init__(self, src_folder=None):
        self.src_folder = src_folder
        self.ratio = .3
        self.thumbnail_folder = "thumbnails"

    def _create_thumbnails_folder(self):
        thumb_path = os.path.join(self.src_folder, self.thumbnail_
folder)
        if not os.path.isdir(thumb_path):
            os.makedirs(thumb_path)
```

```python
    def _build_thumb_path(self, image_path):
        root = os.path.dirname(image_path)
        name, ext = os.path.splitext(os.path.basename(image_path))
        suffix = ".thumbnail"
        return os.path.join(root, self.thumbnail_folder, name + suffix
 + ext)

    def _load_files(self):
        files = set()
        for each in os.listdir(self.src_folder):
            each = os.path.abspath(self.src_folder + '/' + each)
            if os.path.isfile(each):
                files.add(each)
    return files

    def _thumb_size(self, size):
        return (int(size[0] * self.ratio), int(size[1] * self.ratio))

    def create_thumbnails(self):
        self._create_thumbnails_folder()
        files = self._load_files()

        for each in files:
            print "Processing: " + each
            try:
                img = Image.open(each)
                thumb_size = self._thumb_size(img.size)
                resized = img.resize(thumb_size, Image.ANTIALIAS)
                savepath = self._build_thumb_path(each)
                resized.save(savepath)
            except IOError as ex:
                print "Error: " + str(ex)

if __name__ == "__main__":
    # Usage:
    # ch06_rec01_02_pil_thumbnails.py my_images
    assert len(sys.argv) == 2
    src_folder = sys.argv[1]

    if not os.path.isdir(src_folder):
        print "Error: Path '{0}' does not exits.".format((src_folder))
        sys.exit(-1)
    thumbs = Thumbnailer(src_folder)
```

```
    # optionally set the name of each thumbnail folder relative to
*src_folder*.
    thumbs.thumbnail_folder = "THUMBS"

    # define ratio to resize image to
    # 0.1 means the original image will be resized to 10% of its size
    thumbs.ratio = 0.1

    # will create set of images in temporary folder
    thumbs.create_thumbnails()
```

How it works...

For the given folder `src_folder`, we load all the files in this folder and try to load each file using `Image.open()`; this is the logic of the `create_thumbnails()` function. If the file we try to load is not an image, IOError will be thrown, and it will print this error and skip to the next file in the sequence.

If we want to have more control over which files we load, we should change the `_load_files()` function to only include files with a certain extension (file type):

```
    for each in os.listdir(self.src_folder):
        if os.path.isfile(each) and os.path.splitext(each) is in
('.jpg','.png'):
            self._files.add(each)
```

This is not foolproof as the file extension does not define the file type, it just helps the operating system to attach a default program to the file. But it works in the majority of cases and is simpler than reading a file header to determine the file content (which still does not guarantee that the file really is the first couple of bytes it says is).

There's more...

With PIL, although not used very often, we can easily convert images from one format to another. This is achievable with two simple operations: first, open an image in a source format using `open()`, and then save that image in another format using `save()`. The format is defined either implicitly via the filename extension (`.png` or `.jpeg`) or explicitly via the format of the argument passed to the `save()` function.

Plotting with images

Images can be used to highlight the strengths of your visualization in addition to pure data values. Many examples have proven that by using symbolic images, we map deeper into the viewer's mental model, thereby helping the viewer to remember the visualizations better and for a longer time. One way to do this is to place images where your data is, to map the values to what they represent. The `matplotlib` library is capable of delivering this functionality, and here we demonstrate how to do it.

Getting ready

We will use the fictional example from the story *The Gospel of the Flying Spaghetti Monster*, by Bobby Henderson, where the author correlates the number of pirates with the sea-surface temperature. To highlight this correlation, we will display the size of the pirate ship proportional to the value representing the number of pirates in the year the sea-surface temperature is measured.

We will use Python matplotlib library's ability to annotate using images and text with advanced location settings, as well as arrow capabilities.

All the files required in the following recipe are available in the source code repository in the `Chapter06` folder.

How to do it...

The following example shows how to add an annotation to a chart using images and text:

```python
import matplotlib.pyplot as plt
from matplotlib._png import read_png
from matplotlib.offsetbox import TextArea, OffsetImage, \
    AnnotationBbox


def load_data():
    import csv
    with open('pirates_temperature.csv', 'r') as f:
        reader = csv.reader(f)
        header = reader.next()
        datarows = []
        for row in reader:
            datarows.append(row)
```

```
        return header, datarows


    def format_data(datarows):
        years, temps, pirates = [], [], []
        for each in datarows:
            years.append(each[0])
            temps.append(each[1])
            pirates.append(each[2])
        return years, temps, pirates
```

After we have defined helper functions, we can approach the construction of the figure object and add subplots. We will annotate these for every year in the collection of years using the image of the ship, scaling the image to the appropriate size:

```
    if __name__ == "__main__":
        fig = plt.figure(figsize=(16,8))
        ax = plt.subplot(111)  # add sub-plot

        header, datarows = load_data()
        xlabel, ylabel = header[0], header[1]
        years, temperature, pirates = format_data(datarows)
        title = "Global Average Temperature vs. Number of Pirates"

        plt.plot(years, temperature, lw=2)
        plt.xlabel(xlabel)
        plt.ylabel(ylabel)

        # for every data point annotate with image and number
        for x in xrange(len(years)):

            # current data coordinate
            xy = years[x], temperature[x]

            # add image
            ax.plot(xy[0], xy[1], "ok")

            # load pirate image
            pirate = read_png('tall-ship.png')

            # zoom coefficient (move image with size)
```

```
        zoomc = int(pirates[x]) * (1 / 90000.)

        # create OffsetImage
        imagebox = OffsetImage(pirate, zoom=zoomc)

        # create anotation bbox with image and setup properties
        ab = AnnotationBbox(imagebox, xy,
                        xybox=(-200.*zoomc, 200.*zoomc),
                        xycoords='data',
                        boxcoords="offset points",
                        pad=0.1,
                        arrowprops=dict(arrowstyle="->",
                            connectionstyle="angle,angleA=0,angleB=-
30,rad=3")
                        )
        ax.add_artist(ab)

        # add text
        no_pirates = TextArea(pirates[x], minimumdescent=False)
        ab = AnnotationBbox(no_pirates, xy,
                        xybox=(50., -25.),
                        xycoords='data',
                        boxcoords="offset points",
                        pad=0.3,
                        arrowprops=dict(arrowstyle="->",
                            connectionstyle="angle,angleA=0,angleB=-
30,rad=3")
                        )
        ax.add_artist(ab)

    plt.grid(1)
    plt.xlim(1800, 2020)
    plt.ylim(14, 16)
    plt.title(title)

    plt.show()
```

The preceding code should give the following plot:

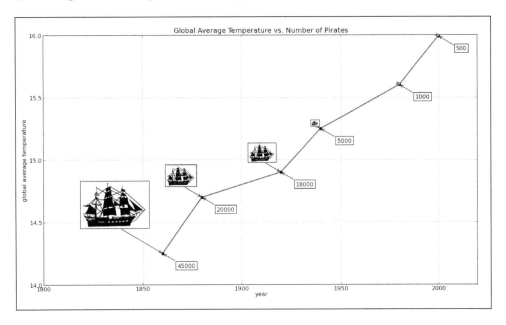

How it works...

We start by creating a figure of a decent size, that is, 16 x 8. We need this size to fit the images we want to display. Now, we load our data from the file, using the csv module. Instantiating the csv reader object, we can iterate over the data from the file row by row. Note that the first row is special, it is the header describing our columns. As we have plotted years on the *x* axis and temperature on the *y* axis, we read that:

```
xlabel, ylabel, _ = header
```

And use the following lines:

```
plt.xlabel(xlabel)
plt.ylabel(ylabel)
```

> We used a neat Python convention here to unpack the header into three variables, where using _ for variable name, we indicate that we are not interested in the value of that variable.

We return the header and datarows lists from the load_data function to the main caller.

Using the format_data() function, we read every item in the list and add each separate entity (year, temperature, and number of pirates) into the relevant ID list for that entity.

Year is displayed along the *x* axis, while temperature is on the *y* axis. The number of pirates is displayed as an image of a pirate ship, and also to add precision the value is displayed.

We plot year/temperature values using the standard `plot()` function, not adding anything more, apart from making the line a bit wider (2 pt).

We proceed then to add one image for every measurement and to illustrate the number of pirates for a given year. For this, we loop over the range of values of length (`range(len(years))`), plotting one black point on each year/temperature coordinate:

```
ax.plot(xy[0], xy[1], "ok")
```

The image of the ship is loaded from the file into a suitable array format using the `read_png` helper function:

```
pirate = read_png('tall-ship.png')
```

We then compute the zoom coefficient (`zoomc`) to enable us to scale the size of the image in proportion to the number of pirates for the current (`pirates[x]`) measurement. We also use the same coefficient to position the image along the plot.

The actual image is then instantiated inside `OffsetImage`—the image container with relative position to its parent (`AnnotationBbox`).

`AnnotationBbox` is an annotation-like class, but instead of displaying just text as with the `Axes.annotate` function, it can display other `OffsetBox` instances. This allows us to load an image or text object in an annotation and locate it at a particular distance from the data point, as well as allowing us to use the arrowing capabilities (`arrowprops`) to precisely point to an annotated data point.

We supply the `AnnotateBbox` constructor with certain arguments:

- ▸ `Imagebox`: This must be an instance of `OffsetBox` (for example, `OffsetImage`); it is the content of the annotation box
- ▸ `xy`: This is the data point coordinate that the annotation relates to
- ▸ `xybox`: This defines the location of the annotation box
- ▸ `xycoords`: This defines what coordinating system is used by `xy` (for example, data coordinates)
- ▸ `boxcoords`: This defines what coordinating system is used by `xybox` (for example, offset from the `xy` location)
- ▸ `pad`: This specifies the amount of padding
- ▸ `arrowprops`: This is the dictionary of properties for drawing an arrow connection from an annotation-bounding box to a data point

We add text annotation to this plot, using the same data items from the pirates list with a slightly different relative position. Most of the arguments of the second `AnnotationBbox` are the same—we adjust `xybox` and pad to locate the text to the opposite side of the line. The text is inside the `TextArea` class instance. This is similar to what we do with the image, but with text `time`. `TextArea` and `OffsetImage` inherit from the same `OffsetBox` parent class.

We set the text in this `TextArea` instance to `no_pirates` and put it in our `AnnotationBbox`.

Displaying images with other plots in the figure

This recipe will show how we can make simple yet effective usage of Python matplotlib library to process image channels and display the per-channel histogram of an external image.

Getting ready

We have provided some sample images, but the code is ready to load any image file, provided it is supported by matplotlib's `imread` function.

In this recipe, you will learn how to combine different matplotlib plots to achieve functionality of a simple image viewer that displays an image histogram for red, green, and blue channels.

How to do it...

To show how to build an image histogram viewer, we are going to implement a simple class named `ImageViewer`, and that class will contain helper methods to:

1. Load image.
2. Separate RGB channels from image matrix.
3. Configure figure and axes (subplots).
4. Plot channel histograms.
5. Plot the image.

The following code shows how to build an image histogram viewer:

```python
import matplotlib.pyplot as plt
import matplotlib.image as mplimage
import matplotlib as mpl
import os


class ImageViewer(object):
```

```python
    def __init__(self, imfile):
        self._load_image(imfile)
        self._configure()

        self.figure = plt.gcf()
        t = "Image: {0}".format(os.path.basename(imfile))
        self.figure.suptitle(t, fontsize=20)

        self.shape = (3, 2)

    def _configure(self):
        mpl.rcParams['font.size'] = 10
        mpl.rcParams['figure.autolayout'] = False
        mpl.rcParams['figure.figsize'] = (9, 6)
        mpl.rcParams['figure.subplot.top'] = .9

    def _load_image(self, imfile):
        self.im = mplimage.imread(imfile)

    @staticmethod
    def _get_chno(ch):
        chmap = {'R': 0, 'G': 1, 'B': 2}
        return chmap.get(ch, -1)
    def show_channel(self, ch):
        bins = 256
        ec = 'none'
        chno = self._get_chno(ch)
        loc = (chno, 1)
        ax = plt.subplot2grid(self.shape, loc)
        ax.hist(self.im[:, :, chno].flatten(), bins, color=ch, ec=ec,\
                label=ch, alpha=.7)
        ax.set_xlim(0, 255)
        plt.setp(ax.get_xticklabels(), visible=True)
        plt.setp(ax.get_yticklabels(), visible=False)
        plt.setp(ax.get_xticklines(), visible=True)
        plt.setp(ax.get_yticklines(), visible=False)
        plt.legend()
        plt.grid(True, axis='y')
        return ax

    def show(self):
        loc = (0, 0)
        axim = plt.subplot2grid(self.shape, loc, rowspan=3)
        axim.imshow(self.im)
```

```
            plt.setp(axim.get_xticklabels(), visible=False)
            plt.setp(axim.get_yticklabels(), visible=False)
            plt.setp(axim.get_xticklines(), visible=False)
            plt.setp(axim.get_yticklines(), visible=False)
            axr = self.show_channel('R')
            axg = self.show_channel('G')
            axb = self.show_channel('B')
            plt.show()

    if __name__ == '__main__':
        im = 'images/yellow_flowers.jpg'
        try:
            iv = ImageViewer(im)
            iv.show()
        except Exception as ex:
            print ex
```

How it works...

Reading from the end of the code, we see hard-coded filenames. These can be swapped by loading the argument from the command line and parsing the given argument into the `im` variable using the `sys.argv` sequence.

We instantiate the `ImageViewer` class with the provided path to an image file. During object instantiation, we try to load an image file into an array, configure the figure via the `rcParams` dictionary, set the figure size and title, and define the object fields (self.shape) to be used inside the object's methods.

The main method here is `show()`, which creates a layout for the figure and loads the image arrays into the main (left column) subplot. We hide any ticks and tick labels as this is the actual image, where we don't have to use the ticks.

We then call the private `show_channel()` method for each of the red, green, and blue channels. This method also creates new subplot axes, this time in the right-hand side column, with each one in a separate row. We plot the histogram for each channel in a separate subplot.

We also set up a little plot to remove unnecessary x ticks, and add a legend in case we want to print this figure in a non-color environment, in which case we can discern channel representation even in those environments.

After we run this code, we will get the following screenshot:

There's more...

The use of the histogram plot type is just a choice for this image viewer example. We could have used any of the matplotlib supported plot types. Another real-world example would be to plot an EEG or similar medical records where we would want to display slice as an image, the time series of the EEG recorded as a line plot, and also additional meta information about the data shown, that would probably go into `matplotlib.text.Text` artists.

Having the ability to interact with the user GUI event, matplotlib's figure allows us also to implement interaction where we would want to zoom into all plots if we manually zoom on one plot only. That would be another usage where we want to display an image and zoom into it while also zooming into other displayed plots in the currently active figure. An idea would be to use `motion_notify_event` to call a function that will update x and y limits for all axes (subplots) in the current figure.

Plotting data on a map using Basemap

Probably the best geospatial visualizations are done by overlaying the data over the map. Whether the whole globe, a continent, a state, or even the sky, it is one of the easiest ways for a viewer to comprehend the relationship between the data and the geography it has displayed.

In this recipe, you will learn how to project data on a map using matplotlib's `Basemap` toolkit.

Getting ready

As we are already familiar with matplotlib as our plotting engine, we can extend that to matplotlib's capability to use other toolkits, one such example being the `Basemap` mapping toolkit.

`Basemap` itself doesn't do any plotting. It just transforms given geospatial coordinates to map projection and gives that data to matplotlib for plotting.

First, we need to install the `Basemap` toolkit. If you are using EPD, `Basemap` is already installed. If you are on Linux, it is best to use native package managers to install the package containing `Basemap`. On Ubuntu, for example, the package is called `python-mpltoolkits.basemap` and can be installed using standard package manager:

```
$ sudo apt-get install python-mpltoolkits.basemap
```

On Mac OS X, it is recommended to use EPD, although installation using popular package managers such as Homebrew, Fink, and pip is also possible.

How to do it...

Here is an example of how to use the `Basemap` toolkit to plot simple Mercator projection within a specific region, specified by longitude, latitude coordinate pairs:

1. We instantiate `Basemap` defining the projection to be used (`merc` for Mercator).
2. We define (in the same `Basemap` constructor) longitude and latitude for the lower-left and upper-right corners of a map.
3. We set up the `Basemap` instance map, to draw coastlines and countries.
4. We set up the `Basemap` instance map to fill continents and draw the map boundary.
5. We instruct the `Basemap` instance map to draw meridians and parallels.

The following code shows how to use `Basemap` toolkit to plot a simple Mercator projection:

```
from mpl_toolkits.basemap import Basemap
import matplotlib.pyplot as plt
import numpy as np

map = Basemap(projection='merc',
              resolution = 'h',
              area_thresh = 0.1,
        llcrnrlon=-126.619875, llcrnrlat=31.354158,
        urcrnrlon=-59.647219, urcrnrlat=47.517613)
```

```
map.drawcoastlines()
map.drawcountries()
map.fillcontinents(color='coral', lake_color='aqua')
map.drawmapboundary(fill_color='aqua')

map.drawmeridians(np.arange(0, 360, 30))
map.drawparallels(np.arange(-90, 90, 30))

plt.show()
```

This will give a recognizable portion of our globe:

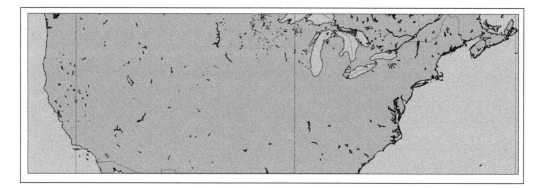

Now that we know how to plot a map, we need to know how to plot data on top of this map. If we recall that `Basemap` is a big transcoder of longitude and latitude pairs into current map projections, we will recognize that all we need is a dataset that contains longitude and latitude that we can pass to `Basemap` for projecting, before plotting over with matplotlib. We use the `cities.shp` and `cities.shx` files to load the coordinates of US cities and project them onto the map.

The file is provided in the `Chapter06` folder of the code repository. Here's the example of how to achieve this:

```
from mpl_toolkits.basemap import Basemap
import matplotlib.pyplot as plt
import numpy as np

map = Basemap(projection='merc',
              resolution = 'h',
              area_thresh = 100,
        llcrnrlon=-126.619875, llcrnrlat=25,
        urcrnrlon=-59.647219, urcrnrlat=55)

shapeinfo = map.readshapefile('cities','cities')
```

```
x, y = zip(*map.cities)

# build a list of US cities
city_names = []
for each in map.cities_info:
    if each['COUNTRY'] != 'US':
        city_names.append("")
    else:
        city_names.append(each['NAME'])

map.drawcoastlines()
map.drawcountries()
map.fillcontinents(color='coral', lake_color='aqua')
map.drawmapboundary(fill_color='aqua')
map.drawmeridians(np.arange(0, 360, 30))
map.drawparallels(np.arange(-90, 90, 30))

# draw city markers
map.scatter(x,y,25, marker='o',zorder=10)

# plot labels at City coords.
for city_label, city_x, city_y in zip(city_names, x, y):
    plt.text(city_x, city_y, city_label)

plt.title('Cities in USA')

plt.show()
```

How it works...

The basics of `Basemap` usage consists of importing the main module and instantiating a `Basemap` class with desired properties. What we must specify during instantiations are the projections to be used and the portion of the globe that we want to work with.

Additional configuration can be applied before drawing the map and displaying the figure window with `matplotlib.pyplot.show()`.

More than a dozen (or 32, to be precise) different projections are supported in `Basemap`. Most of them are very narrow-usage oriented, but some are more general and apply to most common map visualizations.

We can easily see what projections are available by asking the Basemap module itself:

```
import mpl_toolkits.basemap
print mpl_toolkits.basemap.supported_projections
```

`mbtfpq`	McBryde-Thomas Flat-Polar Quartic
`aeqd`	Azimuthal Equidistant
`sinu`	Sinusoidal
`poly`	Polyconic
`omerc`	Oblique Mercator
`gnom`	Gnomonic
`moll`	Mollweide
`lcc`	Lambert Conformal
`tmerc`	Transverse Mercator
`nplaea`	North-Polar Lambert Azimuthal
`gall`	Gall Stereographic Cylindrical
`npaeqd`	North-Polar Azimuthal Equidistant
`mill`	Miller Cylindrical
`merc`	Mercator
`stere`	Stereographic
`eqdc`	Equidistant Conic
`cyl`	Cylindrical Equidistant
`npstere`	North-Polar Stereographic
`spstere`	South-Polar Stereographic
`hammer`	Hammer
`geos`	Geostationary
`nsper`	Near-Sided Perspective
`eck4`	Eckert IV
`aea`	Albers Equal Area
`kav7`	Kavrayskiy VII
`spaeqd`	South-Polar Azimuthal Equidistant
`ortho`	Orthographic
`cass`	Cassini-Soldner
`vandg`	van der Grinten
`laea`	Lambert Azimuthal Equal Area
`splaea`	South-Polar Lambert Azimuthal
`robin`	Robinson

Usually, we plot the whole projection, if nothing is specified, and some reasonable defaults are used.

To zoom in on a specific region of the map, we specify the latitude and longitude of the lower-left and upper-right corners of the region you want to show. For this example, we will use the Mercator projection.

Here we see how the arguments' names are shortened descriptions:

llcrnrlon: This is lower-left corner longitude

llcrnrlat: This is lower-left corner latitude

urcrnrlon: This is upper-right corner longitude

urcrnrlat: This is upper-right corner latitude

There's more...

We have just scratched the surface of the capabilities of Basemap toolkit. More examples can be found in the official documentation at http://matplotlib.org/basemap/users/examples.html.

Most of the data used in the examples in the official Basemap documentation is located on remote servers and in a specific format. To efficiently fetch this data, NetCDF data format is used. NetCDF is a common data format designed with network efficiency in mind. It allows a program to fetch as much data as is needed, even when the whole dataset is very large, which makes using this format very practical. We don't have to download and store large datasets locally every time we want to use them and every time they change.

Plotting data on a map using the Google Map API

In this recipe, we will diverge from the desktop environment and show how we can output for the Web. Although the main language for the web frontend is not Python but HTML, CSS, and JavaScript, we can still use Python for heavy lifting: fetch data, process it, perform intensive computations, and render data in a format(s) suitable for web output, that is, create HTML pages with the required JavaScript version to render our visualization(s).

Getting ready

We will use **Google Data Visualization Library for Python** to help us prepare data for the frontend interface, where we will use another **Google Visualization API** to render data in the desired visualization, that is, a map and a table.

Before we start, we need to install the `google-visualization-python` module. Download the latest stable version from Github and install the module. The following actions demonstrate how to do this:

```
$ git clone https://github.com/google/google-visualization-python.git
```

```
$ cd google-visualization-python/
```

```
$ sudo python setup.py install
```

Note that we have to become a super user (that is, gain administrator privileges) to install this module on our system.

A better option, if you don't want to pollute your OS packages, is to create a `virtualenv` environment to install the packages just for this recipe. We explained how to deal with `virutalenv` environments in *Chapter 1, Preparing Your Working Environment*.

For the frontend library we don't have to install anything, as that library will be loaded from the web page directly from the Google servers.

We need active access to the Internet for this recipe, because the output of it will be a web page that will, when opened in a web browser, pull the JavaScript libraries directly from remote servers.

In this recipe, you will learn how to use Google Data Visualization Library for Python and JavaScript to combine them for creating web visualization.

How to do it...

The following example shows how to visualize **Disposable Median Monthly Salary per Country** on the world map projection using **Google Geochart** and **Table Visualization**, loading the data from a `.csv` file using Python and the `gdata_viz` module. We will:

1. Implement a function to act as a template generator.
2. Use the `csv` module to load the data from the local `.csv` file.
3. Use `DataTable` to describe the data and `LoadData` to load the data from the Python dictionary.
4. Render the output to a web page.

This can be achieved with the following code:

```
import csv
import gviz_api

def get_page_template():
```

```
    page_template = """
    <html>
        <script src="https://www.google.com/jsapi" type="text/
javascript"></script>
        <script>
          google.load('visualization', '1', {packages:['geochart',
'table']});

          google.setOnLoadCallback(drawMap);
          function drawMap() {
              var json_data = new google.visualization.DataTable(%s,
0.6);

              var options = {colorAxis: {colors: ['#eee', 'green']}};
              var mymap = new google.visualization.GeoChart(
                                document.getElementById('map_div'));
              mymap.draw(json_data, options);

              var mytable = new google.visualization.Table(
                                document.getElementById('table_div'));
              mytable.draw(json_data, {showRowNumber: true})
          }
        </script>
        <body>
          <H1>Median Monthly Disposable Salary World Countries</H1>

          <div id="map_div"></div>
          <hr />
          <div id="table_div"></div>

          <div id="source">
          <hr />
          <small>
          Source:
          <a href="http://www.numbeo.com/cost-of-living/prices_by_
country.jsp?displayCurrency=EUR&itemId=105">
          http://www.numbeo.com/cost-of-living/prices_by_country.jsp?dis
playCurrency=EUR&itemId=105
          </a>
          </small>
          </div>
        </body>
    </html>
    """
    return page_template
```

```python
def main():
    # Load data from CVS file
    afile = "median-dpi-countries.csv"
    datarows = []
    with open(afile, 'r') as f:
        reader = csv.reader(f)
        reader.next()  # skip header
        for row in reader:
            datarows.append(row)

    # Describe data
    description = {"country": ("string", "Country"),
                   "dpi": ("number", "EUR"), }

    # Build list of dictionaries from loaded data
    data = []
    for each in datarows:
        data.append({"country": each[0],
                     "dpi": (float(each[1]), each[1])})

    # Instantiate DataTable with structure defined in 'description'
    data_table = gviz_api.DataTable(description)

    # Load it into gviz_api.DataTable
    data_table.LoadData(data)

    # Creating a JSon string
    json = data_table.ToJSon(columns_order=("country", "dpi"),
                             order_by="country", )

    # Put JSON string into the template
    # and save to output.html
    with open('output.html', 'w') as out:
        out.write(get_page_template() % (json,))

if __name__ == '__main__':
    main()
```

This will produce the `output.html` file, which we can open in our favorite web browser. The page should look like the following screenshot:

How it works...

The main entry point here is our `main()` function. First, we use the `csv` module to load our data. This data is obtained from the public website `www.numbeo.com`, and the data is put in the `.csv` format. The final file is available in the repository for this chapter in the `Chapter06` folder. To be able to use Google Data Visualization Library, we need to describe the data to it. We describe data using the Python dictionaries, where we define the ID of the columns, their data type, and an optional label. In the following example, the data is defined in this constraint:

```
{"name": ("data_type", "Label")}:
description = {"country": ("string", "Country"),
                       "dpi": ("number", "EUR"), }
```

Then we need to fit our loaded `.csv` rows in this format. We will build a list of dictionaries in the data variable.

Now we have everything to instantiate our `data_table` with `gviz_data.DataTable` with the described structure. We then load the data into it and output in the JSON format to our `page_template`.

The `get_page_template()` function contains the other part of this equation. It contains a client (frontend) code to produce an HTML web page and a JavaScript code to load Google Data Visualization Library from Google servers. The line that loads the Google JavaScript API is:

```
<script src="https://www.google.com/jsapi"
   type="text/javascript"></script>
```

After this follows another pair of `<script>...</script>` tags that contains an additional setup. First, we load Google Data Visualization Library and the required package—geochart and table:

```
google.load('visualization', '1', {packages:['geochart',
   'table']});
```

Then we set up a function that will be called when the pages are loaded. This event in the web world is registered as `onLoad`, so callback is set up via `setOnLoadCallback` function:

```
google.setOnLoadCallback(drawMap);
```

This defines that when a page is loaded, the Google instance will call the custom function `drawMap()` that we defined. The `drawMap` function loads a JSON string into the JavaScript version of the `DataTable` instance:

```
var json_data = new google.visualization.DataTable(%s, 0.6);
```

Following that, we create a geochart instance in an HTML element with the ID `map_div`:

```
var mymap = new google.visualization.GeoChart(
document.getElementById('map_div'));
```

Draw the map using `json_data` and provided custom options:

```
mymap.draw(json_data, options);
```

Similarly, Google's JavaScript table is rendered below the map:

```
var mytable = new google.visualization.Table(
document.getElementById('table_div'));
mytable.draw(json_data, {showRowNumber: true})
```

We save this output as an HTML file that we can open in a browser. This is not so useful for the dynamic rendering of a web service. There is a better option for this—to output the HTTP response directly from Python, and thus build a background service responding to client web requests with JSON that a client can load and render.

 If you want to understand more on reading HTTP responses, please read more on HTTP Protocol and Response messages at `http://en.wikipedia.org/wiki/Hypertext_Transfer_Protocol#Response_message`.

We do this by replacing the `ToJson()` call with the `ToJSonResponse()` with the same signature. This call will respond with a proper HTTP response containing the payload—our JSON-ified `data_table` ready to be consumed by our JavaScript client.

There's more...

This, of course, is just one example of how we can combine Python as a backend language, sitting on our server, doing the data fetch and processing, while the frontend is left to the universal HTML/JavaScript/CSS set of languages. This enables us to provide interactive and dynamic interfaces with visualizations to a wide audience without requiring them to install anything (well, apart from a web browser, but that is usually installed on a computer or smartphone). Saying that, we must note that the quality of these outputs is not as high as that of matplotlib; the strength of matplotlib lies in its high-quality output.

To work more with the web (and Python), you would have to learn more about the web technologies and languages used. This book does not cover such topics but does give an insight into how to achieve one possible solution using well-known third-party libraries that produce pleasing web outputs, with as little web coding as possible.

 More documentation is available on the Google Developer portal at `https://developers.google.com/chart/interactive/docs/dev/gviz_api_lib`.

Generating CAPTCHA images

Although this is not strictly data visualization in usual terms, the ability to generate images using Python comes in handy in many cases, and this is one of them.

In this recipe, we will be covering the generation of random images to tell humans and computers apart—CAPTCHA image.

Getting ready

CAPTCHA stands for **Completely Automated Public Turing test to tell Computers and Humans Apart**, and is trademarked by Carnegie Mellon University. This test is used to challenge computer programs (usually referred to as bots) that automatically fill various web forms that are primarily targeted at humans and that should not be automated. Usual examples are sign-up forms, login forms, surveys, and similar.

CAPTCHA itself can take various forms, but the most common form consists of a challenge where a human should read an image with distorted characters and numbers and type in the result in the related response field.

In this recipe, you will learn how to harness Python's Imaging Library to generate images, render lines and points, and also render text.

How to do it...

We will show you what is involved in creating a personal and simple CAPTCHA generator by performing the following steps:

1. Define size, text, font size, background color, and CAPTCHA length.
2. Pick random characters from the English alphabet.
3. Draw those on the image using defined font and colors.
4. Add some noise in the form of lines and arcs.
5. Return the image object to the caller together with the CAPTCHA challenge.
6. Show the generated image to the user.

The following code shows how to create a personal and simple CAPTCHA generator:

```python
from PIL import Image, ImageDraw, ImageFont
import random
import string


class SimpleCaptchaException(Exception):
    pass


class SimpleCaptcha(object):
    def __init__(self, length=5, size=(200, 100), fontsize=36,
                 random_text=None, random_bgcolor=None):
        self.size = size
        self.text = "CAPTCHA"
```

```
        self.fontsize = fontsize
        self.bgcolor = 255
        self.length = length

        self.image = None  # current captcha image

        if random_text:
            self.text = self._random_text()

        if not self.text:
            raise SimpleCaptchaException("Field text must not be
empty.")

        if not self.size:
            raise SimpleCaptchaException("Size must not be empty.")

        if not self.fontsize:
            raise SimpleCaptchaException("Font size must be defined.")

        if random_bgcolor:
            self.bgcolor = self._random_color()

    def _center_coords(self, draw, font):
        width, height = draw.textsize(self.text, font)
        xy = (self.size[0] - width) / 2., (self.size[1] - height) / 2.
        return xy

    def _add_noise_dots(self, draw):
        size = self.image.size
        for _ in range(int(size[0] * size[1] * 0.1)):
            draw.point((random.randint(0, size[0]),
                        random.randint(0, size[1])),
                       fill="white")
        return draw

    def _add_noise_lines(self, draw):
        size = self.image.size
        for _ in range(8):
            width = random.randint(1, 2)
            start = (0, random.randint(0, size[1] - 1))
            end = (size[0], random.randint(0,size[1]-1))
            draw.line([start, end], fill="white", width=width)
        for _ in range(8):
            start = (-50, -50)
```

```python
            end = (size[0] + 10, random.randint(0, size[1]+10))
            draw.arc(start + end, 0, 360, fill="white")
        return draw

    def get_captcha(self, size=None, text=None, bgcolor=None):
        if text is not None:
            self.text = text
        if size is not None:
            self.size = size
        if bgcolor is not None:
            self.bgcolor = bgcolor

        self.image = Image.new('RGB', self.size, self.bgcolor)
        # Note that the font file must be present
        # or point to your OS's system font
        # Ex. on Mac the path should be '/Library/Fonts/Tahoma.ttf'
        font = ImageFont.truetype('fonts/Vera.ttf', self.fontsize)
        draw = ImageDraw.Draw(self.image)
        xy = self._center_coords(draw, font)
        draw.text(xy=xy, text=self.text, font=font)

        # Add some dot noise
        draw = self._add_noise_dots(draw)

        # Add some random lines
        draw = self._add_noise_lines(draw)

        self.image.show()
        return self.image, self.text


    def _random_text(self):
        letters = string.ascii_lowercase + string.ascii_uppercase
        random_text = ""
        for _ in range(self.length):
            random_text += random.choice(letters)
        return random_text

    def _random_color(self):
        r = random.randint(0, 255)
        g = random.randint(0, 255)
        b = random.randint(0, 255)
        return (r, g, b)
if __name__ == "__main__":
```

```
sc = SimpleCaptcha(length=7, fontsize=36, random_text=True,
random_bgcolor=True)
    sc.get_captcha()
```

This produces an image similar to the following:

How it works...

This example shows a process for using Python's imaging library to generate predefined images, to create a simple, yet effective, CAPTCHA generator.

We wrapped the functionality into one class `SimpleCaptcha`, because it gives us a safe space for future development. We also created a custom `SimpleCaptchaException` to accommodate future exception hierarchies.

 If you are writing anything more than simple and quick scripts, it is always good to start writing and designing custom exception hierarchies for your domain, rather than using generic Python's standard exceptions. You will gain a lot in the readability and maintenance of the software.

Start reading from the main section. At the end of the code listing, we instantiate class giving settings of our future image as arguments to the constructor. Following that, we call the `get_captcha` method on the sc object. For this recipe's purposes, `get_captcha` shows the image object as a result, but we also return the image object to the potential caller of this method so it could make use of the result. The usage can vary; the caller could either save the image on the file, or if this was a web application, return the image stream and written challenge to the client requesting this CAPTCHA.

The important thing to note is that in order to finish the challenge-response process of the CAPTCHA test, we must return the CAPTCHA string generated on the image as text so that the caller can compare the user's response with the expected values.

The `get_captcha` method first verifies the input arguments, in order to override the class defaults if the user provides custom values. After that, a new image object is instantiated by `Image.new`. This object is saved in `self.image`, where we use it to draw and write text. Having written the text to the image, we add the noise of randomly placed points and lines, as well as some arc segments.

These tasks are carried out by the _add_noise_points and _add_noise_lines methods. The first one loops a few times and adds a point to a random location on the image, not too close to the edges of the image, and the latter one draws lines from the left-hand side of the image to the right-hand side of the image.

There's more...

We constructed this class using some assumptions about its use. We assumed that the user will just want to accept our default settings (that is, a random seven characters on a random background color) and receive the result from it. That is the reasoning behind placing helper functions in the constructor to set random text and random background color. If the most frequent and effective usage is to always override configuration, then we want to remove these operations from the constructor and place them in separate calls.

For example, maybe a user wants to always use English words as the CAPTCHA challenge. If this is the case, we want to be able to just call a method to provide us with results like that. This method could be get_english_captcha and with the random logic of this constructor, we would then construct that method to pick random words from the provided English dictionary. On a Unix system, there is a common English dictionary inside /usr/share/dict/words that we could use for this:

```
def get_english_captcha(self):
    words = '/usr/share/dict/words'
    with open(words, 'r') as wf:
        words = wf.readlines()
        aword = random.choice(words)
        aword = aword.strip()  # remove newline and spaces
    return self.get_captcha(text=aword)
```

Overall, the example of the CAPTCHA generation is not production quality and should not be used without adding more protection and randomness, such as letter rotation.

If you need to protect your web forms from bots, there are already third-party Python modules and libraries that you could use. There are even specialized modules built for the existing web frameworks.

There are event web services such as **reCAPTCHA** (http://www.google.com/recaptcha) with an already proven Python module recaptcha-client (https://pypi.python.org/pypi/recaptcha-client) that you can sign up and use. It does not require any imaging libraries because the image is pulled directly from the reCAPTCHA web service, but it has other dependencies such as **pycrypto**. Using this web service and library, you are also helping books scanned using **Optical Character Recognition** (**OCR**) from the Google Books project or old editions of *The New York Times.* Read more on the reCAPTCHA website.

7
Using the Right Plots to Understand Data

In this chapter, you will cover the following recipes:

- ▶ Understanding logarithmic plots
- ▶ Understanding spectrograms
- ▶ Creating stem plot
- ▶ Drawing streamlines of vector flow
- ▶ Using colormaps
- ▶ Using scatter plots and histograms
- ▶ Plotting the cross correlation between two variables
- ▶ Importance of autocorrelation

Introduction

In this chapter, we will focus more on understanding what we want to say with the data that we are presenting, and how to say it effectively. We will present some new techniques and plots, but all will be underlined by understanding of the information we want to convey to the user. Let's ask the questions. Why do we want to present information in this state? This is the most important question that should be asked during the data exploration phase. If we miss the opportunity to understand the data and present it in a certain way, the viewer, then, is not going to understand the data correctly, for sure.

Understanding logarithmic plots

More often than not, while reading daily newspapers and similar articles, one can find charts that are used by media organizations to misrepresent the facts. One usual example is using linear scales to create, so called, panic charts where constantly growing value is followed for long period of time (years) and starting values are smaller from latest one by several magnitudes. These values when visualized correctly, would (and usually should), produce linear or almost linear charts. This takes some panic out of the articles they illustrate.

Getting ready

With the logarithmic scale, the ratio of consecutive values is constant. This is important when we are trying to read log plots. With linear (arithmetic) scales, the constant is the distance between consecutive values. In other words, logarithmic plots have constant distance in orders of magnitude. We will see this illustrated on the following plots. The code used to produce this figure is explained here.

As a general rule of thumb, logarithmic scales should be used when the data presented has the following:

- ▸ values that span several orders of magnitude
- ▸ skewness toward large values (some points are much larger than the rest of the data)
- ▸ you want to show the rate of change (growth rate) and not value of change

Don't blindly follow these rules, they are more like hints than rules. Always use your own judgment about the data in hand and requirements presented to you by the project or customer.

Depending on the data range, different log bases should be used. The standard base for the log is 10, but if the range of the data is smaller, a base of 2 can prove to be more useful as it will show more "resolution" within the smaller range.

If we have the range of data suitable for display on logarithmic scales, we will note that the values previously being too close to judge any difference are now well apart. This allows us to read the chart much easily than if we would present the data in linear scale.

The growth rate charts, where long-range time series data is collected, are where we want to see, not the absolute value measured at time point, but the *growth in time*. We will still get the absolute value information, but that information is of lower priority.

Also, if the data distribution has positive skew (for example, salaries), taking the logarithm of the value (salary) will help us fit the data into the model, as the logarithm transformation will give us more normal data distribution.

How to do it...

We will exemplify this with a sample code that shows the same two dataset (one linear and one logarithmic in nature) on two different plots (in the same figure) using different scales (linear and logarithmic).

We will be performing the following steps with the help of the code mentioned after the steps:

1. Generate two simple datasets, y—exponential/logarithmic in nature, and z—linear in nature.

2. Create figure containing grid of four subplots.

3. Create two subplots containing the y dataset one in logarithmic scale and one in linear scale.

4. Create another two subplots containing z dataset, again, one logarithmic and the other linear.

Here is the code:

```python
from matplotlib import pyplot as plt
import numpy as np

x = np.linspace(1, 10)
y = [10 ** el for el in x]
z = [2 * el for el in x]

fig = plt.figure(figsize=(10, 8))

ax1 = fig.add_subplot(2, 2, 1)
ax1.plot(x, y, color='blue')
ax1.set_yscale('log')
ax1.set_title(r'Logarithmic plot of $ {10}^{x} $ ')
ax1.set_ylabel(r'$ {y} = {10}^{x} $')
plt.grid(b=True, which='both', axis='both')


ax2 = fig.add_subplot(2, 2, 2)
ax2.plot(x, y, color='red')
ax2.set_yscale('linear')
ax2.set_title(r'Linear plot of $ {10}^{x} $ ')
ax2.set_ylabel(r'$ {y} = {10}^{x} $')
plt.grid(b=True, which='both', axis='both')
```

```
ax3 = fig.add_subplot(2, 2, 3)
ax3.plot(x, z, color='green')
ax3.set_yscale('log')
ax3.set_title(r'Logarithmic plot of $ {2}*{x} $ ')
ax3.set_ylabel(r'$ {y} = {2}*{x} $')
plt.grid(b=True, which='both', axis='both')


ax4 = fig.add_subplot(2, 2, 4)
ax4.plot(x, z, color='magenta')
ax4.set_yscale('linear')
ax4.set_title(r'Linear plot of $ {2}*{x} $ ')
ax4.set_ylabel(r'$ {y} = {2}*{x} $')
plt.grid(b=True, which='both', axis='both')


plt.show()
```

This code will produce the following figure:

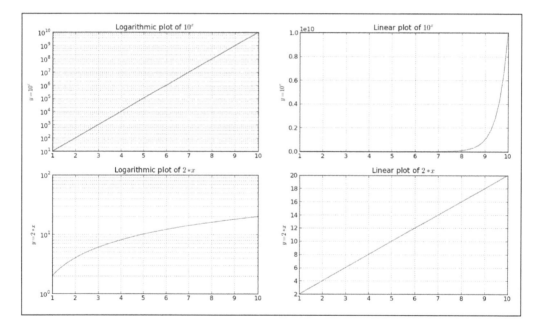

How it works...

We generate some sample data and two dependent variables—y and z. Variable y is expressed as exponential function of data (x), and variable z is simple linear function of x. This helps us illustrate different looks of linear and exponential charts.

We then create grid of four subplots, where the top row subplots are of data (x, y) and bottom row are of data (x, z) pairs.

Looking from left-hand side, columns charts have logarithmic scales on the *y*-axis, while right-hand side columns are in linear scale. We set this using `set_yscale('log')` for each axis separately.

For every subplot, we set a title and label, where label also describes the function plotted.

With `plt.grid(b=True, which='both', axis='both')`, we turn the grid on for both axis and both the major and minor ticks.

We observe how linear functions are straight lines on linear plots, while logarithmic functions are straight lines on logarithmic plots.

Understanding spectrograms

A spectrogram is a time-varying spectral representation that shows how the spectral density of a signal varies with time.

It represents a spectrum of frequencies of the sound or other signal in a visual manner. It is used in various science fields, from sound fingerprinting like voice recognition to radar engineering and seismology.

Usually spectrogram layout is as following: *x*-axis represents time, *y*-axis represents frequency, and the third dimension is amplitude of a frequency-time pair, which is color coded. This is three-dimensional data, therefore, we can also create 3D plot where the intensity is represented as height on the *z*-axis. The problem with 3D charts is that humans are bad at understanding and comparing them. Also, they tend to take more space than 2D charts.

Getting ready

For serious signal processing, we would go into low level details to be able to detect patterns and auto fingerprint certain specific, but for this data visualization recipe we, will leverage a couple of well-known Python libraries to read in audio file, sample it, and spot a spectrogram.

In order to read `.wav` files to visualize sound, we need to do some prep work. We need to install the `libsndfile1` system library for reading/writing audio files. This is done via the favorite package manager. For Ubuntu, you can use:

```
$ sudo apt-get install libsndfile1-dev.
```

It is important to install the dev package, which contains header files so pip can build the `scikits.audiolab` module.

We can also install `libasound`, **ALSA** (**Advanced Linux Sound Architecture**) headers to avoid the runtime warning. This is optional, as we are not going to use features provided by the ALSA library. For Ubuntu, Linux issue the following command:

```
$ sudo apt-get install libasound2-dev
```

To install `scikits.audiolab`, which we will use to read `.wav` files, we will use `pip`:

```
$ pip install scikits.audiolab
```

 Always remember to enter the virtual environment for your current project, as you don't want to dirty system libraries.

How to do it...

For this recipe, we will use prerecorded sound file `test.wav` that can be found in the file repository with this book. But we could also generate a sample, which we will try later.

In this following example, we perform the following steps in this order:

1. Read the `.wav` file that contains recorded sound sample

2. Define the length of the window used for Fourier transform—NFFT

3. Define the overlapping data points while sampling—`noverlap`

 `NFFT` defines the number of data points used for computing the Discrete Fourier Transform in each block. The most efficient computation is then the `NFFT` is the power of two. The windows can overlap and the number of data points that are overlapped (that is, repeated) is defined by the `noverlap` argument.

```
import os
from math import floor, log

from scikits.audiolab import Sndfile
import numpy as np
from matplotlib import pyplot as plt
```

```
# Load the sound file in Sndfile instance
soundfile = Sndfile("test.wav")


# define start/stop seconds and compute start/stop frames
start_sec = 0
stop_sec  = 5
start_frame = start_sec * soundfile.samplerate
stop_frame  = stop_sec * soundfile.samplerate

# go to the start frame of the sound object
soundfile.seek(start_frame)

# read number of frames from start to stop
delta_frames = stop_frame - start_frame
sample = soundfile.read_frames(delta_frames)


map = 'CMRmap'

fig = plt.figure(figsize=(10, 6), )
ax = fig.add_subplot(111)
# define number of data points for FT
NFFT = 128
# define number of data points to overlap for each block
noverlap = 65

pxx,  freq, t, cax = ax.specgram(sample, Fs=soundfile.samplerate,
                                 NFFT=NFFT, noverlap=noverlap,
                                 cmap=plt.get_cmap(map))
plt.colorbar(cax)
plt.xlabel("Times [sec]")
plt.ylabel("Frequency [Hz]")

plt.show()
```

This generates the following spectrogram, with visible "white-like" traces for separate notes.

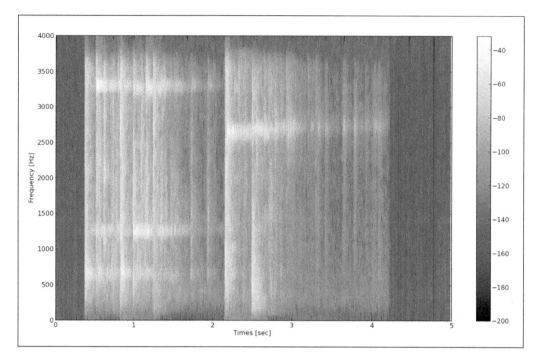

How it works...

We need to load a sound file first. To do this, we use the `scikits.audiolab.SndFile` method and provide it with a filename. This will instantiate sound object, which we can then query for data and call function on.

To read data needed for spectrogram, we need to read the desired frames of data from our sound object. This is done by `read_frames()`, which accepts the start and end frame. We calculate the frame number by multiplying sample rate with the time points (`start`, `end`) we want to visualize.

There's more...

If you can't find audio (wave), you can easily generate one. Here's how to generate it:

```
import numpy


def _get_mask(t, t1, t2, lvl_pos, lvl_neg):
```

```
    if t1 >= t2:
        raise ValueError("t1 must be less than t2")

    return numpy.where(numpy.logical_and(t > t1, t < t2), lvl_pos,
lvl_neg)


def generate_signal(t):
    sin1 = numpy.sin(2 * numpy.pi * 100 * t)
    sin2 = 2 * numpy.sin(2 * numpy.pi * 200 * t)

    # add interval of high pitched signal
    sin2 = sin2 * _get_mask(t, 2, 5, 1.0, 0.0)

    noise = 0.02 * numpy.random.randn(len(t))
    final_signal = sin1 + sin2 + noise
    return final_signal


if __name__ == '__main__':
    step = 0.001
    sampling_freq=1000
    t = numpy.arange(0.0, 20.0, step)
    y = generate_signal(t)

    # we can visualize this now
    # in time
    ax1 = plt.subplot(211)
    plt.plot(t, y)
    # and in frequency
    plt.subplot(212)
    plt.specgram(y, NFFT=1024, noverlap=900,
        Fs=sampling_freq, cmap=plt.cm.gist_heat)

    plt.show()
```

Will give you the following signal where the top subplot represent the signal we generated. Here, the *X* axis is time and *Y* axis is the signal's amplitude. The bottom subplot is the same signal in the frequency domain. Here, while x-axis is the same time as in the top subplot (we matched the time by selecting the sampling rate), the y-axis is the frequency of the signal.

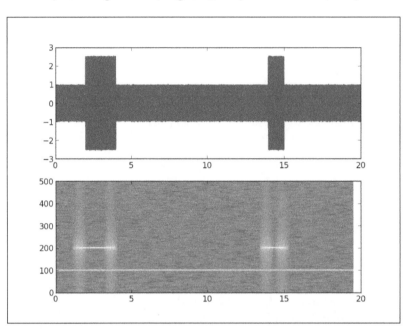

Creating stem plot

A two-dimensional stem plot displays data as lines extending from a baseline along the x-axis. A circle (the default) or the other marker's y-position represents the data value that terminates each stem.

In this recipe, we will be discussing about how to create a stem plot.

Do not confuse stem with stem and leaf plots, which is a method of representing data by separating the last important digit of values as leaves and higher order values as stems.

```
steam | leaf
==============================
    0 | 6 7 8
    1 | 0 2 3 4 7 7 7 8 9
    2 | 1 3 4 4 5 7
    3 | 3 1 1 2 6 6 9
    4 | 1 5 5 6 9
    5 | 0
```

Getting ready

For this kind of plot, we need to use a sequence of discrete data, where ordinary an line plots wouldn't make sense anyway.

Plot discrete sequences as stems, where data values are represented as markers at the end of each stem. Stems extend from baseline (usually at *y=0*) to the data point value.

How to do it...

We will use matplotlib to plot stem plots using the `stem()` function. This function can use just a series of y values when x values are generated as a simple sequence from 0 to `len(y)`−1. If we provide the stem function with both x and y sequences, they will be used for both axes.

What we want to configure with stem plot is several formatters:

- ▶ `linefmt`: This is the line formatter for stem line
- ▶ `markerfmt`: The stems at the end of the line is formatted using this argument
- ▶ `basefmt`: This formats the look of the base line
- ▶ `label`: This defines label for legend for stem plot
- ▶ `hold`: This holds the current graphs on current axis
- ▶ `bottom`: This sets up the location of baseline position on *y* axis, default value is 0

The `hold` argument is used as a usual feature for plots. If it is on (`True`), all the following plotting is added to the current axes. Otherwise, every plot will create a new figure and axes.

To create a stem plot, perform the following steps:

1. Generate random noise data
2. Configure stem options
3. Plot the stem

Here is the code to do it:

```python
import matplotlib.pyplot as plt
import numpy as np


# time domain in which we sample
x = np.linspace(0, 20, 50)

# random function to simulate sampled signal
y = np.sin(x + 1) + np.cos(x ** 2)


# here we can setup baseline position
bottom = -0.1

# True  -- hold current axes for further plotting
# False -- opposite. clear and use new figure/plot
hold = False

# set label for legend.
label = "delta"

markerline, stemlines, baseline = plt.stem(x, y, bottom=bottom,
                                label=label, hold=hold)

# we use setp() here to setup
# multiple properties of lines generated by stem()
plt.setp(markerline, color='red', marker='o')
plt.setp(stemlines, color='blue', linestyle=':')
plt.setp(baseline, color='grey', linewidth=2, linestyle='-')

# draw a legend
plt.legend()

plt.show()
```

This code produces the following plots:

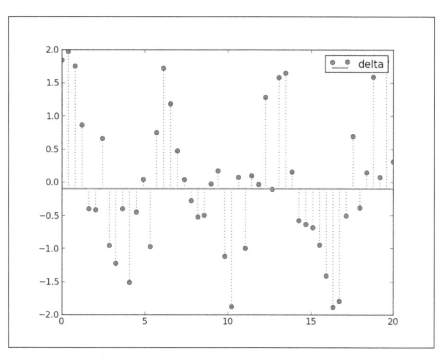

How it works...

First, we need some data. For this recipe, the generated sampled pseudo-signal will suffice. In real world, any discrete sequential data can be properly visualized using stem plot. We generate this signal using Numpy's `numpy.linspace`, `numpy.cos`, and `numpy.sin` functions.

We then set up label for stem plot and position of baseline, which defaults to 0.

If we want to draw multiple stem plots, we will set hold to `True`, and the following plotting calls will be rendered over the same set of axes.

Call to a `matplotlib.stem` returns three objects. First is `markerline`, instance of `Line2D`. This holds the reference to a line representing stems themselves, rendering only markers and not the line connecting the markers. This line can be made visible by the editing property of the `Line2D` instance, which we will explain soon. The last one is also a `Line2D` instance—`baseline`, holding a reference to a horizontal line that represents the source of all `stemlines`. Second object returned—`stemlines`—collection (Python list at the moment) of `Line2D` instances representing stem-lines, of course.

We use these objects returned to manipulate the visual appeal of the stem plot, using the `setp` function to apply properties to all lines (`Line2D` instances) in those objects or collections of objects.

Experiment with the desired settings until you understand how `setp` changes your plot's style.

Drawing streamlines of vector flow

Stream plots are used to visualize flow in vector fields. Examples from science and nature include fields of magnetic and gravitational forces or movement of liquid materials.

Vector field can be visualized in such a way, where we assign a line and one or more arrows to every point. The intensity can be represented by the line length, and direction by arrow pointing in particular direction.

Usually, the intensity of the force is visualized with the length of a particular streamline, but density can also be used for the same purpose.

Getting ready

To visualize vector fields, we will use `matplotlib`'s `matplotlib.pyplot.streamplot` function. This function creates plots from streamlines of a flow uniformly filling the domain. The velocities field is interpolated and streamlines are integrated. The original source for this function is to visualize wind patterns or liquid flow, hence we don't need strict vector lines but uniform representation of the vector field.

Most important arguments for this function are x, y evenly spaced grid of one-dimensional NumPy array, and u, v matching two-dimensional NumPy arrays of x, y velocities. Matrices u and v must be of such dimensions that the number of rows must be of equal length of y, and the number of columns must match the length of x.

Line width of stream plot can be controlled per line, if the `linewidth` argument is given a two-dimensional array matching the shape of u and v velocities, or it, simply can be just one integer value that all lines will accept.

Color, can not only be just one value for all stream line, but also a matrix shaped like the `linewidth` argument.

Arrows (the `FancyArrowPatch` class) are used to indicate vector direction, and we can control them using two params: `arrowsize`—size of the arrow, and `arrowstyle`—format of the arrow (for example, `"simple"`, `"->"`).

How to do it...

We will start with a simple example, just to get the sense of what's going on here. Perform the following steps:

1. Create data vectors

2. Print intermediate values

3. Plot the stream-plot

4. Show the figure with streamlines visualizing our vectors

Here is the code sample:

```
import matplotlib.pyplot as plt
import numpy as np

Y, X = np.mgrid[0:5:100j, 0:5:100j]

U = X
V = Y

from pprint import pprint
print "X"
pprint(X)

print "Y"
pprint(Y)

plt.streamplot(X, Y, U, V)


plt.show()
```

This will give the following textual output:

```
X
array([[ 0.        ,  0.05050505,  0.1010101 , ...,  4.8989899 ,
         4.94949495,  5.        ],
       [ 0.        ,  0.05050505,  0.1010101 , ...,  4.8989899 ,
         4.94949495,  5.        ],
       [ 0.        ,  0.05050505,  0.1010101 , ...,  4.8989899 ,
         4.94949495,  5.        ],
       ...,
       [ 0.        ,  0.05050505,  0.1010101 , ...,  4.8989899 ,
```

```
          4.94949495,  5.           ],
     [ 0.          ,  0.05050505,  0.1010101 ,  ...,  4.8989899 ,
          4.94949495,  5.           ],
     [ 0.          ,  0.05050505,  0.1010101 ,  ...,  4.8989899 ,
          4.94949495,  5.           ]])
Y
array([[ 0.          ,  0.          ,  0.          ,  ...,  0.          ,
          0.          ,  0.          ],
     [ 0.05050505,  0.05050505,  0.05050505,  ...,  0.05050505,
          0.05050505,  0.05050505],
     [ 0.1010101 ,  0.1010101 ,  0.1010101 ,  ...,  0.1010101 ,
          0.1010101 ,  0.1010101 ],

     ...,
     [ 4.8989899 ,  4.8989899 ,  4.8989899 ,  ...,  4.8989899 ,
          4.8989899 ,  4.8989899 ],
     [ 4.94949495,  4.94949495,  4.94949495,  ...,  4.94949495,
          4.94949495,  4.94949495],
     [ 5.          ,  5.          ,  5.          ,  ...,  5.          ,
    5.          ,  5.           ]])
```

This generates the following streamline flow figure:

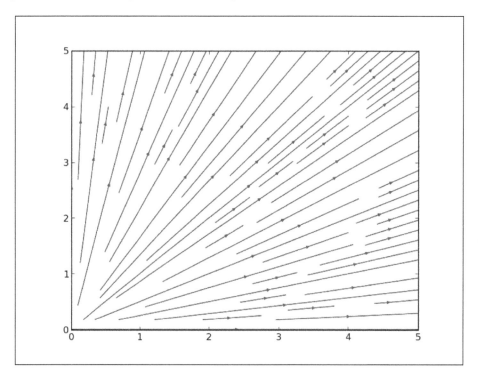

How it works...

We create a vector field of X and Y by indexing the two-dimensional mesh grid, using NumPy's `mgrid` instance. We specify the range of the grid, as start and stop (-2 and 2, respectively). The third index represents a step length. The step length is the number of points to include between start and stop. If you want to include the stop value, use complex numbers for step length, where magnitude is used for the number of points required between start and stop, stop being inclusive.

Mesh grid, fleshed out like this, is then used to compute vector velocities. Here, for the sake of example, we just use the same `meshgrid` as vector velocities.

This generates a plot that clearly shows plain linear dependency and flow of represented vector field.

Play with the values of U and V to get a sense of how values of U and V influence stream plot. For example, make U = `np.sin(X)` or V = `np.sin(Y)`. Following that, try to change the start and stop values. The following figure shows U = `np.sin(X)`:

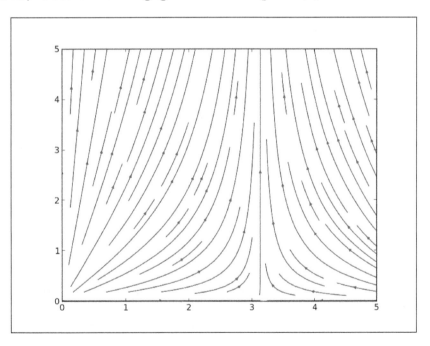

Bare in mind that the plot we plotted is generated by a set of lines and arrow patches; hence, there is no way (currently, at least) to update the existing figure. Lines and arrows know nothing about vectors and fields. Future implementations might bring about this change, but at the moment, this is a known limitation in the current version of matplotlib.

There's more...

Of course this example gives you an opportunity to get to know and understand **matplotlib**'s stream plot features and capabilities.

Real power comes when you have the real data at hand to play with. After understanding this recipe, you will be able to recognize the tools you have. So when you are given the data and you know the domain of it, you will be able to pick the best tool for the job.

Using colormaps

Color coding the data can have great impact on how your visualizations are perceived by the viewer, as they come with assumptions about color and what that color represents.

Being explicit if the color is used to add additional information to the data is always good. To know when and how to use color in your visualizations is even better.

Getting ready

If your data is not naturally color coded (such as earth/terrain altitudes or object temperature), it's better not to make any artificial mappings to natural coloring. We want to understand the data appropriately and make a choice of color to help the reader decode data easily. We don't want readers constantly trying to suppress learned mapping of color for temperatures, if we are representing financial data that has no connection with Kelvins or Celsius.

If possible, avoid the usual red/green associations, if there are no strong correlations in the data to associate them with those colors.

To help you pick the right color mapping, we will explain some colormaps available in the matplotlib package that can save a lot of time and help us, if we know what they are used for and how to find them.

Colormaps, in general, can be categorized as follows:

- ▶ Sequential: Monochromatic colormaps of two color tones from low to high saturation of the same color. For example, from white to bright blue. Ideal for most cases, as they clearly show the change from low to high values.
- ▶ Diverging: The central point here is the median value (some light color usually), but then, ranges go from there to two different color tones in direction for high and for low values. This can be ideal for data with significant median value. For example, when the median is at 0, it clearly shows the difference between negative and positive values.

- ▶ Qualitative: For cases where data has no inherent ordering, and all you want is to make sure different categories are easily discernible from each other.

- ▶ Cyclic: It is used where data can wrap around endpoint values, such as representing time of the day, wind direction, phase angle, or similar.

Matplotlib comes with a lot of predefined maps, and we are able to divide them into several categories. We will suggest when to use some of these colormaps.

The most common and base colormaps are `autumn`, `bone`, `cool`, `copper`, `flag`, `gray`, `hot`, `hsv`, `jet`, `pink`, `prism`, `sprint`, `summer`, `winter`, and `spectral`.

We have another set of colormaps coming from the "Yorick scientific visualization package". This is evolution from GIST package, so all colormaps in this collection have `gist_` as prefix in their name.

 The Yorick is a visualization package and also an interpreted language, written in C, not quite active lately. You can find more information on an official website – `http://yorick.sourceforge.net/index.php`

These colormap set contain following maps: `gist_earth`, `gist_heat`, `gist_ncar`, `gist_rainbow`, and `gist_stern`.

Then, we have the following colormaps based on Color Brewer (`http://colorbrewer.org`), where we can categorize them into: Diverging, where luminance is highest at the midpoint and decreases towards different endpoints; Sequential, where luminance decreases monotonically; Qualitative, where different sets of colors are used to differentiate data categories.

Also, some miscellaneous colormaps are also available:

Colormap	Description
`brg`	This is blue-red-green
`bwr`	Diverging blue-white-red
`coolwarm`	Useful for 3D shading, color blindness, and ordering of colors
`rainbow`	Spectral purple-blue-green-yellow-orange-red colormap with diverging luminance
`seismic`	Diverging blue-white-red
`terrain`	Mapmaker's colors, blue-green-yellow-brown-white, originally from IGOR Pro software

Most of the maps presented here can be reversed by putting `_r` postfix after a name of the colormap, for example, `hot_r` is an inverse cycle colormap of `hot`.

How to do it...

We can set colormap on many items in `matplotlib`. For example, colormap can be set on `image`, `pcolor`, and `scatter`. This is accomplished usually via argument to a function called `cmap`. This argument is an expected instance of `colors.Colormap`.

We can also use `matplotlib.pyplot.set_cmap` to set `cmap` for latest object plotted on the axes.

You can get all available colormaps easily with `matplotlib.pyplot.colormaps`. Fire up IPython and type in the following:

```
In [1]: import matplotlib.pyplot as plt

In [2]: plt.colormaps()
Out[2]:
['Accent',
 'Accent_r',
 'Blues',
 'Blues_r',
 ...
 'winter',
 'winter_r']
```

Note that we have shortened the preceding list because it contains around 140 items and would span across several pages here.

This will import the `pyplot` function interface and allow us to call the `colormaps` function, which returns a list of all registered colormaps.

Finally, we want to show you how to make a nice looking colormap. In the following example, we need to:

1. Use the Color Brewer website to get divergent colormap color values in the hex format
2. Generate a random sample of x and y, where y is cumulative sum of value (simulate stock price variations)
3. Apply customization to scatter plot functions of matplotlib
4. Tweak scatter marker line color and width to make the plot more readable and pleasant for viewers.

```
import matplotlib as mpl
import matplotlib.pyplot as plt
import numpy as np
```

```
# Red Yellow Green divergent colormap
red_yellow_green = ['#d73027', '#f46d43', '#fdae61',
                    '#fee08b', '#ffffbf', '#d9ef8b',
                    '#a6d96a', '#66bd63', '#1a9850']

sample_size = 1000
fig, ax = plt.subplots(1)

for i in range(9):
    y = np.random.normal(size=sample_size).cumsum()
    x = np.arange(sample_size)
    ax.scatter(x, y, label=str(i), linewidth=0.1,
edgecolors='grey',
               facecolor=red_yellow_green[i])

ax.legend()
plt.show()
```

This will render a nice looking figure:

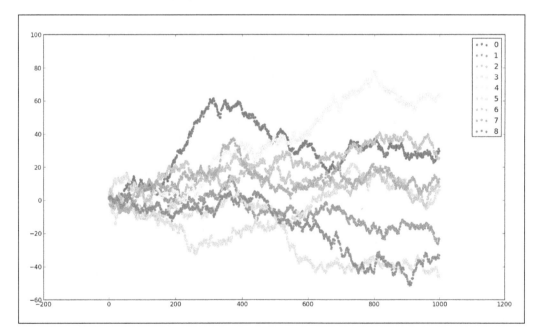

How it works...

We used the ColorBrewer website to find out colors in red, yellow, and green divergent colormap from Colorbrew. Then, we listed those colors in our code and applied them to our scatter plot.

> Colorbrew is a web tool, built by Cynthia Brewer, Mark Harrower, and The Pennsylvania State University as a tool to explore color maps. It is a very handy tool to pick up color maps of different ranges and see them applied on a map using slight variations so that you immediately sense what will they look like on a chart. This particular map is at `http://colorbrewer2.org/index.php?type=diverging&scheme=RdYlGn&n=9`.

Sometimes, we will have to make our customization on `matplotlib.rcParams`, which is the first thing we want to do before we create figure or any of the axes.

For example, `matplotlib.rcParams['axes.cycle_color']` is the configuration setting we want to change in order to set up default colormap for most of the matplotlib functions.

There's more...

Using `matplotlib.pyplot.register_cmap`, we can register a new colormap to matplotlib, so it can be found using the `get_cmap` function. We can use it in two different ways. Here are both signatures:

- `register_cmap(name='swirly', cmap=swirly_cmap)`
- `register_cmap(name='choppy', data=choppydata, lut=128)`

The first signature allows us to specify colormap as an instance of `colors.Colormap` and register it via the `name` argument. The `name` argument can be omitted in which case it will be inherited from the `name` attribute of the `cmap` instance provided.

The latter one, we are passing three arguments to the linear segmented colormap constructor, and registering that colormap afterwards.

Using `maplotlib.pyplot.get_cmap`, we can get the `colors.Colormap` instance using name argument.

Here's how to make your own map using `matplotlib.colors.LinearSegmentedColormap`:

```
from pylab import *
cdict = {'red': ((0.0, 0.0, 0.0),
                 (0.5, 1.0, 0.7),
```

```
              (1.0, 1.0, 1.0)),
      'green': ((0.0, 0.0, 0.0),
                (0.5, 1.0, 0.0),
                (1.0, 1.0, 1.0)),
      'blue': ((0.0, 0.0, 0.0),
                (0.5, 1.0, 0.0),
                (1.0, 0.5, 1.0))}
my_cmap = matplotlib.colors.LinearSegmentedColormap('my_
colormap',cdict,256)
pcolor(rand(10,10),cmap=my_cmap)
colorbar()
```

This is the simplest part, while the hardest part is to actually come with a combination of colors that are informative, do not take away from the data we want to visualize, and that are pleasant for the eyes of the viewer.

For the base map list (colormaps listed in the preceding table), we can use the `pylab` shortcut to set colormap. For example, the following code would set colormap of the image X to `cmap='hot'`:

```
imshow(X)
hot()
```

Using scatter plots and histograms

Scatter plots are very often encountered around, as they are the most common plot to visualize the relation between two variables. If we want to take a quick look at the data and see if there is any relation between those (that is, correlation), we would draw a quick scatter plot. For a scatter plot to exist, we must have one variable that can be systematically changed by, for example, experimenter, so we can inspect the possibilities of influencing another variable.

That's why, in this recipe, you will learn how to understand the scatter plots.

Getting ready

We want to see, for example, how two events are affected by each other or if they are affected at all. This visualization is especially useful on large sets of data, where we cannot make any conclusions by looking at the data in the native form—when it is just numbers.

Correlation between values, if there is any, can be positive and negative. Positive correlation is when, for increasing *X* values, the *Y* values are increasing too. In negative correlation, for increasing *X* values, *Y* values are decreasing. In an ideal case, positive correlation is a line starting from bottom-left corner of axes to top-right corner. Negative ideal correlation is a line starting from top-left corner to the bottom-right corner of axes.

Ideal positive correlation between two data points is given the value of 1 and ideal negative is given the value of -1. Everything inside this interval represents weaker correlation between two values. Usually, everything inside -0.5 to 0.5 is not considered valuable from a perspective of two variables being in real connection.

Example of positive correlation would be the amount of money put in a charity jar being directly positively correlated to number of people seeing the jar. Negative correlation is between the time required to reach place B from place A, depending on the distance between A and B locations. The greater the distance, more time we need to complete the travel.

For example, what we have presented here is a positive correlation, but this is not perfect, as different people might put different amounts of money per visit. But, in general, we can assume that the more people see that jar, more money will be left inside.

Keep in mind, though, that even if the scatter plot displays correlation between two variables, that correlation might not be a direct one. There might be a third variable that influences both plotted variables, so the correlation is just a case that plotted values are correlated with that third variable. In the end, the correlation might be just apparent and no real relation exists behind.

How to do it...

With the following code sample, we will demonstrate how scatter plot can explain the relation between variables.

The data we use is obtained using the Google Trends web portal, where one can download the CSV file containing normalized values of relative search volumes for given parameters.

We will store our data in the ch07_search_data.py Python module, so we can import it in subsequent code recipes.

Here's the content of it:

```
# ch07_search_data


# daily search trend for keyword 'flowers' for a year

DATA = [
 1.04, 1.04, 1.16, 1.22, 1.46, 2.34, 1.16, 1.12, 1.24, 1.30, 1.44,
1.22, 1.26,
 1.34, 1.26, 1.40, 1.52, 2.56, 1.36, 1.30, 1.20, 1.12, 1.12, 1.12,
1.06, 1.06,
 1.00, 1.02, 1.04, 1.02, 1.06, 1.02, 1.04, 0.98, 0.98, 0.98, 1.00,
1.02, 1.02,
```

1.00, 1.02, 0.96, 0.94, 0.94, 0.94, 0.96, 0.86, 0.92, 0.98, 1.08, 1.04, 0.74,

0.98, 1.02, 1.02, 1.12, 1.34, 2.02, 1.68, 1.12, 1.38, 1.14, 1.16, 1.22, 1.10,

1.14, 1.16, 1.28, 1.44, 2.58, 1.30, 1.20, 1.16, 1.06, 1.06, 1.08, 1.00, 1.00,

0.92, 1.00, 1.02, 1.00, 1.06, 1.10, 1.14, 1.08, 1.00, 1.04, 1.10, 1.06, 1.06,

1.06, 1.02, 1.04, 0.96, 0.96, 0.96, 0.92, 0.84, 0.88, 0.90, 1.00, 1.08, 0.80,

0.90, 0.98, 1.00, 1.10, 1.24, 1.66, 1.94, 1.02, 1.06, 1.08, 1.10, 1.30, 1.10,

1.12, 1.20, 1.16, 1.26, 1.42, 2.18, 1.26, 1.06, 1.00, 1.04, 1.00, 0.98, 0.94,

0.88, 0.98, 0.96, 0.92, 0.94, 0.96, 0.96, 0.94, 0.90, 0.92, 0.96, 0.96, 0.96,

0.98, 0.90, 0.90, 0.88, 0.88, 0.88, 0.90, 0.78, 0.84, 0.86, 0.92, 1.00, 0.68,

0.82, 0.90, 0.88, 0.98, 1.08, 1.36, 2.04, 0.98, 0.96, 1.02, 1.20, 0.98, 1.00,

1.08, 0.98, 1.02, 1.14, 1.28, 2.04, 1.16, 1.04, 0.96, 0.98, 0.92, 0.86, 0.88,

0.82, 0.92, 0.90, 0.86, 0.84, 0.86, 0.90, 0.84, 0.82, 0.82, 0.86, 0.86, 0.84,

0.84, 0.82, 0.80, 0.78, 0.78, 0.76, 0.74, 0.68, 0.74, 0.80, 0.80, 0.90, 0.60,

0.72, 0.80, 0.82, 0.86, 0.94, 1.24, 1.92, 0.92, 1.12, 0.90, 0.90, 0.94, 0.90,

0.90, 0.94, 0.98, 1.08, 1.24, 2.04, 1.04, 0.94, 0.86, 0.86, 0.86, 0.82, 0.84,

0.76, 0.80, 0.80, 0.80, 0.78, 0.80, 0.82, 0.76, 0.76, 0.76, 0.76, 0.78, 0.78,

0.76, 0.76, 0.72, 0.74, 0.70, 0.68, 0.72, 0.70, 0.64, 0.70, 0.72, 0.74, 0.64,

0.62, 0.74, 0.80, 0.82, 0.88, 1.02, 1.66, 0.94, 0.94, 0.96, 1.00, 1.16, 1.02,

1.04, 1.06, 1.02, 1.10, 1.22, 1.94, 1.18, 1.12, 1.06, 1.06, 1.04, 1.02, 0.94,

0.94, 0.98, 0.96, 0.96, 0.98, 1.00, 0.96, 0.92, 0.90, 0.86, 0.82, 0.90, 0.84,

0.84, 0.82, 0.80, 0.80, 0.76, 0.80, 0.82, 0.80, 0.72, 0.72, 0.76, 0.80, 0.76,

0.70, 0.74, 0.82, 0.84, 0.88, 0.98, 1.44, 0.96, 0.88, 0.92, 1.08, 0.90, 0.92,

0.96, 0.94, 1.04, 1.08, 1.14, 1.66, 1.08, 0.96, 0.90, 0.86, 0.84, 0.86, 0.82,

```
    0.84, 0.82, 0.84, 0.84, 0.84, 0.84, 0.82, 0.86, 0.82, 0.82, 0.86,
0.90, 0.84,
    0.82, 0.78, 0.80, 0.78, 0.74, 0.78, 0.76, 0.76, 0.70, 0.72, 0.76,
0.72, 0.70,
    0.64]
```

We need to perform the following steps:

1. Use a cleaned dataset of Google Trend search volume for 1 year for keyword 'flowers'. We will import this dataset into variable d.

2. Use a random normal distribution of the same length (365 data points) as our Google Trend dataset. This will be dataset d1.

3. Create a figure containing four subplots.

4. In the first subplot, plot scatter-plot of d and d1.

5. In the second subplot, plot scatter-plot of d1 with d1.

6. In the third subplot, render scatter-plot of of d1 with inverted d1.

7. In the fourth subplot, render scatter-plot of d1 with similar dataset constructed of (d1+d).

This code will illustrate the relation as we explained them earlier in this recipe:

```python
import matplotlib.pyplot as plt
import numpy as np

# import the data

from ch07_search_data import DATA

d = DATA

# Now let's generate random data for the same period
d1 = np.random.random(365)
assert len(d) == len(d1)

fig = plt.figure()

ax1 = fig.add_subplot(221)
ax1.scatter(d, d1, alpha=0.5)
ax1.set_title('No correlation')
ax1.grid(True)

ax2 = fig.add_subplot(222)
ax2.scatter(d1, d1, alpha=0.5)
```

```
ax2.set_title('Ideal positive correlation')

ax2.grid(True)

ax3 = fig.add_subplot(223)
ax3.scatter(d1, d1*-1, alpha=0.5)
ax3.set_title('Ideal negative correlation')
ax3.grid(True)

ax4 = fig.add_subplot(224)
ax4.scatter(d1, d1+d, alpha=0.5)
ax4.set_title('Non ideal positive correlation')
ax4.grid(True)

plt.tight_layout()

plt.show()
```

This is the figure we should get when the preceding code is executed:

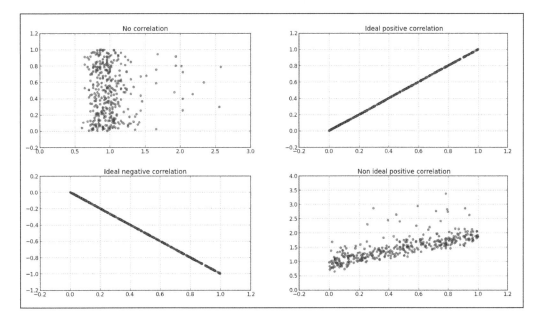

How it works...

The preceding sample we see, clearly displays if there is any correlation between different datasets. While the second (top right) subplot shows ideal or perfect, positive correlation of dataset d1 with d1 itself (obviously). We can see that the fourth subplot (bottom right) hints that there is a positive correlation, although not ideal. We constructed this dataset from d1 and d (random) to simulate two similar signals (events), where the second one (d + d1) has certain randomness (or noise) in it, but still can be comparable with the original (d) signal.

There's more...

We can also add histograms to scatter plots in such a way that they can tell us more about the data plotted. We can add horizontal and vertical histograms to show frequencies of data points on the X and Y axes. Using this, we can, at the same time, see the summary of the whole dataset (histogram) and individual data points (scatter-plot).

Here is the example of the code to generate a scatter-histogram combination, using the same two datasets we introduced in this recipe. The meat of the code is the scatterhist() function that is given here to be reusable to different datasets, trying to set some of the variables based on the dataset provided (number of bins in histogram, limits for axes and similar).

We start with the usual imports:

```
import numpy as np
import matplotlib.pyplot as plt
from mpl_toolkits.axes_grid1 import make_axes_locatable
```

This is the definition of our function to generate scatter histograms given x,y dataset and, optionally, a figsize parameter:

```
def scatterhist(x, y, figsize=(8,8)):
    """
    Create simple scatter & histograms of data x, y inside given plot

    @param figsize: Figure size to create figure
    @type figsize: Tuple of two floats representing size in inches

    @param x: X axis data set
    @type x: np.array

    @param y: Y axis data set
    @type y: np.array
    """
```

```
_, scatter_axes = plt.subplots(figsize=figsize)

    # the scatter plot:
    scatter_axes.scatter(x, y, alpha=0.5)
    scatter_axes.set_aspect(1.)

    divider = make_axes_locatable(scatter_axes)
    axes_hist_x = divider.append_axes(position="top", sharex=scatter_
axes,
                                        size=1, pad=0.1)
    axes_hist_y = divider.append_axes(position="right",
sharey=scatter_axes,
                                        size=1, pad=0.1)

    # compute bins accordingly
    binwidth = 0.25

    # global max value in both data sets
    xymax = np.max([np.max(np.fabs(x)), np.max(np.fabs(y))])
    # number of bins
    bincap = int(xymax / binwidth) * binwidth

    bins = np.arange(-bincap, bincap, binwidth)
    nx, binsx, _ = axes_hist_x.hist(x, bins=bins,
histtype='stepfilled',
                        orientation='vertical')
    ny, binsy, _ = axes_hist_y.hist(y, bins=bins,
histtype='stepfilled',
                        orientation='horizontal')

    tickstep = 50
    ticksmax = np.max([np.max(nx), np.max(ny)])
    xyticks = np.arange(0, ticksmax + tickstep, tickstep)

    # hide x and y ticklabels on histograms
    for tl in axes_hist_x.get_xticklabels():
        tl.set_visible(False)
    axes_hist_x.set_yticks(xyticks)

    for tl in axes_hist_y.get_yticklabels():
        tl.set_visible(False)
    axes_hist_y.set_xticks(xyticks)

    plt.show()
```

Now, we proceed with loading of the data and function call to generate and render the desired chart:

```
if __name__ == '__main__':     # import the data
    from ch07_search_data import DATA as d

    # Now let's generate random data for the same period
    d1 = np.random.random(365)
    assert len(d) == len(d1)

    # try with the random data
#       d = np.random.randn(1000)
#       d1 = np.random.randn(1000)

    scatterhist(d, d1)
```

This should generate the following figure:

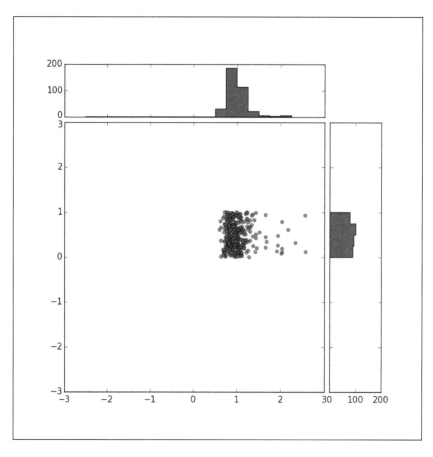

Plotting the cross correlation between two variables

If we have two different datasets from two different observations, we want to know if those two event sets are correlated. We want to cross correlate them and see if they match in any way. We are looking for a pattern of a smaller data sample in a larger data sample. The pattern does not have to be an obvious or simple pattern.

Getting ready

We can use the `matplotlib`'s function from `pyplot` lab—`matplotlib.pyplot.xcorr`. These functions can plot correlation between two datasets in such a way that we can see if there is any significant pattern between the plotted values. It is assumed that x and y are of the same length.

If we pass the `normed` argument as `True`, we can normalize by cross correlation at 0-th lag (that is, when there is no time delay or time lag).

Behind the scenes, correlation is done using NumPy's `numpy.correlate` function.

Using the `usevlines` argument (setting it to True), we can instruct matplotlib to use `vlines()` instead of `plot()` to draw lines of the correlation plot. The main difference is, if we are using `plot()`, we can style the lines using standard `Line2D` properties passed in the `**kwargs` argument to the `matplotlib.pyplot.xcorr` function.

How to do it...

In this following example, we need to:

1. Import the `matplotlib.pyplot` module.
2. Import the `numpy` package.
3. Use cleaned dataset of Google search volume trend for a year for the keyword `'flowers'`.
4. Plot the datasets (real one and artificial one) and cross correlation diagram.
5. Tighten the layout in order to have better overview of labels and ticks.
6. Add appropriate labels and grids for easier understanding of the plot.

This is the code that will perform the previously mentioned steps:

```
import matplotlib.pyplot as plt
import numpy as np

# import the data

from ch07_search_data import DATA as d

total = sum(d)
av = total / len(d)
z = [i - av for i in d]

# Now let's generate random data for the same period
d1 = np.random.random(365)
assert len(d) == len(d1)

total1 = sum(d1)
av1 = total1 / len(d1)
z1 = [i - av1 for i in d1]

fig = plt.figure()

# Search trend volume
ax1 = fig.add_subplot(311)
ax1.plot(d)
ax1.set_xlabel('Google Trends data for "flowers"')

# Random: "search trend volume"
ax2 = fig.add_subplot(312)
ax2.plot(d1)
ax2.set_xlabel('Random data')

# Is there a pattern in search trend for this keyword?
ax3 = fig.add_subplot(313)
ax3.set_xlabel('Cross correlation of random data')
ax3.xcorr(z, z1, usevlines=True, maxlags=None, normed=True, lw=2)
ax3.grid(True)
plt.ylim(-1, 1)

plt.tight_layout()

plt.show()
```

This code will render the following figure:

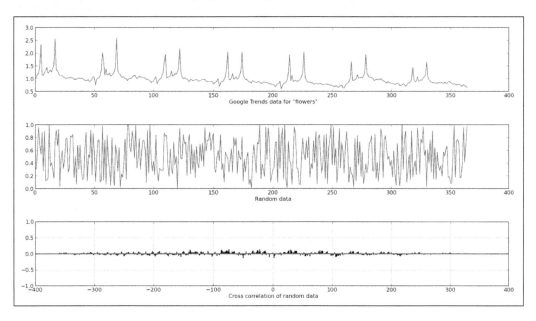

How it works...

We used real data set with a recognizable pattern in it (two peaks repeating in similar manner across the dataset—see the preceding figure). The other dataset is just a random normal distributed data of the same length as real accrued data from public service Google Trends.

We plotted both datasets over the top half of the figure to visualize the data.

Using matplotlib's `xcorr`, which in turn uses NumPy's `correlate()` function, we computed cross correlation and plotted it on the bottom half.

Cross-correlation computation in NumPy returns correlation coefficients array that represent degree of similarity of two datasets (or signals, as usually referred to if used in signal processing field).

The cross-correlation diagram—**correlogram**—tells us that these two signals are not correlated, which is represented by the height of correlation values (vertical lines at certain time lags). We see that there is no one vertical line (correlation coefficient at time lag n) that is the preceding 0.5 value.

If, for example, two datasets would have correlation at time lag 100 (for example, 100 seconds shift between same object observed by two different sensors), we would see vertical line (representing correlation coefficient) at x = 100 in this preceding figure.

Importance of autocorrelation

Autocorrelation represents the degree of similarity between a given time series and a lagged (that is, delayed in time) version of itself over successive time intervals. It occurs in time series studies when the errors associated with a given time period carry over into future time periods. For example, if we are predicting the growth of stock dividends, an overestimate in 1 year is likely to lead to overestimates in the succeeding years.

The time series analysis data arise in lots of different scientific applications and in lots of financial processes. Some of the examples include: generated reports of financial performance, prices over time, computing volatility, and others.

If we are analyzing unknown data, autocorrelation can help us detect if the data is random or not. For that, we can use a **correlogram**. It can help provide answers to questions such as: is the data random, is this time series data a white noise, is it sinusoidal, is it autoregressive, what is the model of this time series data?

Getting ready

We will use matplotlib to compare two sets of data. One is Google day trend of search volume for a certain keyword for 1 year (365 days). The other set is 365 random measurements (generated with random data) with normal distribution.

We will autocorrelate both datasets and compare how the correlograms visualize patterns in data.

How to do it...

In this section, we will perform the following steps:

1. Import the `matplotlib.pyplot` module
2. Import the `numpy` package
3. Use a cleaned dataset of Google search volume for a year
4. Plot the data set and plot its autocorrelation diagram
5. Generate the same-length random dataset using NumPy
6. Plot the random dataset on the same figure and plot its autocorrelation diagram
7. Add appropriate labels and grids for easier understanding of the plot

This is the code:

```
import matplotlib.pyplot as plt
import numpy as np

# import the data

from ch07_search_data import DATA as d

total = sum(d)
av = total / len(d)
z = [i - av for i in d]

fig = plt.figure()
# plt.title('Comparing autocorrelations')

# Search trend volume
ax1 = fig.add_subplot(221)
ax1.plot(d)
ax1.set_xlabel('Google Trends data for "flowers"')

# Is there a pattern in search trend for this keyword?
ax2 = fig.add_subplot(222)
ax2.acorr(z, usevlines=True, maxlags=None, normed=True, lw=2)
ax2.grid(True)
ax2.set_xlabel('Autocorrelation')

# Now let's generate random data for the same period
d1 = np.random.random(365)
assert len(d) == len(d1)

total = sum(d1)
av = total / len(d1)
z = [i - av for i in d1]

# Random: "search trend volume"
ax3 = fig.add_subplot(223)
ax3.plot(d1)
ax3.set_xlabel('Random data')

# Is there a pattern in search trend for this keyword?
ax4 = fig.add_subplot(224)
ax4.set_xlabel('Autocorrelation of random data')
ax4.acorr( z, usevlines=True, maxlags=None, normed=True, lw=2)
ax4.grid(True)

plt.show()
```

This code will render following figure:

How it works...

Looking at the left-hand side plots it is easy to spot patterns in search volume data, where bottom left plot is normally distributed random data—where patterns are not obvious, but still might exist.

Computing and plotting autocorrelation over the random data, we see that there is a high correlation at 0—which is expected, data is correlated with itself in no time lag. But going before or after no time lag, the signal is almost 0, so we can safely conclude that there is no correlation between the signal in original time and any time lags examined.

Looking at the real data—Google search volume trend—we can see the same behavior at 0 time lag, still something we can expect for any autocorrelated signal. But, we have strong signals at around 30, 60, and 110 days after 0 time lag. This indicates that there is a pattern with this particular search term and a way people search for it on the Google search engine.

Explaining why is this is a very different story, and we will leave this exercise to the reader. Remember that correlation and causation are two very different things.

There's more...

Autocorrelation is used very often when we want to identify model for unknown data, and try to fit data into a model. How data correlates to itself is sometimes a first step to identifying an appropriate model for a dataset we are presented with. This requires more than Python; it requires knowledge of mathematical modeling. Various statistical tests (Ljung-Box test, Box-Pierce test, and so on) will help us answer these questions.

8
More on matplotlib Gems

In this chapter, we will cover:

- ▶ Drawing barbs
- ▶ Making a box-and-whisker plot
- ▶ Making Gantt charts
- ▶ Making error bars
- ▶ Making use of text and font properties
- ▶ Rendering text with LaTeX
- ▶ Understanding the difference between pyplot and OO API

Introduction

In this chapter, we will explore some less frequently used features of the matplotlib package. Some of these examples stretch the matplotlib original target, but they show what can be done with a little creativity, and prove that matplolib is full featured and generically oriented.

Drawing barbs

A **barb** is a representation of the speed and direction of wind, and is mainly deployed by meteorology scientists. In theory, they can be used to visualize any type of two-dimensional vector quantities. They are similar to arrows (**quivers**), but the difference is that arrows represent vector magnitude by the length of the arrow, while barbs give more information about the vector's magnitude by employing lines or triangles as increments of magnitude.

We will explain what barbs are, how to read them, and how to visualize them using Python and matplotlib. Here's a typical set of barbs:

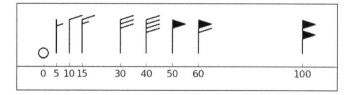

In the preceding diagram, the triangle, also known as flag, represents the largest increment.

A full line or barb represents a smaller increment; a half line is the smallest increment.

The increments are in the order of **5, 10**, and **65** for a half-line, line, and triangle, respectively. The values here represent, for meteorologists at least, wind speed in nautical miles per hour (knots).

We ordered the barbs from left to right to represent the following magnitudes: **0, 5, 10, 15, 30, 40, 50, 60**, and **100** knots. The direction here is the same for each barb and is from north to south, because the east-west speed component is **0** for each barb.

Getting ready

A barb can be created using a matplotlib function from `matplotlib.pyplot.barbs`.

The barbs function accepts various arguments, but we can also only specify X and Y coordinates, representing locations of observed data points. The second pair of arguments—U, V—represents the magnitude of the vector in north-south and east-west directions in knots.

Other arguments that can be useful are pivots, sizes, and various coloring arguments.

A pivot argument (`pivot`) represents the part of the arrow represented on the grid point. We get a pivot argument when the arrow rotates around this point. The arrow can rotate around the tip or middle, which are valid values for the pivot argument.

Because barbs consist of several parts, we can set up the coloring of any of those parts. So, we have a few color-related arguments that we can set up:

- ▶ `barbcolor`: This defines the color of all the parts for a barb, except for flags
- ▶ `flagcolor` This defines the color of any flag on the barb
- ▶ `facecolor`: This argument is used if none of the preceding color arguments are specified (or the default value is read from `rcParams`)

If any of the preceding color-related arguments are specified, the argument `facecolor` is overridden. The `facecolor` argument is the one used in coloring polygons.

The size argument (`sizes`) specifies the ration of a feature to the length of the barb. This is a collection of coefficients that can be specified using any or all of the following keys:

- ▶ `spacing`: This defines the space among features of the flag/barb
- ▶ `height`: This defines the distance from the shaft to the top of a flag or barb
- ▶ `width`: This defines the width of a flag
- ▶ `emptybarb`: This defines the circle radius used for low magnitudes

How to do it...

Let's demonstrate how to use a barb function by performing the following steps:

1. Generate a grid of coordinates to simulate observations.
2. Simulate observational values for wind speed.
3. Plot barb diagrams.
4. Plot quivers to demonstrate different appearances.

The following code will generate the figure:

```
import matplotlib.pyplot as plt
import numpy as np

x = np.linspace(-20, 20, 8)
y = np.linspace(  0, 20, 8)

# make2D coordinates
X, Y = np.meshgrid(x, y)

U, V = X+25, Y-35


# plot the barbs
plt.subplot(1,2,1)
plt.barbs(X, Y, U, V, flagcolor='green', alpha=0.75)
plt.grid(True, color='gray')

# compare that with quiver / arrows
plt.subplot(1,2,2)
plt.quiver(X, Y, U, V, facecolor='red', alpha=0.75)

# misc settings
plt.grid(True, color='grey')
plt.show()
```

The preceding code renders two subplots as shown in the following figure:

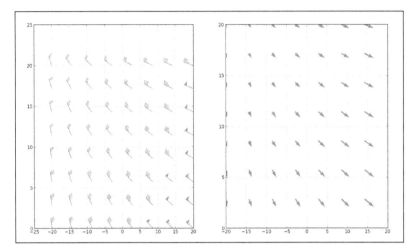

How it works...

To illustrate how the same data can bring different information to light, we used barbs and quiver plots from matplotlib to visualize simulated observed wind data.

First, we used NumPy to generate samples of variations for x and y arrays. Then we used NumPy's `meshgrid()` function to create a 2D grid of coordinates where our observed data is sampled at certain coordinates. Finally, U and V are wind speed values in NS (north-south) and EW (east-west) directions in knots (nautical miles per hours). For the purpose of the recipe, we adjusted some values from the already available X and Y matrices.

We then divided the figure into two subplots, plotting barbs in the leftmost plot and arrow-patches in the rightmost plot. We adjusted the color and transparency of both the subplots slightly, as well as turned the grid on both the subplots.

There's more...

This is all fine on the northern hemisphere where the wind rotates in a counter-clockwise direction and the feathers (triangles, full lines, and half lines of the barb) point in the direction of lower pressure. On the southern hemisphere, this is inverted so our wind barb graph would not represent the data we are visualizing correctly.

We have to invert this direction of feathers. Luckily, the barbs function has the argument `flip_barb`. This argument can be of one single Boolean value (`True` or `False`) or a sequence of Boolean values such as the shape of other data arrays, when each item in the sequence specifies a flip decision for each barb.

Making a box-and-whisker plot

Do you want to visualize a series of data measurement (or observations) to show several properties of the data series (such as the median value, the spread of the data, and the distribution of the data) in one plot? And would you want to do that in a way where you can visually compare several similar data series? How would you visualize them? Welcome to the **box-and-whisker plot**! Probably the best plot type for comparing distributions, if you are talking to people used to information density.

The box-and-whisker plot usage examples range from comparing test scores between schools to comparing process parameters before and after changes (optimization).

Getting ready

What are the elements of box-and-whisker plots? As we see in the following diagram, we have several important elements that carry information in the box-and-whisker plot. The first component is the box that carries information about the interquartile range going from lower to upper quartile values. The median value of the data is represented by a line across the box.

The whiskers extend from the box on both sides going from the first quartile (25 percentile) to the last quartile (75 percentile) of the data. In other words, the whiskers extend 1.5 times from the base of the inter-quartile range. In the case of a normal distribution, whiskers will cover 99.3% of the total data range.

If there are values outside the whiskers range, they will be displayed as fliers. Otherwise, the whiskers will cover the total range of the data.

Optionally, the box can also carry information about confidence intervals around the median. This is represented by a notch in the box. This information can be used to indicate whether the data in the two series is of the similar distribution. However, this is not rigorous and is just an indication that can be visually inspected.

How to do it...

In the following recipe, you will learn how to create a box-and-whisker plot using matplotlib.

We will perform the following steps:

1. Sample some comparative process data, where a single integer number represents the occurrence of an error during the observed period of the running process.

2. Read data from the PROCESSES dictionary into DATA.

3. Read labels from the PROCESSES dictionary into LABELS.

4. Render the box-and-whisker plot using `matplotlib.pyplot.boxplot`.

5. Remove some chart junk from the figure.

6. Add `axes` labels.

7. Show the figure.

The following code implements these steps:

```
import matplotlib.pyplot as plt
# define data
PROCESSES = {
    "A": [12, 15, 23, 24, 30, 31, 33, 36, 50, 73],
    "B": [6, 22, 26, 33, 35, 47, 54, 55, 62, 63],
    "C": [2, 3, 6, 8, 13, 14, 19, 23, 60, 69],
    "D": [1, 22, 36, 37, 45, 47, 48, 51, 52, 69],
    }

DATA = PROCESSES.values()
LABELS = PROCESSES.keys()


plt.boxplot(DATA, notch=False, widths=0.3)

# set ticklabel to process name
plt.gca().xaxis.set_ticklabels(LABELS)

# some clean up(removing chartjunk)
# turn the spine off
for spine in plt.gca().spines.values():
spine.set_visible(False)

# turn all ticks for x-axis off
plt.gca().xaxis.set_ticks_position('none')
# leave left ticks for y-axis on
plt.gca().yaxis.set_ticks_position('left')
```

```
# set axes labels
plt.ylabel("Errors observed over defined period.")
plt.xlabel("Process observed over defined period.")

plt.show()
```

The preceding code generates the following figure:

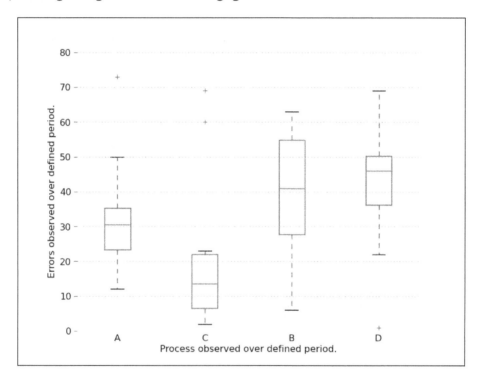

How it works...

The box-and-whisker plot is rendered by first computing quartiles for the given data in DATA.

These quartile values are used to compute lines to draw boxes and whiskers.

We adjusted the plot removing all the unnecessary lines (referring to superfluous lines such as chart junk, as mentioned in the famous book, *The Visual Display of Quantitative Information*, by Edward R. Tufte). Those lines do not carry information and just put more pressure on the mental models in a viewer's brain to decode all the lines before discovering real valuable information.

Making Gantt charts

One form of very widely used visualization of time-based data is a **Gantt chart**. Named after the mechanical engineer Henry Gantt who invented it in 1910s, it is almost exclusively used to visualize work breakdown structures in project management. This chart is loved by managers for its descriptive value and not so loved by employees, especially when the project deadline is near.

This kind of chart is very straightforward, almost every one can understand and read it, even if it is overloaded with additional (related and unrelated) information.

A basic Gantt chart has a time series on the *X* axis and a set of labels that represent tasks or subtasks on the *Y* axis. Task duration is usually visualized either as a line or as a bar chart, extending from the start to end time of a given task.

If subtasks are present, one or many subtasks have a parent task, in which the case total time of a task is aggregated from subtasks in such a way that overlapping and gap time is accounted for.

So, in this recipe, we will be covering the creation of the Gantt chart using Python.

Getting ready

There are many full-fledged software applications and services that allow you to make very flexible and complicated Gantt charts. We will try to demonstrate how you could do it in pure Python, not relying on external applications, yet achieving neat looking and informative Gantt charts.

The Gantt chart shown in the example does not support nested tasks, but it is sufficient for simple work breakdown structures.

How to do it...

The following code example will allow us to demonstrate how Python can be used together with matplotlib to render the Gantt chart. We will perform the following steps:

1. Load `TEST_DATA` that contains a set of tasks and instantiate the Gantt class with `TEST_DATA`.

2. Each task contains a label and the start and end time.

3. Process all tasks by plotting horizontal bars on the axes.

4. Format the *x* and *y* axes for the data we are rendering.

5. Tighten the layout.

6. Show the Gantt chart.

The following is a sample code:

```
from datetime import datetime
import sys

import numpy as np
import matplotlib.pyplot as plt
import matplotlib.font_manager as font_manager
import matplotlib.dates as mdates

import logging


class Gantt(object):
    '''
Simple Gantt renderer.
    Uses *matplotlib* rendering capabilities.
    '''

    # Red Yellow Green diverging colormap
    # from http://colorbrewer2.org/
RdYlGr = ['#d73027', '#f46d43', '#fdae61',
                '#fee08b', '#ffffbf', '#d9ef8b',
                '#a6d96a', '#66bd63', '#1a9850']

POS_START = 1.0
POS_STEP = 0.5

def __init__(self, tasks):
self._fig = plt.figure()
self._ax = self._fig.add_axes([0.1, 0.1, .75, .5])

self.tasks = tasks[::-1]

def _format_date(self, date_string):
        '''
        Formats string representation of *date_string* into
*matplotlib.dates*
instance.
        '''
try:
date = datetime.strptime(date_string, '%Y-%m-%d %H:%M:%S')
exceptValueError as err:
logging.error("String '{0}' can not be converted to datetime object:
{1}"
```

```
                            .format(date_string, err))
        sys.exit(-1)
    mpl_date = mdates.date2num(date)
    returnmpl_date


    def _plot_bars(self):
        '''
        Processes each task and adds *barh* to the current *self._ax*
    (*axes*).
        '''
        i = 0
    for task in self.tasks:
    start = self._format_date(task['start'])
    end = self._format_date(task['end'])
    bottom = (i * Gantt.POS_STEP) + Gantt.POS_START
    width = end - start
            self._ax.barh(bottom, width, left=start, height=0.3,
    align='center', label=task['label'],
    color = Gantt.RdYlGr[i])
            i += 1


    def _configure_yaxis(self):
        '''y axis'''
    task_labels = [t['label'] for t in self.tasks]
    pos = self._positions(len(task_labels))
    ylocs = self._ax.set_yticks(pos)
    ylabels = self._ax.set_yticklabels(task_labels)
    plt.setp(ylabels, size='medium')


    def _configure_xaxis(self):
        ''''x axis'''
        # make x axis date axis
        self._ax.xaxis_date()

        # format date to ticks on every 7 days
    rule = mdates.rrulewrapper(mdates.DAILY, interval=7)
    loc = mdates.RRuleLocator(rule)
    formatter = mdates.DateFormatter("%d %b")

    self._ax.xaxis.set_major_locator(loc)
        self._ax.xaxis.set_major_formatter(formatter)
    xlabels = self._ax.get_xticklabels()
    plt.setp(xlabels, rotation=30, fontsize=9)
```

```
def _configure_figure(self):
    self._configure_xaxis()
  self._configure_yaxis()

    self._ax.grid(True, color='gray')
    self._set_legend()
    self._fig.autofmt_xdate()

def _set_legend(self):
    '''
    Tweak font to be small and place *legend*
in the upper right corner of the figure
    '''
font = font_manager.FontProperties(size='small')
    self._ax.legend(loc='upper right', prop=font)

def _positions(self, count):
    '''
    For given *count* number of positions, get array for the
positions.
    '''
end = count * Gantt.POS_STEP + Gantt.POS_START
pos = np.arange(Gantt.POS_START, end, Gantt.POS_STEP)
return pos
```

The main function that drives the Gantt chart generation is defined in the following code. In this function, we load the data into an instance, plot bars accordingly, set up the date formatter for the time axis (x axis), and set values for the y axis (the project's tasks).

```
def show(self):
    self._plot_bars()
    self._configure_figure()
plt.show()


if __name__ == '__main__':
TEST_DATA = (
{ 'label': 'Research',      'start':'2013-10-01 12:00:00', 'end':
'2013-10-02 18:00:00'},  # @IgnorePep8
{ 'label': 'Compilation',   'start':'2013-10-02 09:00:00', 'end':
'2013-10-02 12:00:00'},  # @IgnorePep8
{ 'label': 'Meeting #1',    'start':'2013-10-03 12:00:00', 'end':
'2013-10-03 18:00:00'},  # @IgnorePep8
{ 'label': 'Design',        'start':'2013-10-04 09:00:00', 'end':
'2013-10-10 13:00:00'},  # @IgnorePep8
```

```
{ 'label': 'Meeting #2',        'start':'2013-10-11 09:00:00', 'end':
'2013-10-11 13:00:00'},  # @IgnorePep8
{ 'label': 'Implementation', 'start':'2013-10-12 09:00:00', 'end':
'2013-10-22 13:00:00'},  # @IgnorePep8
{ 'label': 'Demo',              'start':'2013-10-23 09:00:00', 'end':
'2013-10-23 13:00:00'},  # @IgnorePep8
                        )

gantt = Gantt(TEST_DATA)
gantt.show()
```

This code will render a simple, neat looking Gantt chart like the following one:

How it works...

We can start reading the preceding code from the bottom after the condition that checks if we are in "__main__".

After we instantiate the Gantt class giving it TEST_DATA, we set up the necessary fields of our instance. We save TASK_DATA in the self.tasks field, and we create our figure and axes to hold the charts we create in future.

Then, we call show() on the instance that walks us through the steps required to render the Gantt chart:

```
def show(self):
        self._plot_bars()
        self._configure_figure()
    plt.show()
```

Plotting bars requires iteration where we apply the data about the name and duration of each task to the matplotlib.pyplot.barh function, adding it to the axes at self._ax. We place each task in a separate channel by giving it a different (incremental) bottom argument value.

Also, to make it easy to map tasks to their names, we cycle over the divergent color maps that we generated using the `colorbrewer2.org` tool.

The next step is to configure the figure, which means that we set up the format date on the x axis and tickers' positions and labels on the y axis to match the tasks plotted by `matplotlib.pyplot.barh`.

Finally, we add a `grid` and a `legend`.

At the end, we call `plt.show()` to show the figure.

Making error bars

Error bars are useful to display the dispersion of data on a plot. They are relatively simple as a form of visualization; however, they are also a bit problematic because what is shown as an error varies across different sciences and publications. This does not lessen the usefulness of error bars, it just imposes the need to always be careful and explicitly state the nature of the error visualized as an error bar.

Getting ready

To be able to plot an error bar in the raw observed data, we need to compute the mean and the error we want to display.

The error we compute represents the 95% confidence interval that the mean we get from our observation is stable, which means our observations are good estimates of the whole population.

Matplotlib supports these type of plots via `matplotlib.pyplot.errorbar function`.

It offers several kinds of error bars. They can be vertical (`yerr`) or horizontal (`xerr`) and symmetrical or asymmetrical.

How to do it...

In the following code we will:

1. Use some sample data that consists of four sets of observations.
2. For each set of observations, compute the mean value.
3. For each set of observations, compute the 95% confidence interval.
4. Render bars with vertical symmetrical error bars.

Here is the code for this:

```
import matplotlib.pyplot as plt
import numpy as np
import scipy.stats as sc

TEST_DATA = np.array([[1,2,3,2,1,2,3,4,2,3,2,1,2,3,4,4,3,2,3,2,3,2,1],
                      [5,6,5,4,5,6,7,7,6,7,7,2,8,7,6,5,5,6,7,7,7,6,5],
                      [9,8,7,8,8,7,4,6,6,5,4,3,2,2,2,3,3,4,5,5,5,6,1],
                      [3,2,3,2,2,2,2,3,3,3,3,4,4,4,4,5,6,6,7,8,9,8,5],
                      ])

# find mean for each of our observations
y = np.mean(TEST_DATA, axis=1, dtype=np.float64)
# and the 95% confidence interval
ci95 = np.abs(y - 1.96 * sc.sem(TEST_DATA, axis=1))

# each set is one try
tries = np.arange(0, len(y), 1.0)

# tweak grid and setup labels, limits
plt.grid(True, alpha=0.5)
plt.gca().set_xlabel('Observation #')
plt.gca().set_ylabel('Mean (+- 95% CI)')
plt.title("Observations with corresponding 95% CI as error bar.")
plt.bar(tries, y, align='center', alpha=0.2)
plt.errorbar(tries, y, yerr=ci95, fmt=None)

plt.show()
```

The preceding code will render a plot with error bars that display 95% confidence intervals as whiskers extending along the y axis. Remember, the wider the whiskers, the lesser are the probability that the observed mean is true. The following graph is the output for the preceding code:

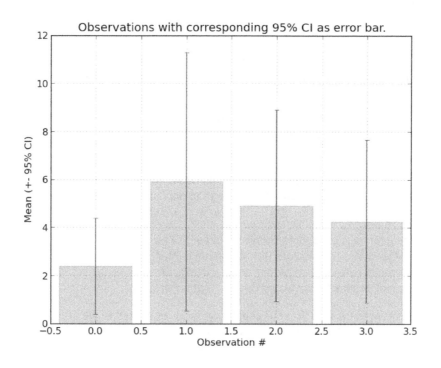

How it works...

In order to avoid iterating over each set of observations, we use NumPy's vectorized methods to compute means and standard errors, which we use for plotting and computing error values.

Using NumPy's vectorized implementations, which are written in C language (and called from Python), allows us to speed up computations by several magnitudes.

This is not very important for a few data points but, for millions of data points, it can either make or break our efforts to create responsive applications.

Also, you may note that we explicitly specified `dtype=np.float 64` in the `np.mean` function call. According to the official NumPy documentation reference (`http://docs.scipy.org/doc/numpy/reference/generated/numpy.mean.html`),`np.mean` can be inaccurate if used in single precision; it's better to compute it with `np.float32`, or if performance is not an issue, use `np.float 64`.

There's more...

There is an ongoing issue with what to show on error bars. Some advise on using *SD, 2SD, SE,* or *95%CI.* We must understand what the difference between all these values and what they are used for, in order to be able to give reasoning on what to use and when.

Standard Deviation informs us about the distribution of individual data points around the mean value. If we assume normal distribution, then we know that *68.2% (~2/3)* of data values will fall between *±SD,* and *95.4%* of values will be between *±2*SD.*

Standard Error is calculated as *SD* divided by the square root of *N (SD/√N),* where *N* is the number of data points. Standard Error (SE) informs us about variability of mean values, if we are able to perform the same sampling more than once (like performing the same study hundreds of times).

The confidence interval is calculated from SE, similar to how the range of values is calculated from Standard Deviation. To calculate 95% confidence interval, we must add/subtract *1.96 * SE* to/from our mean value or use proper notation: *95% CI = M ± (1.96 * SE).* The wider the confidence interval, the lesser we would be sure that we are right.

We see that in order to be sure that our estimation is correct and that we are giving its proof to our reader, we should display the confidence interval, which in turn carries the standard error; this, if small, proves that our means are stable.

Making use of text and font properties

You already learned how to annotate the plot by adding legends, but sometimes we want more with text. This recipe will explain and demonstrate more features of text manipulation in matplotlib, giving a powerful toolkit for even advanced typesetting needs.

We will not cover LaTeX support in this recipe, as there is a recipe named *Rendering text with LaTeX* in this chapter.

Getting ready

We start with listing of the most useful set of functions that matplotlib offers. Most of the functions are available via `pyplot` module's interface, but we map their origin function here to allow you to explore more if a particular text feature is not covered in this recipe.

Basic text manipulations and their mapping in matplotlib OO API is presented in the following table:

matplotlib. pyplot	Matplotlib API	Description
text	matplotlib.axes.Axes.text	Adds text to the axes at the location specified by (*x*, *y*). Argument fontdict allows us to override generic font properties, or we can use kwargs to override a specific property.
xlabel	matplotlib.axes.Axes.set_xlabel	Sets the label for the x axis. Specifies the spacing between the label and the x axis in accordance with labelpad.
ylabel	matplotlib.axes.Axes.set_ylabel	Similar to xlabel, but intended for the y axis.
title	matplotlib.axes.Axes.set_title	Sets the title for the axes. Accepts all the usual text properties such as fontdict and kwargs.
suptitle	matplotlib.figure.Figure. suptitle	Adds a centered title to the figure. Accepts all the usual text properties via kwargs. Uses figure coordinates.
figtext	matplotlib.figure.Figure.text	Puts text anywhere on the figure. The location is defined using (*x,y*), using figure's normalized coordinates. Override font properties using fontdict, but also support kwargs to override any text-related property.

The base class for text storing and drawing inside windows or data coordinates is the matplotlib.text.Text class. It supports the definition of the location of text objects as well as a range of properties that we can define, to tune how our strings are going to appear on a figure or a window.

The font properties supported by the `matplotlib.text.Text` instances are:

Property	Values	Description
family	'serif', 'sans-serif', 'cursive', 'fantasy', 'monospace'	Specifies the font name or font family. If this is a list, then it is ordered by priority, so the first matched name will be used.
size or fontsize	12, 10,... or 'xx-small', 'x-small', 'small', 'medium', 'large', 'x-large', 'xx-large'	Specifies the size in relative or absolute points or specifies the relative size as a size string.
style or fontstyle	'normal', 'italic', 'oblique'	Specifies the font style as a string.
variant	'normal', 'small-caps'	Specifies the font variant.
weight or fontweight	0-1000 or 'ultralight', 'light', 'normal', 'regular', 'book', 'medium', 'roman', 'semibold', 'demibold', 'demi', 'bold', 'heavy', 'extra bold', 'black'	Specifies the font weight or using a specific weight string. Font weight is defined as the thickness of character outline relative to its height.

Property	Values	Description
`stretch` or `fontstretch`	`0-1000 or 'ultra-condensed', 'extra-condensed', 'condensed', 'semi-condensed', 'normal', 'semi-expanded', 'expanded', 'extra-expanded', 'ultra-expanded'`	Specifies the stretch of the font. Stretch is defined as horizontal condensation or expansion. This property is not currently implemented.
`fontproperties`	-	Defaults to the `matplotlib.font_manager.FontProperties` instance. This class stores and manages font properties as described in W3CCSSLevel1 specification at `http://www.w3.org/TR/1998/REC-CSS2-19980512/`.

We can also specify the background box that will contain the text, and which can be further specified in color, borders, and transparency.

The basic text color is read from `rcParams['text.color']`, if not specified on the current instance, of course.

Specified text can also be aligned according to visual needs. There are the following alignment properties:

▶ `horizontalalignment` or `ha`: This allows alignment of text horizontally to `center`, `left`, and `right`.

▶ `verticalalignment` or `va`: The allowed values for this are `center`, `top`, `bottom`, and `baseline`.

▶ `multialignment`: This allows alignment of text strings that span multilines. The allowed values are `left`, `right`, and `center`.

How to do it...

So far all is good, but we have a hard time visualizing all these variations in the fonts we can create. So, this is going to illustrate what we can do. In the next code, we will perform the following steps:

1. List all the possible properties we want to vary on the font.

2. Iterate over the first set of variations: font family and size.

3. Iterate over the second set of variations: weight and style.

4. Render text samples for both the iterations and print the variation combination as a text on the plot.

5. Remove axes from the figure, as they serve no purpose.

The following is the code:

```python
importmatplotlib.pyplot as plt
frommatplotlib.font_manager import FontProperties

# properties:
families = ['serif', 'sans-serif', 'cursive', 'fantasy', 'monospace']
sizes   = ['xx-small', 'x-small', 'small', 'medium', 'large',
           'x-large', 'xx-large']
styles  = ['normal', 'italic', 'oblique']
weights = ['light', 'normal', 'medium', 'semibold', 'bold', 'heavy',
'black']
variants = ['normal', 'small-caps']

fig = plt.figure(figsize=(9,17))
ax = fig.add_subplot(111)
ax.set_xlim(0,9)
ax.set_ylim(0,17)
```

```
    # VAR: FAMILY, SIZE
y = 0
size = sizes[0]
style = styles[0]
weight = weights[0]
variant = variants[0]

forfamily in families:
    x = 0
    y = y + .5
for size in sizes:
        y = y + .4
sample = family + " " + size
ax.text(x, y, sample, family=family, size=size,
style=style, weight=weight, variant=variant)
# VAR: STYLE, WEIGHT
y = 0
family = families[0]
size = sizes[4]
variant = variants[0]

for weight in weights:
    x = 5
    y = y + .5
for style in styles:
        y = y + .4
sample = weight + " " + style
ax.text(x, y, sample, family=family, size=size,
style=style, weight=weight, variant=variant)

ax.set_axis_off()
plt.show()
```

The preceding code will produce the following screenshot:

```
monospace xx-large
monospace x-large
monospace large
monospace medium
monospace small
monospace x-small
monospace xx-small
```

fantasy xx-large
fantasy x-large
fantasy large
fantasy medium   *black oblique*
fantasy small   *black italic*
fantasy x-small   **black normal**
fantasy xx-small

                                        heavy oblique
cursive xx-large   *heavy italic*
cursive x-large   **heavy normal**
cursive large
cursive medium   *bold oblique*
cursive small   *bold italic*
cursive x-small   **bold normal**
cursive xx-small

sans-serif xx-large   ***semibold oblique***
sans-serif x-large   ***semibold italic***
sans-serif large   **semibold normal**
sans-serif medium
sans-serif small   *medium oblique*
sans-serif x-small   *medium italic*
sans-serif xx-small   medium normal

serif xx-large   *normal oblique*
serif x-large   *normal italic*
serif large   normal normal
serif medium
serif small   *light oblique*
serif x-small   *light italic*
serif xx-small   light normal

How it works...

The code is really straightforward, as we just iterate twice over tuples of properties printing their values.

The only trick employed here is the positioning of text on the figure canvas, as that allows us to have a nice layout of text samples we can easily compare.

Keep in mind that the default font matplotlib will use is dependent on the operating system you are running, so the preceding screenshot might look slightly different. This screenshot was rendered using standard Ubuntu 13.04 installed fonts.

Rendering text with LaTeX

If we want to plot more scientific graphics and explain math as it should be using scientific notations and complex equations on the figures, we need support from the best.

Although matplotlib has support for math text rendering, the best support comes from the LaTeX community, proven in the task being used for many decades.

LaTeX is a high-quality typesetting system for the production of scientific and technical documentation, being a *de facto* standard for scientific typesetting or publication. It is a free software, available on majority of desktop platforms used today as prepackages binary installation; hence, it is easy to install.

The basic syntax of LaTeX is similar to markup languages; so to produce satisfactory content, one would write focusing more on the structure than on the look and style. For example:

```
\documentclass{article}
\title{This here is a title of my document}
\author{Peter J. S. Smith}
\date{September 2013}
\begin{document}
    \maketitle
    Hello world, from LaTeX!
\end{document}
```

We see how this is different from the usual word processor, where the WYSIWYG editor environment and the style is already applied to your text. Sometimes this is good but, for scientific publications, style is a secondary concern; the primary focus is having the right, correct, and valid content. Here, by content, we also mean mathematical notations (usually a lot of it), including graphs.

Apart from this, there are many more features such as automatic generation of bibliographies and indexes, which are important for medium to large publications. These are the main focus points of the LaTeX system.

Since this is not a book about LaTeX, we will stop with the quick introduction here. A lot more documentation is available on the project's website at `http://latex-project.org/`.

Getting ready

Before we start demonstrating matplotlib's support for rendering text using LaTeX, we need to have the following packages installed on our system:

- **LaTeX system**: The most common one is the TeX Live prepackaged distribution
- **DVI to PNG converter**: This makes PNG graphics from DVI files as obtained from TeX, by producing anti-aliased screen-resolution images
- **Ghost script**: This is required, unless already installed by TeX Live distribution

There are different prepackaged systems of the **LaTeX** environment for different operating systems. For Linux-based systems, **TeX Live** is a complete TeX system. For Mac OS, the recommended environment is the **MacTeX** distribution; for the Windows environment, the **proTeX** system is going to install all the TeX supports, including LaTeX.

Whichever package you install, make sure it comes with font libraries and programs for typesetting, previewing, and printing of TeX documents in many different languages.

We will install our package for Linux using the `texlive` and `dvipng` packages for Ubuntu. We can install this using the following command:

```
$ sudo apt-get install texlivedvipng
```

The next step is to tell our matplotlib to use LaTeX by setting `text.usetex` to `True`. We can do that either in our custom `.matplotlibrc` inside our home directory (`/home/<user>/.matplotlibrc` on Unix-based systems, or `C:\Documents and Settings\<user>\.matplotlibrc`) via `rcParams['text']`, or using the following code:

```
matplotlib.pyplot.rc('text', usetex=True)
```

The start of the code will tell matplotlib to go back to LaTeX for all text rendering. It is important to do this before we add any figure and axis.

Not all backends support LaTeX rendering. Only the Agg, PS, and PDF backends support text rendering via LaTeX.

How to do it...

What we want to do here is demonstrate the basic usage properties of LaTeX. We will perform the following steps:

1. Generate some sample data.
2. Set up matplotlib to use LaTeX for this plotting session.

3. Set up the font and font properties to be used.

4. Write out the equation syntax.

5. Demonstrate the usage of Greek symbols' syntax.

6. Draw math notations of fractions and fractals.

7. Write some limits and exponential expressions.

8. Write possible range expressions.

9. Write expressions with text and formatted text in them.

10. Write some math expressions on x and y labels as figure titles.

The following code will perform these steps:

```
import numpy as np
import matplotlib.pyplot as plt


# Example data
t = np.arange(0.0, 1.0 + 0.01, 0.01)
s = np.cos(4 * np.pi * t) * np.sin(np.pi*t/4) + 2

plt.rc('text', usetex=True)
plt.rc('font',**{'family':'sans-serif','sans-serif':['Helvetica'],
'size':16})

plt.plot(t, s, alpha=0.25)

# first, the equation for 's'
# note the usage of Python's raw strings
plt.annotate(r'$\cos(4 \times \pi \times {t}) \times \sin(\pi \times \
frac {t} 4) + 2$', xy=(.9,2.2), xytext=(.5, 2.6), color='red', arrowpr
ops={'arrowstyle':'->'})

# some math alphabet
plt.text(.01, 2.7, r'$\alpha, \beta, \gamma, \Gamma, \pi, \Pi, \phi, \
varphi, \Phi$')
# some equation
plt.text(.01, 2.5, r'some equations $\frac{n!}{k!(n-k)!} = {n \choose
k}$')
# more equations
plt.text(.01, 2.3, r'EQ1 $\lim_{x \to \infty} \exp(-x) = 0$')
# some ranges...
plt.text(.01, 2.1, r'Ranges: $( a ), [ b ], \{ c \}, | d |, \| e \|, \
langle f \rangle, \lfloor g \rfloor, \lceil h \rceil$')
# you can multiply apples and oranges
```

```
plt.text(.01, 1.9, r'Text: $50 apples \times 100 oranges = lots of
juice$')
plt.text(.01, 1.7, r'More text formatting: $50 \textrm{ apples} \times
100 \textbf{ apples} = \textit{lots of juice}$')
plt.text(.01, 1.5, r'Some indexing: $\beta = (\beta_1,\beta_2,\dotsc,\
beta_n)$')
# we can also write on labels
plt.xlabel(r'\textbf{time} (s)')
plt.ylabel(r'\textit{y values} (W)')
# and write titles using LaTeX
plt.title(r"\TeX\ is Number "
          r"$\displaystyle\sum_{n=1}^\infty\frac{-e^{i\pi}}{2^n}$!",
fontsize=16, color='gray')
# Make room for the ridiculously large title.
plt.subplots_adjust(top=0.8)

plt.savefig('tex_demo')
plt.show()
```

The preceding code will render the following text-saturated figure that demonstrates LaTeX rendering:

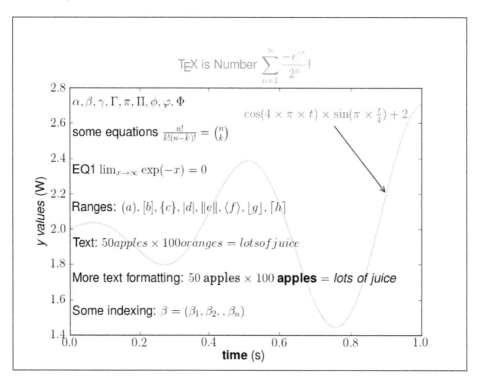

How it works...

After we set up the rendering engine and font properties, we basically used standard matplotlib calls for text rendering, such as `matplotlib.pyplot.annotate`, `matplotlib.pyplot.text`, `matplotlib.pyplot.xlabel`, `matplotlib.pyplot.ylabel`, and `matplotlib.pyplot.title`.

The difference here is that all the strings are so-called raw strings, meaning that Python will not interpret them and no string substitution will occur; hence, the LaTeX engine is going to receive exactly the same strings as commands to act upon.

More examples of how to use TeX and how to integrate it in matplotlib can be found on the official matplotlib documentation at `http://matplotlib.org/users/mathtext.html#writing-mathematical-expressions`.

Note that this URL is not on LaTeX but on matplotlib's own integrated TeX parser. This parser supports almost the same syntax, and it can even be sufficient for your needs.

There's more...

If you run into a problem while setting up this environment or have different problems with fonts that either look bad or are not able to produce the LaTeX rendering, make sure that you have installed all required packages, your `$PATH` environment variable (if on Windows) is set up to include all the required binaries, and matplotlib is set to use LaTeX for text rendering.

If all of the given instructions are followed and the results cannot be replicated, refer to the official matplotlib website at `http://matplotlib.org/users/usetex.html#possible-hangups` and the LaTeX community on `http://tex.stackexchange.com/` for further assistance.

It is known that this setup is not as streamlined as it should be, and some quirks may occur for various reasons.

Understanding the difference between pyplot and OO API

This recipe will try to explain some of the programming interfaces in matplotlib and make a comparison of pyplot and object-oriented **API (Application Programming Interface)**. Depending on the task at hand, this will allow us to decide why and when to use either of these interfaces.

Getting ready

When the matplotlib library was introduced, it was similar to many open source projects—there was no proper (free) solution to the problem a person had, so he wrote one. The problem encountered with MATLAB® was with respect to performance for the task in hand (http://www.aosabook.org/en/matplotlib.html), and the original author already had knowledge of both MATLAB® and Python, so he started writing matplotlib as a solution for his need for the current project.

This is the main reason matplotlib has a MATLAB®-like interface that allows one to quickly plot data without worrying about background details, such as which platform matplotlib is running on, what are the underlying rendering libraries (is it with GTK, Qt, Tk, or wxWidgets either on Linux or Windows), or are we running on Mac OS with the help of Cocoa toolkits. This is all hidden inside matplotlib under a nice procedural interface in the `matplotlib.pyplot` module, a stateful interface handling logic for creating figures and axes to connect them with the configured backend. It also keeps data structures for the current figure and axes, which are called upon with the plot commands.

This is the interface (`matplotlib.pyplot`) we have been using through most of this book as it is simple, straightforward, and good enough for most of the tasks we were trying to accomplish. The matplotlib library was designed with this philosophy in mind. We must be able to draw plots with as few commands as possible, even just one command (for example, `plt.plot([1,2,3,4,5]); plt.show()` works). For these tasks, we don't want to be forced into thinking about objects, instances, methods, properties, rendering backends, figures, canvases, lines, and other graphical primitives.

If you are reading this book from the start, you probably note that some classes started appearing in various examples, such as, `FontProperties` or `AxesGrid`, where we needed more than what is provided by the `matplotlib.pyplot` module.

This is the object-oriented programming interface that implements all the hidden hard stuff, such as rendering graphical elements, rendering those to the platform's graphical toolkit, and handling user inputs (mouse and keystrokes). There is nothing to stop us from using OO API, and that is what we are going to do.

So if we take a look at matplotlib as software, it consists of three parts:

- **matplotlib.pyplot interface**: This is a set of functions for the user to create plots like in MATLAB®
- **matplotlib API (also called matplotlib frontend)**: This is a set of classes for the creation and management of figures, text, lines, plots, and so on
- **backends**: These are drawing drivers. They transform front abstract representation into a file or a display device

This backend layer contains concrete implementations of abstract interface classes. There are classes, such as `FigureCanvas` (a surface to draw onto paper), `Renderer` (a paintbrush that does the drawing on the canvas), and `Event` (a class that handles the user's keystrokes and mouse events).

The code is also separated. The base abstract classes are in `matplotlib.backend_bases` and every concrete implementation is in a separate module. For example, the GTK 3 backend is in `matplotlib.backends.backend_gkt3agg`.

In this stack, there is an `Artist` classes' hierarchy where most of the hard stuff is done. `Artist` knows about `Renderer` and how to use it to draw images on `FigureCanvas`. Most of the stuff, we are interested in (text, lines, ticks, tick labels, images, and so on) are `Artist` or subclasses of the `Artist` class (located in the `matplotlib.artist` module).

The `matplotlib.artist.Artist` class contains all the shared properties of its children: coordinates transformation, clip box, label, user event handlers, and visibility.

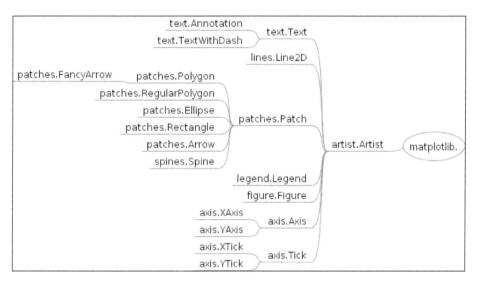

In this figure, `Artist` is the base for most of the other classes. There are two basic categories of classes that are inherited from `Artist`. The first category is of primitive artists that are visible objects such as `Line2D`, `Rectangle`, `Circle`, and `Text`. The second category is of composite artists that are collections of other `Artists`, such as `Axis`, `Tick`, `Axes`, and `Figure`. For example, `Figure` has the background of the primitive artist `Rectangle`, but also contains at least one composite artist, `Axes`.

Most of the plotting is happening on the `Axes` class (`matplotlib.axes.Axes`). The figure background elements such as ticks, axis lines, and the grid and color of the background patch is contained in `Axes`. Another important feature of `Axes` is that all the helper methods create other primitive artists and add them to the `Axes` instance; for example, `plot`, `hist`, and `imshow`.

`Axes.hist`, for example, creates many `matplotlib.patch.Rectangle` instances and stores them in the `Axes.patches` collection.

`Axes.plot` creates one or more `matplotlib.lines.Line2D` and stores them in the `Axes.lines` collection.

How to do it...

As an illustration, we will:

1. Instantiate the matplotlib `Path` object for custom drawing.
2. Construct the vertices of our object.
3. Construct the path's command codes to connect those vertices.
4. Create a patch.
5. Add it to the `Axes` instance of `figure`.

The following code implements our intentions:

```python
import matplotlib.pyplot as plt
from matplotlib.path import Path
import matplotlib.patches as patches

# add figure and axes
fig = plt.figure()
ax = fig.add_subplot(111)

coords = [
    (1., 0.),   # start position
    (0., 1.),
    (0., 2.),   # left side
    (1., 3.),
    (2., 3.),
    (3., 2.),   # top right corner
    (3.,1.),    # right side
    (2., 0.),
    (0., 0.),   # ignored
    ]

line_cmds = [Path.MOVETO,
Path.LINETO,
Path.LINETO,
Path.LINETO,
Path.LINETO,
Path.LINETO,
```

```
Path.LINETO,
Path.LINETO,
Path.CLOSEPOLY,
          ]

# construct path
path = Path(coords, line_cmds)
# construct path patch
patch = patches.PathPatch(path, lw=1,
facecolor='#A1D99B', edgecolor='#31A354')
# add it to *ax* axes
ax.add_patch(patch)

ax.text(1.1, 1.4, 'Python', fontsize=24)
ax.set_xlim(-1, 4)
ax.set_ylim(-1, 4)
plt.show()
```

The preceding code will generate the following:

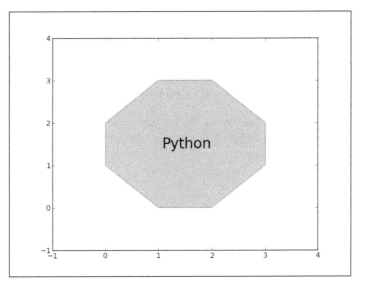

How it works...

For this octagon, we used the base patch `matplotlib.path.Path`, which supports the basic set of primitives for drawing lines and curves (`moveto` and `lineto`). These can be used to draw simple and also more advanced polygons using Bezier curves.

First, we specified a set of coordinates in the data coordinates that we match with a set of path commands to act upon those coordinates (or vertices, if you like). With that, we instantiate `matplotlib.path.Path`. We then construct the patch instance `matplotlib.patched.PathPatch` with that path, which is a general polycurve path patch.

This patch can now be added to the figure's axes (the `fig.axes` collection), and we can render the figure to show the polygon.

What we didn't want to do in this example is use `matplotlib.figure.Figure` directly in place of the `matplotlib.pyplot.figure()` call. The reason for this is that the `pyplot.figure()` call does a lot in the background, such as reading the `rc` parameters from the `matplotlibrc` file (to load default `figsize`, `dpi`, and figure color settings), setting up the figure manager class (`Gcf`), and so on. We could do all that, but until we really know what we are doing, this is the recommended way to create the figure.

As a general rule of thumb, unless we cannot achieve something via the `pyplot` interface, we should not reach for direct classes such as `Figure`, `Axes`, and `Axis`, because there is a lot of state managing going on in the background; unless we are developing matplotlib, we should avoid bothering about it.

There's more...

If you want interactivity and exploration, it would be the best to use matplotlib via the Python interactive shell. For this purpose, probably the most well known is IPython. This gives you all the matplotlib features in a powerful and introspective shell with rich set features such as history, inline plotting, and the possibility to share your work if you use the IPython Notebook.

The IPython Notebook is an interface to the IPython shell that can be accessed through the browser. Matplotlib has a strong integration with this interface, indeed the plots can be directly embedded in the browser interface.

9
Visualizations on the Clouds with Plot.ly

In this chapter, you will cover the following recipes:

- ▸ Creating line charts
- ▸ Creating bar charts
- ▸ Plotting a 3D trefoil knot
- ▸ Visualizing maps and bubbles

Introduction

Plot.ly is an online data visualization tool. It makes it possible for us to create and share interactive charts. Plot.ly can be used in two ways: you can either login into the website, upload your data, and use the web interface to create a chart, or use their API. In this chapter, we will focus on how to use their API.

The difference with matplotlib is that our charts are now created online and not on our machine. This means that we will be able to access them from the Plot.ly website. With a free account, all the charts that you make are made public and anyone can access them.

To try the recipes that will be presented in this chapter, you need a Plot.ly account and an API key. You can create a Plot.ly account by going on `https://plot.ly/` and clicking on **Sign in**. After the account is created, you can go in the **Settings** section and generate an API key.

After this, the API binding for Python can be installed using `pip`, as we saw in the first chapter:

```
$ pip install plotly
```

Now we're ready to go!

Creating line charts

In this recipe, we will see how to create a line chart. We have already introduced this kind of chart in *Chapter 3, Drawing Your First Plots and Customizing Them*, and we have seen how to make the plots with matplotlib. This time we'll focus on how to create and share them with Plot.ly.

Getting ready

Before starting, you need to set up your credentials for the Plot.ly platform in the programming environment:

```
$ python -c "import plotly; plotly.tools.set_credentials_
file(username='DemoAccount', api_key='mykey')"
```

Replace Demo Account and mykey with your Plotly username and API key.

How to do it...

The following code example demonstrates how to plot two curves. In particular, we will:

1. Generate the data to plot (a sine and a cosine wave).
2. Organize the data in the format required by Plot.ly.
3. Send a request to the server.
4. Receive a URL that points to our chart.
5. Run the following code:

```
import plotly.plotly as py
from plotly.graph_objs import Scatter
import numpy as np

x = np.linspace(-2*np.pi, 2*np.pi, 50)

trace0 = Scatter(x=x.tolist(),
    y=np.sin(x).tolist(),
    name='sin(x)'
)
trace1 = Scatter(
    x=x.tolist(),
    y=np.cos(x).tolist(),
    name='cos(x)'
)
```

```
data = [trace0, trace1]

unique_url = py.plot(data, filename = 'sin-cos')
```

How it works...

Here, we used the `Scatter` object twice. The first instance of `Scatter` (`trace0`) represents the points of the sine curve, while the second instance (`trace1`) represents the cosine curve. The parameters `x` and `y` of the constructor of these objects are used to specify the data points to plot, while the parameter name is used for the legend of the chart.

After building the objects that represent the curves, we wrapped all the data in a list that was then passed to the `py.plot` method. This method invokes Plot.ly and creates the chart for us. Right after invoking this method, your default browser opens automatically on a page that shows the chart. Here's what I got:

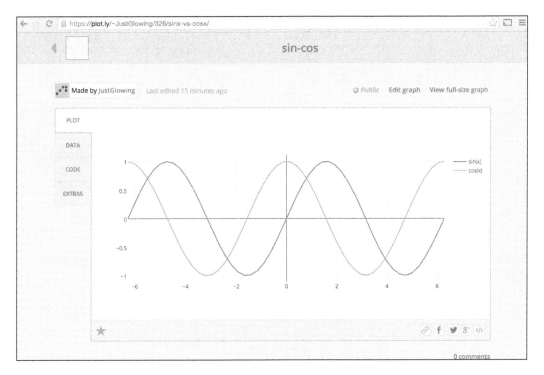

Now, the chart (and also the data) is stored on the Plot.ly servers, and we can access it through the URL returned by the method plot. Every chart has a unique name specified through the parameter filename of the method plot (in this case, the name of the chart is sin–cos).

The peculiarity of the Plot.ly interface is that the charts are interactive. If we hover the mouse pointer on the curves, we see a tooltip box that shows the information of the point we're on. We can also zoom out and zoom in using the scrolling wheel of the mouse.

There's more...

Following the link **DATA**, we also have the opportunity to inspect the data:

This feature enables us to share the chart and the data at the same time. If we go into the **CODE** section, we can also view the data in the JSON format:

We even get a script (in Python, MATLAB, Javascript, R, or Julia) that recreates the chart. Here's the Python version:

Also, going into the **Edit graph** section, we are able to modify many aspects of the chart, such as the theme and layout, and to add notes and so on without going back to the code:

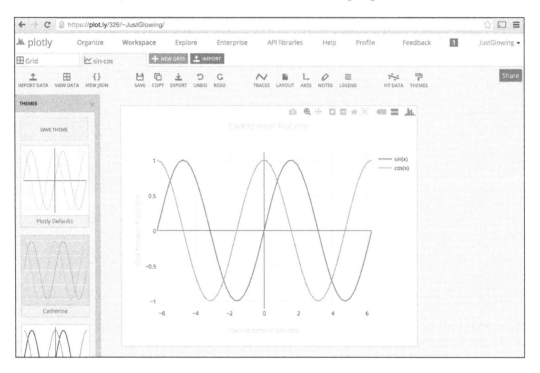

This very handy because it allows us to sketch a chart with a very simple code snippet and then improve its appearance with a point-and-click interface.

Creating bar charts

In this recipe, we will focus on how to create a bar chart to compare the occurrences of different crimes in Germany, Italy, and Spain in the year 2012. In particular, we will create a bar chart where we have three bars for each country, one with the number of burglaries, another with the number of robberies, and a third with the number of motor vehicle thefts.

Getting ready

For this recipe, we need the `crim_gen.tsv` file which comes with this book. This file contains the number of crimes reported to the police by year and by country. This data has been downloaded from the Eurostat website (`http://ec.europa.eu/eurostat`).

We assume that this file is in the same directory as the code using it.

How to do it...

The following code example demonstrates how to create a bar chart. We will:

1. Open a **tsv** (**tab separated values**) file.

2. Isolate and organize the data that we want to plot.

3. Invoke `plotly` to make the chart.

```
# bar charts
import pandas as pd
crimes = pd.read_csv('crim_gen.tsv', sep=',|\t', na_values=': ')
crimes = crimes[crimes.country.isin(['IT', 'ES', 'DE'])]

burglary = crimes.query('iccs == "burglary"')[['country', '2012
']].sort(columns='country').values
robbery = crimes.query('iccs == "robbery"')[['country', '2012 ']].
sort(columns='country').values
motor_theft = crimes.query('iccs == "theft_motor_vehicle"')
[['country', '2012 ']].sort(columns='country').values

import plotly.plotly as py
from plotly.graph_objs import *

trace1 = Bar(
    x=burglary[:,0].tolist(),
    y=burglary[:,1].tolist(),
    name='burglary'
)

trace2 = Bar(
    x=motor_theft[:,0].tolist(),
    y=motor_theft[:,1].tolist(),
    name='motor_theft'
)

trace3 = Bar(
    x=robbery[:,0].tolist(),
    y=robbery[:,1].tolist(),
    name='robbery'
)


data = Data([trace1, trace2, trace3])
layout = Layout(
```

```
        barmode='group'
    )
    fig = Figure(data=data, layout=layout)
    plot_url = py.plot(fig, filename='bars-crimes')
```

How it works...

In this recipe, we have used pandas (which were introduced in the first chapters of this book) to import and query the data. First, we isolated the data by the countries that we were interested in using the `isin` method, and then by the types of crimes that we were interested in. In particular, we have the three matrices `burglary`, `robbery`, and `motor_theft`, where the first column is the country code and the second is the number of times that crime has been reported in the country. Here's what the matrix `motor_theft` looks like:

```
[['DE', 70511.0],
 ['ES', 55197.0],
 ['IT', 196589.0]]
```

For each of the matrices, we instantiated a bar object, just like we did for the scatter object, but this time the parameter `x` is the first column of the matrix and `y` is the second. The data was again organized in a list and passed to the method plot. The result should be as follows:

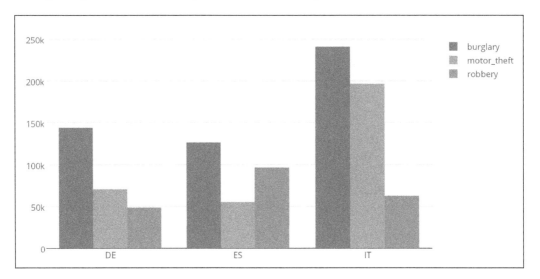

As we can see, we have three groups of bars, and each group contains three bars.

There's more...

In this snippet, we also used a new object: layout. This object enables us to specify the layout properties of the chart. Setting the parameter of this object bar mode as `group`, we specified that the bars needed to be grouped. If we set this attribute to `stack`, we get something like this:

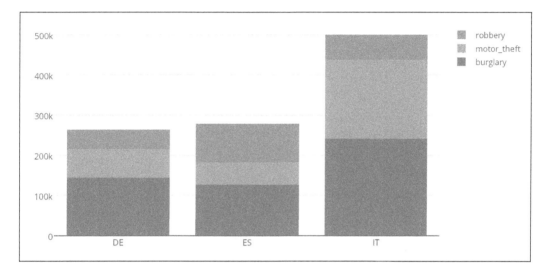

This means that now we also know how to stack the bars instead of just grouping them.

Plotting a 3D trefoil knot

In this recipe, we will see how to plot a 3D **trefoil knot**. A trefoil knot is a closed curve with three crossings. In this recipe, we will draw not just a curve, but a solid 3D curve. This is beyond the plotly capabilities, and we will implement this functionality using a trick.

How to do it...

In this recipe, we will:

1. Generate all the points of the knot using parametric equations.
2. Organize the data as required by `plotly`.
3. Define a clean layout.

4. Invoke `plotly` to draw the chart:

```
import numpy as np
import plotly.plotly as py
from plotly.graph_objs import Scatter3d, Data, Layout
from plotly.graph_objs import Figure, Line, Margin, Marker

from numpy import linspace,pi,cos,sin
phi = linspace(0,2*pi,250)
x = sin(phi)+2*sin(2*phi)
y = cos(phi)-2*cos(2*phi)
z = -sin(3*phi)

traces = list()
colors = ['rgb(%d,50,210)' % c for c in np.abs(z / max(z)) * 255]
for i in linspace(-np.pi,np.pi,50):
    trace = Scatter3d(x=x+np.cos(i)*.5, y=y+np.sin(i)*.5, z=z,
                      mode='markers',
                      marker=Marker(color=colors, size=13))
    traces.append(trace)

data = Data(traces)

layout = Layout(showlegend=False, autosize=False,
                width=500, height=500,
                margin=Margin(l=0,r=0,b=0,t=65))

fig = Figure(data=data, layout=layout)
plot_url = py.plot(fig, filename='3d-trifoil')
```

How it works...

First, we generated all the points of our knot curve using the following parametric equations:

```
x = sin(phi)+2*sin(2*phi)
y = cos(phi)-2*cos(2*phi)
z = -sin(3*phi)
```

This means that x, y, and z are parallel vectors, and the point (x[i], y[i], z[i]) is a point of our curve in the 3D space. To generate a solid curve, we created a series of other curves around the main one. Indeed, we generated a set of Scatter3d objects (each one is a curve).

To give to the knot a 3D effect, we draw each point of each curve with a different color. The color is the function of the z coordinate, and it is blue when z is equal to 0 and gradually becomes purple when z moves away from 0.

The colors were specified with a list of RGB triplets. Indeed, if we take a look at the values of the list colors, it will look like this:

```
['rgb(0,50,210)',
 'rgb(19,50,210)',
 'rgb(38,50,210)',
 'rgb(57,50,210)',
 'rgb(76,50,210)',
 ...
```

Each element is a string that contains the RGB value of one of the points of the curve.

The results are as follows:

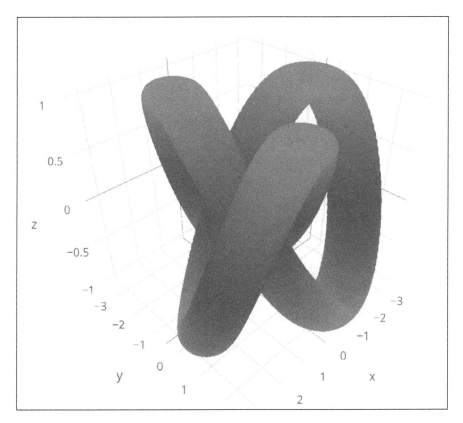

Here, we can not only zoom in and out, but also rotate the figure.

Visualizing maps and bubbles

In this recipe, we will see how to visualize a map and place a bubble on each country, in this case some European countries. The size of each bubble will be proportional to the number of total reported crimes in that country.

Getting ready

Here we will again use the `crim_gen.tsv` file, which comes with this book, assuming that this file is in the same directory as the code using it.

How to do it...

For the following recipe, we will proceed as follows:

1. Import and query the data.
2. Define the coordinates of each country.
3. Create an entry for each country.
4. Define the layout for the chart.
5. Invoke `plotly`.

```
import plotly.plotly as py
from plotly.graph_objs import *

import pandas as pd
crimes = pd.read_csv('crim_gen.tsv', sep=',|\t', na_values=': ')
crimes = crimes[crimes.country.isin(['IT','ES','DE','FR','NO','FI'])]

total_crimes = crimes.query('iccs == "TOTAL"')[['country', '2012
']].sort(columns='2012 ').values
coords = {'IT': (13.007813, 42.553080), 'ES': (-3.867188,
39.909736), 'DE': (9.316406,50.736455),
        'FR': (2.636719, 46.195042), 'NO': (8.613281,
61.100789), 'FI': (25.839844, 62.431074)}
scale = 300000
countries = []


for info in total_crimes:
    c = coords[info[0]]
    country = dict(
```

```
            type = 'scattergeo',
            lon = [c[0]],
            lat = [c[1]],
            text = info[0]+':'+str(info[1]),
            sizemode = 'diameter',
            name= info[0],
            marker = dict(
                size = info[1] / scale,
                color = 'red',
                line = dict(width = 1,color = 'red')
            ))
        countries.append(country)

    layout = dict(
            title = '2012 Reported crimes',
            showlegend = True,
            geo = dict(
                scope='europe'
            ),
        )

    fig = dict( data=countries, layout=layout )
    url = py.plot( fig, validate=False, filename='bubble-map-crimes' )
```

How it works...

Here, we have isolated the data for six countries: Spain, Italy, Germany, France, Norway, and Finland. For each of these countries, we defined the coordinate to place the bubble in the dictionary `coords`. Then, for each country, we created a dictionary with the details of the bubble to show the size, string in the tooltip, color, and geographical coordinates.

Then, we created the layout for the chart. What tells Plot.ly that this chart contains a map is the parameter `geo`. When Plot.ly finds this parameter in the specifications of the layout, it automatically assumes that it is a map. With this parameter, we specify the scope of the map, which in this case is Europe.

The resulting figure should be as follows:

Index

Symbols

3D bars
creating 143-147
3D histograms
creating 147-150
3D trefoil knot
about 269
plotting 269-271

A

**Advanced Linux Sound Architecture
(ALSA) 196**
alignment properties
horizontalalignment (ha) 247
multialignment 247
verticalalignment (va) 247
Anaconda 9
animation
in matplotlib 150-153
OpenGL, using 154-158
annotations
about 90
adding 91, 92
antenna radiation pattern
reference link 134
Application Programming Interface (API) 255
areas, between two contours
filling 102-104
array slicing 53
arrows (quivers) 229
ArtistAnimation class 153
autocorrelation
about 224
using 226, 227
Axes.annotate function 170

axis labels
size, setting of 112, 113
transparency, setting of 112, 113
axis lengths
defining 79-82
axis limits
defining 79-82

B

background color
defining 87
barb
about 229, 230
drawing 230-232
emptybarb 231
height 231
spacing 231
using 231, 232
width 231
bar charts
creating 97-100, 266-269
bar charts, parameters
bottom 98
ecolor 98
edgecolor 98
linewidth 98
orientation 98
width 98
xerr 98
yerr 98
Basemap
used, for plotting data on map 174-179
basic plot, matplotlib
plotting area 71
x and y axes 71
x and y tickers 71

setting, of axis labels 112, 113

U

under-plot area
filling 131-134

V

vector flow
streamlines, drawing 204-208
virtualenv
about 4
installing 5-7
virtualenvwrapper
about 5
installing 5-7
reference link 5

W

whisker plot
creating 233-235
Windows
matplotlib, installing on 9, 10
WYSIWYG
URL 160

Y

Yorick
URL 209

Thank you for buying
Python Data Visualization Cookbook
Second Edition

About Packt Publishing

Packt, pronounced 'packed', published its first book, *Mastering phpMyAdmin for Effective MySQL Management*, in April 2004, and subsequently continued to specialize in publishing highly focused books on specific technologies and solutions.

Our books and publications share the experiences of your fellow IT professionals in adapting and customizing today's systems, applications, and frameworks. Our solution-based books give you the knowledge and power to customize the software and technologies you're using to get the job done. Packt books are more specific and less general than the IT books you have seen in the past. Our unique business model allows us to bring you more focused information, giving you more of what you need to know, and less of what you don't.

Packt is a modern yet unique publishing company that focuses on producing quality, cutting-edge books for communities of developers, administrators, and newbies alike. For more information, please visit our website at www.packtpub.com.

About Packt Open Source

In 2010, Packt launched two new brands, Packt Open Source and Packt Enterprise, in order to continue its focus on specialization. This book is part of the Packt open source brand, home to books published on software built around open source licenses, and offering information to anybody from advanced developers to budding web designers. The Open Source brand also runs Packt's open source Royalty Scheme, by which Packt gives a royalty to each open source project about whose software a book is sold.

Writing for Packt

We welcome all inquiries from people who are interested in authoring. Book proposals should be sent to author@packtpub.com. If your book idea is still at an early stage and you would like to discuss it first before writing a formal book proposal, then please contact us; one of our commissioning editors will get in touch with you.

We're not just looking for published authors; if you have strong technical skills but no writing experience, our experienced editors can help you develop a writing career, or simply get some additional reward for your expertise.

[PACKT] open source ✶
PUBLISHING   community experience distilled

Learning Python Data Visualization

ISBN: 978-1-78355-333-4   Paperback: 212 pages

Master how to build dynamic HTML-5 ready SVG charts using Python and the pygal library

1. A practical guide that helps you break into the world of data visualization with Python.

2. Understand the fundamentals of building charts in Python.

3. Packed with easy-to-understand tutorials for developers who are new to Python or charting in Python.

Python Data Visualization Cookbook

ISBN: 978-1-78216-336-7   Paperback: 280 pages

Over 60 recipes that will enable you to learn how to create attractive visualizations using Python's most popular libraries

1. Learn how to set up an optimal Python environment for data visualization.

2. Understand the topics such as importing data for visualization and formatting data for visualization.

3. Understand the underlying data and how to use the right visualizations.

Please check **www.PacktPub.com** for information on our titles